The Earliest African American Literatures

EDITED BY
ZACHARY MCLEOD HUTCHINS
AND CASSANDER L. SMITH

The Earliest African American Literatures
A Critical Reader

The University of North Carolina Press *Chapel Hill*

This book was published with the assistance of the Anniversary Fund of the University of North Carolina Press.

© 2021 Zachary McLeod Hutchins and Cassander L. Smith
All rights reserved
Set in Arno Pro by Westchester Publishing Services
Manufactured in the United States of America

The University of North Carolina Press has been a member of the Green Press Initiative since 2003.

Library of Congress Cataloging-in-Publication Data
Names: Hutchins, Zachary McLeod, editor. | Smith, Cassander L., 1977– editor.
Title: The earliest African American literatures : a critical reader / edited by Zachary McLeod Hutchins and Cassander L. Smith.
Description: Chapel Hill : University of North Carolina Press, [2021] | Includes bibliographical references.
Identifiers: LCCN 2021041596 | ISBN 9781469665597 (cloth ; alk. paper) | ISBN 9781469665603 (paperback ; alk. paper) | ISBN 9781469665610 (ebook)
Subjects: LCSH: American literature—African American authors—17th century. | American literature—African American authors—18th century. | American literature—African American authors—History and criticism. | African Americans—Biography—Sources. | African Americans in literature. | LCGFT: Autobiographies. | Biographies.
Classification: LCC PS508.B53 E18 2021 | DDC 810.8/0896073—dc23
LC record available at https://lccn.loc.gov/2021041596

Cover illustration: Background pattern © Shutterstock.com/Desirede; fan pattern over table © Shutterstock.com/kirkchai benjarusameeros; Kente pattern over woman's silhouette © 123rf.com/Elena Leonova; white paper texture © freepik.com/kues1.

Contents

Acknowledgments vii

A Note on the Text ix

Introduction: Toward a Theory of Black African Mediation, Authorship, and the Early American Literary Archives 1

Part I Spiritual Accounts 19

ONE Conversion Narrative of a Blackmore Maid, 1643 21

TWO Narrative of Ben, a Negro, 1699 23

THREE Execution of Joseph Hanno, a "Miserable African," 1721 27

FOUR A Letter from Black Enslaved Christians on a Virginia Plantation, 1723 34

FIVE The Confession of Flora Negro, 1748 37

SIX The Antislavery Argument of Negro Greenwich, 1754 42

Part II In the Legal Records 45

SEVEN Anthony Johnson and the Casor Suit, 1655 47

EIGHT The Case of Elizabeth Key Grinstead, 1656 50

NINE The Salem Witch Trials, the Testimony of Candy and Mary Black, 1692 57

TEN Adam Negro's Tryal, 1701 61

ELEVEN The Deposition of Lydia Draper in Dedham, MA, 1723 68

TWELVE Testimony on the New York Arson Conspiracy, 1741 72

THIRTEEN Petition of Jethro Boston for Divorce, 1741 88

FOURTEEN Last Will and Testament of Peter, 1743 91

FIFTEEN The Trial and Execution of Mark and Phillis, 1755 94

Part III Runaways 113

SIXTEEN Penelope, 1704 117

SEVENTEEN George, 1704 119

EIGHTEEN Mother of Four, 1706 120

NINETEEN Peter, 1705–1714 121

TWENTY Daniel, 1712–1714 125

TWENTY-ONE Jethro, 1719–1720 127

TWENTY-TWO John, 1719–1720 129

TWENTY-THREE Richard Molson, 1720 131

TWENTY-FOUR Fransh Manuel, 1722 133

TWENTY-FIVE Quam, 1722–1723 135

TWENTY-SIX Tom, 1723 137

TWENTY-SEVEN Timothy, 1726–1727 139

TWENTY-EIGHT Chocolate Grinder, 1727–1728 141

TWENTY-NINE Stephen, 1728–1729 143

THIRTY John Mallott, 1729 145

THIRTY-ONE Boy, 1729 147

THIRTY-TWO Cora and Joe, 1728–1751 149

Part IV Life and Travel Writing 153

THIRTY-THREE Jethro and King Philip's War, 1676 155

THIRTY-FOUR Onesimus and the Small Pox, 1711–1716 159

THIRTY-FIVE Titus in the Caribbean, 1714–1716 163

THIRTY-SIX John Williams and the Atlantic World, 1724 167

THIRTY-SEVEN A Short Account of the Life of
Elizabeth Colson, 1727 174

THIRTY-EIGHT Ayuba Suleiman Diallo, 1734 177

Notes 189   *Index* 195

Acknowledgments

This book is the product of long conversations, deep contemplations, and breakfast meetings for the coeditors at the biennial meetings of the Society of Early Americanists (SEA). We are grateful to our colleagues in SEA and those at our respective home institutions (Colorado State University and the University of Alabama) who readily engaged and informed our thinking about the literary significance of black Africans in an early American context. We benefited greatly from panel discussions, email exchanges, and teaching brown bags that afforded us the opportunity to discuss the primary documents gathered in this reader. We thank especially Tara Bynum, Brigitte Fielder, Steven Thomas, Lauren Cardon, Trudier Harris, Yolanda Manora, Kristina Bross, Vincent Carretta, John Ernest, Louann Reid, Bill Andrews, Mike Millner, James Coleman, and Joycelyn Moody. Research for this volume was supported by a 2016 Fellowship from the National Endowment for the Humanities, and we express gratitude for that institution and its important work.

We equally are grateful to those students in our African American literature survey, special topics, and graduate courses, who were our first audiences for presenting this material in a pedagogical context. We have been fortunate to encounter students who engaged the materials with enthusiasm, intellectual curiosity, and in some cases outrage because they had not heard of these figures earlier. It is our fervent hope that students and teachers alike will find *The Earliest African American Literatures* a source of provocative, transformative classroom discussions as did we.

We also thank the editorial staff at the University of North Carolina Press, especially acquisitions editor Lucas Church, whose immediate enthusiasm for the project energized us each step of the way. We thank, too, the anonymous readers for the press. Their feedback proved vital in helping us hone the final product.

A Note on the Text

The texts in this reader have been drawn from a diverse array of sources with differing editorial standards. Some are transcribed here, for the first time, from manuscript sources employing abbreviations and spelling practices that would make them illegible to many twenty-first-century readers. In these cases, we have expanded abbreviations, inserted missing punctuation, and corrected spellings. All other texts have been presented as they appear in the published sources from which they have been drawn, with differing approaches to grammatical matters such as capitalization, punctuation, and spelling. We view the resulting diversity of styles as a strength, introducing readers to many of the different ways in which texts were composed, presented, and read by those living in colonial North America.

The Earliest African American Literatures

Introduction
Toward a Theory of Black African Mediation, Authorship, and the Early American Literary Archives

When interrogating the origins of African American literature, scholars almost uniformly focus on the mid-eighteenth century, when those of African descent living in British North America emerged as writing subjects. Scholars, for example, turn to the autobiographical accounts of Briton Hammon and Olaudah Equiano or the poetry of Lucy Terry Prince, Jupiter Hammon, and Phillis Wheatley Peters. These figures, scholars argue, initiate a centuries-long tradition of African American literature.[1] Some have even referred to these early texts as a "pre-history," or in the words of Jeannine Marie DeLombard, "fits and starts" before the tradition "commenced in political and aesthetic earnest" with the slave narrative in the nineteenth century.[2]

This critical reader aims to expand current conversations about the origins of African American literature by examining the literary footprint of black Africans in early America prior to 1760.[3] The reader highlights the narrative presence and textual contributions of some three dozen black Africans who, through processes of dictation and other means, found their words and deeds captured in a range of printed texts and manuscripts, including newspapers, ministerial notes, diaries, and court records. These literary black Africans, as we call them, illustrate the extent to which those of African descent were intervening in American literature long before 1760.[4] Literary black Africans appear in the early American textual archives mostly as mediated representations produced through the writing efforts of European (-American) missionaries and ministers, merchants, travel writers, slaveholders, court transcribers, and so forth. In many cases, those early texts represent black Africans as marginal and incidental. Nonetheless, the representations are crucial textual sites that preserve a record of black African literary authority and agency. This reader, then, reveals an archive of literary black Africans who appeared in and helped to shape American literature prior to the age of Equiano and Wheatley Peters. Our aim is to broaden discussions about how, when, and in what forms those of African descent intervened in early American literature and initiated an African American literary tradition. Specifically, this anthology challenges readers of early American literature to reconsider three terms in relationship to black Africans: mediation, authorship, and archive.

Mediation and the Critical Impasse

Prior to the mid-eighteenth century, black Africans overwhelmingly appear in early American texts as mediated subjects considered from a white, Western perspective and situated at the narrative margins of missionary tracts, captivity narratives, Puritan sermons, spiritual diaries, newspapers, and court records, among other written forms. On occasion, they take center stage in runaway advertisements or gallows confessions. Their textual presence results from the representational machinations of what Toni Morrison calls a white literary imagination.[5] Based on conventional literary paradigms, most of the figures featured in this reader are objects of writing, of authorial control. In the 1990s, Stephen Greenblatt memorably insisted that the process of mediation was akin to the "recording of alien voices" representing those "who have no power to leave literate traces of their existence."[6] For Greenblatt, mediation is a discursive trick, a slight of the authorial hand that appears to provide historical data about cultures and people who left behind no written records of their own. Mediation is an act of appropriation that is most valuable, Greenblatt argues, for what it can tell us about a writer. Mediated figures are bound up with the author, revealing more about the author's ambitions, privileges, preferences—and prejudices—than about the figures being represented. Put another way, the lens of mediation obscures, or refracts, the presence of black Africans in early America, impeding our ability to access meaningful information about those black Africans represented in the texts. Scholars have largely agreed that we cannot assess, for example, a mediated figure's racial consciousness or voice, the very features that have shaped African American literature as a field. These mediated moments lack the "racial realism" that Gene Jarrett argues defined early African American literature.[7] Mediation, then, is a kind of critical impasse that has for decades limited our ability to craft deeper, richer literary histories of black Africans in early America.[8]

This critical reader endeavors to push past that impasse by emphasizing the role of black Africans as both literary figures and human agents whose actions in the material world shaped their textual presence.[9] We operate on the assumption that the mediated textual presences of black Africans can be correlated with material world referents whose actions provided important source material for literary representations. In this way, the reader follows a recent turn in early American studies that has begun to examine the effect of black African (and Native) material presences on the development of early American literary culture.[10] A number of historical and material culture studies have already excavated the material contributions of black Africans in early America.[11] Here, we present a body of texts that can help us excavate their textual and literary legacy. We ask students and scholars to consider literary black Africans in early America before 1760 as more than merely objects of representation or of print but also as subjects and cocreators of the written word.

On Authorship

Readers often treat mediation as an exercise of power and intentionality located solely within the purview of the author, who writes and owns the text. We have an idea of the author that is driven by modern notions of copyright and possession; these notions belie the social reality of imaginative construction, the ways in which texts took shape, particularly in early America, leading us to overdetermine the role of the author in seventeenth- and eighteenth-century writing processes. Our modern conception of authorship emerged in England and America during the eighteenth century, in tandem with ideas about copyright and property ownership and transformations in print culture. Prior to this development, authorship was a status more often associated with acts of imitation, translation, or compilation that a writer performed toward humanist ends, such as communal enrichment. Authorship as we commonly understand it today really began to crystallize, as Andrew Bennett notes, at the turn of the nineteenth century with Romantic poets who understood textual output as a manifestation of subjectivity. According to this Romantic notion of authorship, the identity and labor of an author became just as important as the text itself. Writers increasingly claimed text as a form of personal property reflecting their intellectual capacities.[12] Early African American literature certainly reflects this authorial turn as those first generations of Black writers challenged the dehumanizing effects of the transatlantic slave trade and the racism it engendered by representing themselves as writing subjects. Authorship empowered early African Americans to advocate for citizenship, democracy, and the very notion of Black humanity. It is why Equiano included the words "written by himself" on the cover of his 1789 autobiography.[13] Wheatley Peters confronted the stakes of being a black African writer when her only published volume of poetry in 1773 required the authenticating structure of eighteen white, male Boston elites, "some of the best judges," who could attest to the fact that Wheatley Peters was "qualified to write."[14] In short, writing ensured civic presence for black Africans.

Consequently, the idea of authorship as ownership has been a prevailing paradigm shaping the study of African American literature. Assiduously, scholars track the dates and means and motives by which individuals of African descent began producing texts.[15] This preoccupation with the circumstances of textual production differs from the biographical attentions lavished on canonical white authors because scholars have recognized that for black African authors, writing for publication often constituted a claim of subjectivity and self-possession made in opposition to racist ideologies embedded in editorial and print processes. For example, the question of authorship consumed John Sekora in 1987, when he determined that early slave narratives were so heavily influenced by editors and amanuenses that they were mostly Black messages wrapped inside white envelopes. These accounts, he argues, lack the authority and authenticity of Black authorship—a claim that would be nonsensical if made about white writers, whose belief in their own racial superiority was reaffirmed by their ready access to the means of textual production.[16] Much recent scholarship is still wedded to this authorship paradigm. Studies map the ways in which African Americans embody the role of author toward racial advancement. Kenneth Warren, for example, posits that the very arc of African American literature coincides with the rise and fall of Jim Crow. African Americans wrote, he argues, as "an imaginative response" to a "lived reality" and to "legal" structures of racism and discrimination."[17] Jarrett, too, notes that early African American writing was an inherently political act.[18]

Unfortunately, this concern for authorship over the years has simultaneously rendered illegible the strategies black Africans employed before 1760 to make themselves visible in early American culture. For sure, paradigms that privilege authorship illuminate the agentive, subversive, accommodationist tactics of early Black writers. We cannot, therefore, concede the death of the author or understand authorship simply as an abstract function of language and power, as Roland Barthes and Michel Foucault do in their influential theoretical approaches to authorship.[19] To do so undermines the cultural energy that compels African American literature. Yet, to focus solely on authorship disregards those black Africans who might not have put pen to paper but who, through their interactions with people who did have access to print technologies, found themselves subjects of writing. Without abandoning the apparatus of authorship, we can rethink its meaning in earlier periods. Moving beyond a view of authorship as the creative expression of a lone writer who owns the text enables us to construct richer cultural histories of black Africans in early America.

In advocating for the study of women in early modern literature, Heather Hirschfeld argues, "It is incumbent on scholars who wish to reclaim lost or forgotten female voices to move beyond the dominant Romantic definition of the individual author and to recognize, in the diversified processes of textual production, alternative formulations or experiences of authorship."[20] The same might be said for recovering Black voices in the earliest textual records of America. Scholars invested in a reclamation of literary black Africans must free Greenblatt's conception of mediation from the tyranny of authorship by treating textual production as the collaborative social process it was throughout the early modern period. As David Hall notes, "to be a writer was to enter into a relationship of dependence." Speaking specifically about the literary landscape of the seventeenth-century Chesapeake Bay area, Hall explains that writers were bound up with "patrons, booksellers, coteries, and religious communities."[21] What Hall observes about the collaborative literary landscape of the early Chesapeake Bay applies elsewhere in the early Americas and is an important factor in how and why black Africans appear in the earliest textual records. To think about black Africans as collaborative presences in the early American literary landscape is to acknowledge black African agency. It is the case that some of the black subjects in this reader did, in fact, actively enter into collaborative relationships with white writers. See, for example, the memoirs of Ayuba Suleiman Diallo (Job Ben Solomon) and Elizabeth Colson, included in part 4. In other instances, the collaboration appears more the product of circumstances and interaction. In these cases, collaboration connotes those external factors that coalesce into the shaping of a text.

What Constitutes a Literary Archive

The early modern emphasis on corporate authorship documented by Hall should shift our sense of what constituted a literary object in the seventeenth and early eighteenth centuries. The novel's rise, as a genre, and our own preference for extended prose narratives penned by a single author have long relegated the period's best-selling print forms to obscurity. For instance, the sea providence narrative, in which common sailors related stories of their miraculous deliverance from maritime dangers, was quite popular at the time but has been neglected by early Americanists because, as Julie Sievers notes, "most were originally told by individuals not usually recognized as authors—ordinary people speaking from personal experience, not from positions of privilege, and often relying on others to record and publish their narratives."²² The stories of literary black Africans in colonial North America, like the tales of Sievers's travelers and sailors, have been overlooked at least in part because they are embedded in other texts. Likewise, the genre we now call the African American slave narrative had until recently overlooked the voices and narratives of enslaved people, mainly in the Caribbean, whose stories appear at the margins of narratives of white writers.²³ Accounts of literary black Africans appeared in court records, ship logs, newspapers, broadsides, and other corporately authored texts long before the publication of separately bound books penned by black African authors. Such multivocal productions may be dismissed by twenty-first-century readers on aesthetic grounds because they lack a coherent artistic vision, but they were treated as literary works by contemporaries, who considered their style as well as their substance.²⁴

To wit: in eighteenth-century North America, newspapers were, by far, the most widely read form of text, but scholars rarely scrutinize the pages of colonial newspapers with the attention that fact would seem to warrant.²⁵ Charles Clark attests that "by 1790, it could be said that newspaper issues had comprised 80 percent of all American publications to that point," and each issue was produced with the intent to entertain as well as inform.²⁶ Thus, when the *New-England Weekly Journal* published its first issue on 20 March 1727, Samuel Kneeland announced that the paper would "*Entertain the Publick every Monday with a Collection of the most Remarkable Occurrences*," publishing everything "*worthy of the Publick View; whether of Remarkable Judgments, or Singular Mercies, more private or publick, Preservations & Deliverances by Sea or Land, together with some other Pieces of History of our own, &c. that may be profitable & entertaining both to the Christian and Historian.*"²⁷ Included among the many items in any particular issue were notices publicizing the achievements of black African inventors, accounts of black Africans attacking white slave traders off the coast of Guinea, autobiographical accounts of black Africans condemned to hang, and advertisements offering enslaved black Africans for sale or offering a reward for the capture of runaways, among others. The fragmentary narratives preserved in an advertisement or foreign news bulletin may seem banal to modern eyes, but eighteenth-century readers received such accounts and news appreciatively and imaginatively.

In the eighteenth century, the word *invention* meant not the creation of something new but the discovery and arrangement of extant texts; readers, as well as writers, exercised creative faculties in their consumption and collation of micronarratives. In this way, readers anticipated what we now refer to as "the death of the author." What we propose, in this anthology, is the rememory of strategies deployed by eighteenth-century readers to contemplate the agency and subjectivity of literary black Africans. By imaginatively reintegrating the living presence of enslaved and deceased Africans into our reading practices, as Morrison asks readers to do in her Pulitzer Prize–winning novel *Beloved*, we hope to stimulate creative new approaches to fragmentary and forgotten texts.[28] This expansive, writerly digestion of the printed word is often identified with Barthes, but it shaped the reading of eighteenth-century texts and lives long before the rise of literary theory.[29]

In 1710, for instance, Joseph Addison confessed that

> It is my custom, in a dearth of news, to entertain myself with those collections of advertisements that appear at the end of all our public prints. These I consider as accounts of news from the little world, in the same manner that the foregoing parts of the paper are from the great. If in one we hear that a sovereign prince has fled from his capital city, in the other we hear of a tradesman who hath shut up his shop, and run away. If in the one we find the victory of a general, in the other we see the desertion of a private soldier. I must confess, I have a certain weakness in my temper, that is often very much affected by these little domestic occurrences, and have frequently been caught with tears in my eyes over a melancholy advertisement.[30]

Given that their original readers consumed slave-for-sale advertisements and other notices in the newspaper as literary objects worthy of contemplation and imaginative expansion, we, too, should regard these narrative fragments as texts of aesthetic import. Doing so is both an endorsement of David Waldstreicher's argument that runaway slave advertisements are among the earliest slave narratives and a reminder to look beyond these advertisements to other, comparably neglected textual forms preserving similar stories.[31]

Runaways excited the fancy of readers like Addison, but so, too, did notices such as that published in the *Boston News-Letter* on 24 December 1724. An advertisement in that issue explained that

> Thursday the 17th Instant, A Negro Boy, (seeming to be a Gentlemans Servant) who had an old Bever Hat, bound with Lace, came into a Shop here to buy a Pen knife, had a large Bill of Credit: They being Suspecious of the Boy ask'd him some Questions, have found since that he was false: That therefore may signify, That whoever shall give a true Account of the abovesaid Boy, and what the Bill is, may have it again, paying the Charges.[32]

The tale told here is one of deception and assumed identity, as the anonymous young man dons apparel signifying wealth in order to pass as a "*Gentlemans Servant.*" This act of economic passing, like the racial passing practiced by lighter-skinned African Americans in the nineteenth and twentieth centuries, transgressed cultural norms and demonstrated the multiplicity of identity categories performed by literary black Africans. Posing as a member of the upper class placed racial and economic classifications in conflict, forcing the shopkeepers from whom he stole the penknife to decide which identity category was more important in their consideration of his claim to credit. As Elaine Ginsberg writes, performances such as this one, with which colonial newspapers abound, "expose the contingencies of all identities as well as the 'politics' inherent in their construction and imposition."[33] Even in its abbreviated form, and even though it was not written by the literary black African whose actions it describes, this micronarrative anticipates the work of much later texts penned and published by African American authors, and the performance of class, by this anonymous young man, is comparable to the performance of literary value whereby authors with aesthetic pretentions make overtures to readers with a specific educational and economic background.

Although Addison, like most colonial readers, was white, black African readers also participated in the literary reconstruction of fragmentary narratives such as that of the "*Gentlemans Servant,*" providing their own imagined but nonetheless "*true Account*" in response to the advertisement's call. Thus, the present rememory of those readings by scholars and students is not an anachronistic imposition on the texts in question but the recovery of historical readers and interpretive responses unacknowledged in our current reading practices. Many Africans in colonial North America never had an opportunity to learn how to read and write in English, but these individuals still had access to the news and to the verbal accounts preserved in legal documents. In the eighteenth century, the daily oral performance of newspapers, broadsides, and other popular texts provided illiterate black Africans (and individuals of all races) access to the printed word, making "readers" of men and women who might not even know the alphabet. However, some could read, and many of these texts presuppose a black African audience. In relating the story of "A Negro Man" who allegedly attempted to rape "an English Woman" in Connecticut, for example, the printer notes that "a very remarkable thing fell out, (which we here relate as a caveat for all Negroes medling for the future with any white Women, least they fare with the like treatment,)."[34] Schools promoting the literacy of black Africans were opened by Elias Neau in New York, Cotton Mather in Massachusetts, Samuel Keimer in

Pennsylvania, and Alexander Garden in South Carolina. Those educated in these schools could use their literacy for mundane purposes and to process warnings such as this one, but they also read imaginatively.

The best evidence for these creative and writerly readings may be a broadside published by Thomas Fleet in 1741, commemorating the capture of Spanish fortifications in Cartagena de Indias on the coast of present-day Colombia. The broadside features a poem, "Some Excellent VERSES on Admiral VERNON's taking the Forts and Castles of *Carthagena*," and a woodcut illustrating the battle. The poem celebrates the role of black African labor, which made possible the British assault by cutting down trees and clearing a path of fire for Vernon's artillery:

> *Wenworth* commands, down go the Trees,
>   With horrible Report;
> Agast, the trembling *Spaniard* sees
>   The Negroes and the Fort.
>
> Our Picture shows all this with Art,
>   (Was ever Work so pretty!)
> And soon you'l see the second Part,
>   When we have took the City.

These verses suggest that "the Picture," which shows black African bodies at work, predates the poem, and the woodcut in question was carved by Black Peter—an enslaved man who delivered and helped to produce the *Boston Evening-Post*. Having read, in the *Post*, how "the Wood was cut down and clear'd in one night by 1500 Negroes," Peter responded with a work of art imaginatively re-creating the events narrated in the newspaper and celebrating the contributions made by other black Africans in this important battle; he cut wood to commemorate the wood cut by his countrymen, inserting himself into the narrative.[35] When Peter read this and other textual fragments featuring literary black Africans, he responded creatively. Both white and black African readers participated in the enlargement of these micronarratives.

There are thousands of texts like those we have presented here as examples. In preparing *The Earliest African American Literatures*, we have read more than five thousand issues of colonial American newspapers, including every one of the 2,690 issues published before 1730 and preserved digitally in the Readex series *Early American Newspapers, 1690–1922*. These issues included more than 3,100 passages related to slavery, which means that on average, each issue contained at least one advertisement, editorial, or news item featuring a literary black African or discussing the peculiar institution that curtailed their freedom. And in addition to this vast print archive, hundreds of narratives documenting the bondage and resistance of literary black Africans have been preserved in diaries, letters, and the manuscript records of municipal and colonial governments. In other words, the corpus of texts sampled in this anthology is vast, and its farthest reaches are still undocumented. *The Earliest African American Literatures* points to the interpretive possibilities opened up by an examination of these texts, but it is hardly exhaustive; indeed, a key purpose of its compilation is to stimulate a reexamination of newspapers, court records, and other texts where readers might encounter these forgotten figures and their stories.[36]

Genre and Context as Guiding Principles

In selecting texts from this vast archive to present here, we have prioritized public, narrative accounts that might have been consumed contemporaneously, by creative colonial auditors and readers like Peter. Thus, although we include passages describing the life of an enslaved man named Titus from letters that were entered into the public record, as evidence in a lawsuit, we have not reproduced Samuel Sewall's private remembrance of marrying two enslaved black Africans from his *Diary*.[37] Although we include runaway slave advertisements that recount stories of escape—and, in many cases, serial escapes—from the hands of enslavers, we have not reproduced slave-for-sale advertisements lacking a comparable narrative element. We include Elizabeth Colson's execution-day autobiography, which argues for education reform, but we have omitted strictly polemical texts by white authors, such as John Woolman's *Some Considerations on the Keeping of Negroes* (1754), which treat black Africans as a racial group without offering portraits of their particularized humanity. Because many of the narratives we have located in the archive were produced within the same few rhetorical contexts, we have chosen to use genre as an organizing principle, rather than presenting them in a strictly chronological order.

We and other scholars have described a range of eighteenth-century texts as slave narratives, but the genre only became recognizable as a standardized literary form in the nineteenth century, when the number of lengthy, autobiographical accounts by formerly enslaved men and women dramatically increased. Prior to that point, texts written by or about black Africans were often identified with other genres whose conventions shaped their representations of slavery and the experience of black Africans in North America. For instance, the *Narrative of the Surprizing Deliverance of Briton Hammon, a Negro Man,—Servant to General Winslow, of Marshfield, in New-England* (1760), which some scholars identify as the first slave narrative, features a protagonist in bondage.[38] However, it was clearly marketed as an Indian captivity narrative and adventure story, rather than an account of chattel slavery and racism.[39] For this reason Hammon's *Narrative* identifies his Indian captors, who held him captive for five weeks, as "barbarous and inhuman Savages," but does not use similarly derogatory language to describe the Spanish, who held him for nearly a decade, or Winslow, the "*good Master*" who regarded Hammon as a servant for the duration of his life.[40] Generic conventions dictated the relative morality of white masters and Indian captors in Hammon's *Narrative*, and they also shaped the accounts we have collected in *The Earliest African American Literatures*.

Each of the four parts in this anthology groups together texts produced within a similar rhetorical context. Although their form often differs—a conversion narrative, a letter, a record of oral testimony—similarities in subject matter, style, and perspective make it appropriate to regard the various texts collected in each part as constitutive of distinct subgenres within the broader field of early American literature. Thus, in part 1, we present writings based in Christian doctrine and lived religious experience that document the conversion and spiritual views of black Africans. In part 2, we share texts that situate black Africans within the common-law legal culture of colonial British North America, presenting arguments about the rights and responsibilities of enslaved persons. In part 3, we offer a series of runaway slave advertisements that memorialize, however inadvertently, the resistance of black Africans seeking bodily autonomy. Finally, in part 4, we have gathered auto/biographical accounts of black Africans living and traveling throughout the Atlantic basin. By organizing these texts according to genre, we hope to help students recognize the recurring patterns through which black Africans entered and shaped the textual record of colonial British North America. That the black African writers and protagonists in these relations are often characterized as rebellious or criminal is a reminder of the systemic racism behind slave codes and other statutes that made it unlawful to be Black in the eighteenth century. Laurel Thatcher Ulrich famously observed that "well-behaved women seldom make history," and it is equally true that white colonists seldom allowed black Africans whom they considered well behaved into their narratives of life in the New World.[41] White colonists who controlled the publication process rarely demonstrated an interest in recording and publicizing the normative behaviors of black Africans, and grouping texts generically helps readers to see the social strictures within which black Africans lived and wrote in early America.

Reading generically also foregrounds the ways in which a genre's conventions and formulae influence the contours of its prose. To wit: the functions of a runaway slave advertisement are to help readers identify a specific human being as the property of another human being and to incentivize the participation of readers in returning that property to its owner. To those ends, they typically include the following features:

- First, a declaration that someone has escaped from bondage: "Ran-away from his master . . ." This formulaic opening is a generic code announcing the nature and purpose of the text.
- Second, a description of the body and clothing of an enslaved individual. These words provide identifying features by which the runaway might be recognized.
- Third, an acknowledgment of skills, knowledge, or past deeds that might influence the runaway's escape plans. An ability to write or past service as a merchant sailor might provide clues to the methods whereby a runaway plans to escape capture.
- Fourth and finally, a declaration as to how readers can contact the owner and what remuneration they might hope for in return for information about the runaway's whereabouts or the delivery of his body.

Readers might profitably examine any runaway advertisement by asking how it fulfills these expectations. But because these features of the genre are so consistent, deviations from this expected language, organization, and content imbue an advertisement with additional meaning that may not be obvious to readers unfamiliar with the form's conventions.

For example, this advertisement introduces variations on the form both suggesting a premeditated plan for escape and offering a reason to question the legitimacy of chattel slavery:

> Ran-away from his Master Rebert Rumsey at Fairfield in Connecticut Colony, on the 27th of March last, a Negro man call'd Jack, a tall thin fac'd Fellow, exceeding black, a considerable scarr in his face, can play on a Violin, he hath carried his Fiddle with him, and a considerable bundle of Cloaths. Whoever shall apprehend the said Runaway Negro man, and him safely Convey to his said Master, or give any true Intelligence of him, so as his Master may have him again, shall be sufficiently Rewarded, besides all necessary Charges paid.[42]

Because clothing was a form of wealth in the eighteenth-century world, most runaways only managed to escape with the shirt on their backs and the shoes on their feet; an advertisement's description of that clothing made it possible for readers to identify an escaped slave from a distance. But the man "call'd Jack" escaped with several changes of clothing, meaning that readers would be forced to identify him primarily by the scar on his face, from close range. With a variety of clothes, Jack could present himself as a servant of some upper-class household or a common laborer. His bundle of clothes represented both a disguise and, potentially, a bribe with which he might purchase passage on a vessel. Rumsey's inability to describe Jack's clothing marks a divergence from the generic expectations of a runaway slave advertisement, indicating that when Jack ran he did so with a plan and after significant preparation.

But the more extraordinary detail of this advertisement is its declaration that "he hath carried his Fiddle with him." Words documenting Jack's ability to play the fiddle are of a piece with other advertisements that describe enslaved individuals as carpenters, cooks, and coopers; knowledge of a runaway's skills might plausibly help readers guess where that runaway might seek refuge or employment. However, this advertisement concedes Jack's ownership of property, describing a fiddle that is "his." Such an admission undermines the core premise of an advertisement, that the runaway is property. To acknowledge the right of an enslaved person to property, such as a fiddle, is to acknowledge that this property does not belong to the supposed owner of that person and to grant the enslaved a right to withhold their time, body, or labor from such an owner; for this reason, the slave codes of various states generally included language forbidding the enslaved from inheriting or transmitting property.[43] Accordingly, runaway advertisements did not, as a rule, recognize that the enslaved owned any of the possessions with which they escaped, and in this text, a single possessive pronoun threatens to disrupt the genre.[44]

The will of Black Peter, which is included in *The Earliest African American Literatures*, similarly challenges the fundamental premises of slavery. The white witnesses to Peter's will acknowledged Peter's claim to property, just as Rebert Rumsey acknowledged Jack's ownership of a fiddle. In this case, Peter's stipulation that funds should be disbursed to the individuals he names is a predictable and normal part of any document disposing of an estate, and yet his adherence to the conventions of a last will and testament works to undermine the genre's foundational premise, that one man's right to property can be clearly defined and transmitted. Only through a careful attention to the customary forms of the various genres in which literary black Africans make an appearance is the extraordinary nature of these texts manifest. For these texts, more than most, generic codes and conventions are key to their interpretation.

Appreciating the full import of these accounts likewise depends on locating each within a particular historical context. For example, the confessions of literary black Africans accused of plotting to burn New York in 1741 document the motives of several men charged with setting the city ablaze, who alleged that they undertook this act of war with an expectation that military aid would be forthcoming from France or Spain. In 1741, England was embroiled in the War of Jenkins' Ear, which was fought between England and Spain over the right of British traders to sell enslaved people and merchandise in American ports, and for years it was rumored that France would join this conflict as an ally of Spain.[45] For this reason, "Spanish negroes," or Africans enslaved in Caribbean and American colonies administered by Spain, were automatically suspect in New York and other British colonies and considered potential spies. Thus, when an enslaved man known as Bastian or Tom Peal heard of their involvement in the plot, he assumed "that war would be proclaimed in a little time against the French, and that the French and Spaniards would come here, and that they (meaning the negroes present and the Hughsons) would join with them to take the place." Absent a knowledge of this war, it might be difficult for readers to imagine why the alleged conspirators would have thought French and Spanish forces would soon arrive or why the arsonists thought they could successfully overthrow the city and hold it against British forces. Looking to France and Spain as potential allies, the enslaved envisioned themselves as geopolitical power brokers and planned to convert their vulnerable status into a position of strength from which they could bargain for their freedom. The confessions of Bastian and others suggest that arson was not, primarily, a response to the cruelties of individual enslavers but a calculated bet on international affairs largely taking place outside the text.

In order to help readers appreciate both the historical context within which these confessions and other texts were produced and the generic conventions against which they might be read, we provide a brief introduction to each text and suggestions for further reading.[46] These introductions draw attention to the distinguishing features of the various accounts and model strategies for considering the lives of the literary black Africans they feature. As Lisa Lindsay and John Sweet have observed, the life stories of these individuals often "serve as a corrective to some of the more generalizing tendencies of cultural and demographic history," and attention to the peculiarities of the texts in this anthology will demonstrate the need to rethink truisms about slavery and the black African experience in colonial North America more broadly.[47] Some of the literary black Africans featured in these texts escaped south, inverting the moral geography typically associated with slavery. Others ran away with their owners, in a joint escape attempt, or fled with white companions, demonstrating that a shared experience of unfreedom sometimes mattered more than a shared racial or national identity. Still others, born free, sought to gain social visibility through methods such as religious conversion and entrepreneurship, and in doing so, they created textual traces. Each provides a reason to reconsider long-standing assumptions about the origins, extents, and conventions of African American literature. Each offers a reason to rethink the significance of mediation, authorship, and the archive as terms that shape our engagement with these texts.[48]

Origins and Transitions in Early African American Literature

The literary black Africans highlighted in this reader mostly have left behind mediated and truncated textual footprints. It might be tempting to consider them outliers or deem them a vanguard that *anticipates* the more recognizably literary efforts of those black Africans in the latter eighteenth century who more typically begin the canon of early African American literature. More than a vanguard, literary black Africans, we argue, are part and parcel of early African American literature. That is to say, the study of these literary black Africans is the study of early African American literature. The mid-eighteenth century might mark a point of departure, but it is not a point of origin for early African American literature. It is important, for example, to acknowledge the significance of Briton Hammon's captivity narrative as an early illustration of self-making for black Africans in colonial Massachusetts. The narrative's genre-bending qualities and its configuration of a Black body at the center of a Puritan captivity experience mark its exceptionalism. As an early form of Black life writing, though, the narrative echoes the efforts of Ayuba Suleiman Diallo, who told his own story of enslavement and restoration to Thomas Bluett, a sympathetic, white amanuensis. In 1730, Diallo was kidnapped by slave traders along the Gambia River and forced across the Atlantic, where he was sold into slavery on a Maryland plantation. Due to a series of serendipitous events, mostly resulting from the fact that he was literate and a devout Muslim, Diallo navigated his way from Maryland to London and back to his home in present-day Senegal within the span of about three years. In 1734, Bluett published his memoir. Like Hammon, Diallo appreciated the power of narrative to shape identity. We include his narrative as the final text in this anthology. Examining Hammon within the context of Diallo and the other literary black Africans that compose part 4 of this anthology can illuminate the evolutionary nature of a Black life writing tradition from the beginning of the eighteenth century to 1760.

A focus on literary black Africans offers a more nuanced approach to early African American literature. To amplify this point with another example, consider Lucy Terry Prince. Scholars of early (African) American literature mostly agree that Prince is the earliest known Black writer—writing in English—in what would become the United States. As a small girl, she was kidnapped from her home somewhere in Africa and sold into slavery, arriving at a port in Rhode Island around 1730. Subsequently, she was sold to an enslaver in Deerfield, Massachusetts. In 1744 she joined the congregation of that enslaver's church in Deerfield. Some twelve years later she married a formerly enslaved man named Abijah Prince and soon after gained her freedom. Among her neighbors, Prince enjoyed a reputation for piety and good character. For sure, Prince was a beneficiary of the First Great Awakening, a period of intense religious revival in the British American colonies between 1730 and 1770. The Great Awakening was particularly consequential for black Africans, as it advocated a more egalitarian approach to religion and spiritual authority, allowing even socially marginalized groups to publicly testify about their salvation and exhort. The acquisition of literacy also allowed Prince to conceive the sole literary work we ascribe to her, a broadside ballad titled "Bars Fight," which she composed in 1746 though it was not published until a century later. The ballad recounts an attack by Abenaki on two white families living in Deerfield, Massachusetts. It memorializes the slain members of those families, calling them by name and portraying as heroic and noble the manner in which they died:

Bars Fight

August, 'twas the twenty-fifth,
Seventeen houndred forty-six,
The Indians did in ambush lay,
Some very valiant men to slay.
'Twas nigh unto Sam Dickinson's mill,
The Indians there five men did kill.
The names of whom I'll not leave out,
Samuel Allen like a hero foute,
And though he was so brave and bold,
His face no more shall we behold.
Eleazer Hawks was killed outright,

Before he had time to fight,
Before he did the Indians see,
Was shot and killed immediately.
Oliver Amsden he was slain,
Which caused his friends much grief pain.
Simeon Amsden they found dead
Not many rods from Oliver's head.
Adonijah Gillett, we do hear,
Did lose his life which was so dear,
John Sadler fled across the water,
And thus escaped the dreadful slaughter.
Eunice Allen see the Indians comeing
And hoped to save herself by running;
And had not her petticoats stopt her,
The awful creatures had not cotched her,
Nor tommyhawked her on the head,
And left her on the ground for dead.
Young Samuel Allen, Oh! lack-a-day!
Was taken and carried to Canada.

The ballad is notable as a historical document because it is the only surviving contemporary account of the attack. In that way, Prince records her community's history. As a work of literature, it reflects the popular eighteenth-century genre of the prose Indian captivity narrative. These narratives were the often harrowing accounts of (mostly) white, Puritan New Englanders captured by Natives, then restored to their communities through some act of divine providence. Many of those narratives, including that of Briton Hammon, begin by describing an attack like the one in Deerfield. The narratives and Prince's ballad recount gruesome captivity stories and perpetuate racialized images of Natives, here the Abenaki in particular, as brutal savages. Importantly, Prince employs her ballad as an integrationist tool.[49] That is to say that through her poetic effort, she does not emphasize her own racial or cultural difference; instead the ballad unites Prince with her Deerfield neighbors in a communal suffering and memorialization. We could—in fact we do—recognize Prince as a Black literary *first*. This designation sheds light on early Black authorship, telling us how, when, and under what circumstances black Africans started writing in early America.

We deepen considerations of Prince's literary significance, though, when we consider her within the context of those literary black Africans who decades earlier employed integrationist strategies of their own. In part 1 of this reader, for instance, we present the ever-so-brief spiritual narratives of several literary black Africans, including a "Blackmore maid," who converts to Christianity and then proselytizes Natives in seventeenth-century Massachusetts. A Puritan missionary narrates her story in a pamphlet designed to raise funds for further missionary work in Native communities and for the development of what was then Harvard College. The Blackmore maid's spiritual testimony so moved her neighbors that she was "admitted a member" of the church in Dorchester and became one of its most faithful congregants. Her piety all but subsumes her racial difference, enabling her integration into the local community. Her successful conversion compels the anonymous writer of the pamphlet, titled "New England's First Fruits," to include her story. She is the only literary black African presence in the text. The other texts in part 1 of this anthology reflect a similar integrationist theme, an impulse to belong. The black Africans they feature assimilate to navigate oppression and improve social standing. The point here is that the rhetorical, imaginative moves Prince makes in her ballad by deemphasizing her racial difference are part of a longer literary tradition. Black Africans, like the Blackmore maid mentioned above, worked to incorporate themselves into colonial American spaces; their efforts resulted in textual presences that helped to shape the literary record. From the Blackmore maid to Prince, an integrationist theme runs through early African American literature; that theme also appears later in the captivity narrative of Hammon, the poetry of Phillis Wheatley Peters, the poetry and speeches of Jupiter Hammon, and the life writing of Equiano and John Marrant, to identify a few examples. Within the context of the literary black Africans highlighted in this anthology, Prince and other early black African writers extend rather than begin African American literature and transform it by donning the mantle of authorship.

The earliest literary traces of black Africans can tell us a great deal about the compulsions and impulses that shaped the constructions of texts both about and by people of African descent living in early America. Granted, these figures and texts present especially complex questions about Black consciousness and subjectivity and how we define an *African American* literature. Those complexities demand different critical apparatuses and approaches to concepts like authorship, mediation, and archive, as we have explained in this introduction, in order to move beyond the critical impasse that has led us to overlook these early figures and texts. In doing so, we can appreciate more fully the earliest African American literatures.

Part I
Spiritual Accounts

Spiritual conversion and Indian captivity narratives were two of the earliest genres to emerge in British North America, initiated by the spiritual fervor of the Puritans, then transformed by those Protestant denominations that appeared amid the First Great Awakening in the early eighteenth century. It makes sense, then, that some of the earliest African American literatures would come in these generic forms. In this first part of *The Earliest African American Literatures*, we highlight literary black Africans in a range of spiritual contexts that stretch the generic borders of the captivity and conversion narratives. They appear in these spiritual accounts as criminals, converts, and saviors. They proselytize, supplicate, censure, repent, condemn slavery, and, in one case, negotiate for improved living conditions. Several are as-told-to narratives that position black African lives as front and center in the texts.

Often, black Africans understood religious assimilation, specifically, conversion to Christianity, as a route to better treatment; for those enslaved, conversion held out the possibility for freedom based on common-law practice that discouraged the enslavement of Christians. In his 1789 autobiography *The Interesting Narrative*, Olaudah Equiano alludes to this common law in his attempts to thwart one enslaver's efforts to sell him; he declares, "I have been baptized; and by the laws of the land no man has a right to sell me."[1] Sold shortly after making that declaration, Equiano discovered what his black African predecessors featured in this reader discovered decades earlier. Christian conversion did not immunize black Africans from racial oppression. The texts included here illustrate black African efforts to integrate, to model the virtues and customs of the predominately Anglo-American communities in which they found themselves. In some cases, their efforts strained the pre-Enlightenment conceptions of race that located human difference in cultural markers like language, religion, and behavior. For example, a group of mixed-race men and women enslaved on a plantation in Virginia in 1723 appealed to the Anglican Church in London to emancipate them. They complained that their enslavement prohibited them from exercising good Christian values. In the effort to distance themselves from the Blackness that justified their enslavement, they argued that they were just as much white as Black, the brothers and sisters of those enslavers who held them in bondage. By emphasizing their faith, they also made claims about their commonality with their brothers and sisters in Christ. Their petition is included in this part, along with several other texts that employ a similar rhetorical strategy of racial elision. Presumably, living life as a good Christian could render one less "black." Religion was one way early black Americans navigated enslavement and other forms of racism. Their efforts created a literary footprint.

CHAPTER ONE

Conversion Narrative of a Blackmore Maid, 1643

Introduction

"New England's First Fruits" is the first in a collection of seventeenth-century missionary writings known as the *Eliot Tracts*, named after the Puritan minister and teacher John Eliot. The tracts are a series of eleven texts, written between 1643 and 1675, that detail the efforts of Puritan missionaries to convert Native populations, mainly in the Massachusetts Bay Colony. A key feature of the tracts are the transcriptions—in the form of summaries, paraphrases, and quoted speech—of the conversion testimonies that Natives presented orally before church officials as proof of their conversion to Christianity. Those narratives have become rich source material for scholars of early American and Native American studies, who argue that even though the conversion narratives in the tracts are heavily mediated by English writers, they offer some of the earliest representations of Native agency in early American literature. Although the *Tracts* largely focus on the interactions between colonists and Natives, this first tract represents a black African woman convert living in Dorchester, Massachusetts. She is the only black African described in the text, which implies that her piety garnered her a measure of esteem among her white, Puritan counterparts. Rhetorically, her narrative seems anomalous, an odd digression. In the seventeenth century, American Puritans debated whether black Africans had souls and whether they could be converted. Therefore, with the inclusion of this woman's testimony, the scope, the rhetorical aims of the entire tract expand, leading to questions about how black Africans fit into the colony's larger missionary efforts. The moment also offers another perspective on black African agency and the experiences of black African women in colonial Massachusetts.

Text

From "New England's First Fruits" (1643). In *The Eliot Tracts: With Letters from John Eliot to Thomas Thorowgood and Richard Baxter*, edited by Michael P. Clark, 55–78. Westport, CT: Praeger, 2003.

> There is also a Blackmore maid, that hath long lived at *Dorchester* in *New-England*, unto whom God hath so blessed the publique and private means of Grace, that she is not only indued with a competent measure of knowledge in the mysteries of God, and conviction of her miserable estate by sinne; but hath also experience of the saving work of grace in her heart, and a sweet savour of Christ breathing in her; insomuch that her soule hath longed to enjoy Church fellowship with the Saints there, and having propounded her desire to the Elders of the Church after some triall of her taken in private, she was called before the whole Church, and there did make confession of her knowledge in the Mysteries of Christ and of the work of Conversion upon her Soule: And after that there was such a testimony given of her blamelesse and godly Conversation, that she was admitted a member by the joynt consent of the Church, with great joy to all their hearts. Since which time, we have heard her much admiring Gods free grace to such a poore wretch as she was; that God leaving all her friends and Kindred still in their sinnes, should cast an eye upon her, to make her a member of Christ, and of his Church also: and hath with teares exhorted some other of the *Indians* that live with us to embrace *Iefus Chrijl*, declaring how willing he would be to receive them, even as he had received her.

Suggested Reading

Bassard, Katherine Clay. *Spiritual Interrogations: Culture, Gender, and Community in Early African American Women's Writing*. Princeton, NJ: Princeton University Press, 1999.

Bellin, Joshua. "John Eliot's Playing Indian." *Early American Literature* 42, no. 1 (2007): 1–30.

Caldwell, Patricia. *The Puritan Conversion Narrative*. Cambridge: Cambridge University Press, 1985.

Gray, Kathryn N. "Christian Indian Women in Seventeenth-Century New England." In *John Eliot and the Praying Indians of Massachusetts Bay: Communities and Connections in Puritan New England*, 89–120. Lewisburg, PA: Bucknell University Press, 2013.

Hartman, Saidiya. "Venus in Two Acts." *Small Axe* 12, no. 2 (June 2008): 1–14.

Peterson, Carla. *Doers of the Word: African-American Women Speakers and Writers in the North (1830–1880)*. New Brunswick, NJ: Rutgers University Press, 1995.

Smith, Cassander L. "Race." In *A History of American Puritan Literature*, edited by Kristina Bross and Abram Van Engen, 211–24. Cambridge: Cambridge University Press, 2020.

CHAPTER TWO

Narrative of Ben, a Negro, 1699

Introduction

Jonathan Dickinson was a seventeenth-century Quaker and sea merchant from Philadelphia. In 1696, he was returning from a voyage to Jamaica when his ship wrecked off the coast of Florida. He, his wife and infant son, a score of sailors and other passengers, ten enslaved black Africans, and a Native girl were taken captive by Ais along the South Florida coast. In 1699, he published the journal he had kept during the ordeal. Of particular interest to readers and scholars of Dickinson's journal are his descriptions of the Ais and other Native groups as animal-like, his fear of acculturation as a result of captivity, his use of religious rhetoric, and the cultural exchange between the (mostly) English colonists and the Natives. Throughout this text, Dickinson represents the enslaved black Africans as submissive, dutiful. He references them as a collective, anonymous body that works at the margins of the text. In addition, he portrays them as objects of commercial exchange between Ais caciques and himself. Some moments in the narrative, though, contradict that representational pattern. At times, Dickinson finds himself negotiating with enslaved black Africans much as he does with the Ais—and eventually the Spanish—on his way north to St. Augustine. At one point in the narrative, he portrays the actions of an enslaved man named Ben, listed on the title page as the property of the ship's captain. As members of the shipwrecked party make their escape and flee up the coast toward St. Augustine, Ben endeavors to save one of Dickinson's relatives who has fallen behind, but he does so only after Dickinson bribes him with undisclosed enticements. The excerpt below describes their exchange. On the face of it, the moment appears rather insignificant. Dickinson mentions it without reflection or additional commentary. It would seem that Ben simply fulfills the expected roles of submission and service. The passage is remarkable, though, because it suggests the level of autonomy and self-possession that Ben experienced during their mutual captivity ordeal. The moment is a reminder that black Africans were not merely objects but active agents in building the multicultural networks that characterized Dickinson's captivity experience and his narrative.

Text

From Jonathan Dickinson, *God's Protecting Providence Man's Surest Help and Defence in the times of the greatest difficulty and most Imminent danger Evidenced in the Remarkable Deliverance of divers Persons, from the devouring Waves of the Sea, amongst which they Suffered Shipwreck*. Philadelphia, 1699. Early English Books Online Text Creation Partnership, 2011, accessed March 03, 2020, http://name.umdl.umich.edu/N05268.0001.001.

The 13th of the 9th Month; the 6th of the Week

> T[his] Morning we were loth to part with our Fires, but to stay here it could not be; so we went to our Boats, wading in the Water, till it was ready to b[e]num us: But we put forward, and rowing about 2 Leagues, came to an old House, where the *Spaniard* told us, we must leave the Boats, and Travel by Land; we had a Boggy Marsh to wade through for a Mile, to get to the Sea-Shore, and had about five or six Leagues, along the Bay or Strand, to the *Spanish* Sentinal's House: The *North-West-Wind* was violent, and the Cold such, that the strongest of us thought we should not out-live that Day. Having got through the Boggy Marsh, and on the Sea-Shore, our People, Black and White, made all Speed, one not staying for another that could not Travel so fast: none but I, with my Wife and Child, *Robert Barrow*, my Kinsman *Benjamin Allen*, and my Negro *London*, whom I kept to help carry my Child, keeping together; the rest of our Company had left us, not expecting to see some of us again; especially *Robert Barrow*, my Wife and Child. We travelled after as well as we could, having gone about two Miles, the Cold so seized on my Kinsman, *Benjamin Allen*, that he began to be st[i]ff in his Limbs, and staggered and fell, grieviously complaining that the Cold would kill him: Our Negro having our young Child, I and my Wife took our Kinsman under each Arm, and helped him along; but at length his Limbs were quite stiff, his Speech almost gone, and he began to Foam at the Mouth: In this strait we knew not what to do; to stay with him we must perish also, and we were willing to strive as long as we could. We carried our Kinsman, and laid him under the Bank, not being Dead; I resolved to run after our People, some of them not being out of Sight; which I did, and left my Wife and Child, with the Negro, to follow as fast as they could. I run about two Miles, making signs to them, thinking if they should look

behind them, and see me running, they would stop till I got up with them. I was in hopes, if I could have accomplished this my design, to have got help to have carried my Kinsman along; but they stopp'd not, and I ran until the Wind pierced me, so that my Limbs failed, and I fell; yet still I strove and getting up, walked backwards to meet my Wife; as I was going, I met with the *Spaniard* coming out of the Sand-Hills, and *Joseph Kirle's Negro Ben*. I made my Complaint to the *Spaniard*, but he not being able to understand me well, went forward. I then apply'd my self to the Negro, making large Promises, if he would fetch my Kinsman; he offered to go back, and used his endeavour, which he did. At length my *Wife* and *Child* came up with me, she was almost overcome with Grief, expressing in what Manner we were forced to part with our Kinsman; and expecting that she and the Child should go next.

. . . When we got to the House, we found four Sentinals, and the *Spaniard* our Guide, with three of our Men, viz. *Joseph Buckley, Nathaniel Randal,* and *John Shires*. The *Spaniards* bid us welcome, and made Room for us to sit down by the Fire. The chiefest Man of the Sentinals took a *Kersey-Coat* and gave my Wife to cover her, and gave each of us a piece of Bread, made of *Indian-Corn*, which was pleasant unto us; after it we had plenty of hot *Cas|seena-Drink*. It was dark, and we endeavoured to prevail with the *Spaniards* to go seek for *Robert Barrow* and my Kinsman, offering them considerable; but they seemed not fully to understand me, yet I could make them sensible, that my *Kinsman* was almost dead, if not quite; and that the *Old Man* was in a bad Condition. They made me to understand, that the Weather was not fit to go out, but they would watch if *Robert* would pass by. About an Hour or two after, one of the *Spaniards* being walking out on the Bay, met with *Robert*, and brought him into the House: We rejoiced to see him, and enquired concerning our *Kinsman* and Negro Ben. He said, our *Kinsman* was striving to get up, and could not; he came to him, and spake unto him; he could not answer, but cry'd, and he could not help him. But coming along, at some considerable distance, met Negro *Ben*, who said he was going for *Benjamin Allen*, so he past him.

The 16th of the 9th. Month; the 2d of the Week

This Day came *Joseph Kirle's* Negro Ben, he gave us this Account, That after we had sent him back, he having looked, and not finding my

Kinsman, went to seek for a place to shelter himself from the Cold, and some place he found to creep in, where he lay down, and continued there all Night, but by Morning, was so stiff with Cold that he could not use his Legs, but halled himself towards the Bay. The *Spaniard*, our Guide, from the first Sentry-house, the Morning after we went thence, returned along the Bay, to see if any of our People were living; but he found all dead, except Negro *Ben*. And he getting a Fire made, Negro *Ben* was recovered, and got the use of his Limbs.

Suggested Reading

Berlin, Ira. *Generations of Captivity: A History of African American Slaves*. Cambridge, MA: Belknap Press, 2003.

Bushnell, Amy Turner. "Escape of the Nickaleers: European-Indian Relations on the Wild Coast of Florida in 1696 from Jonathan Dickinson's Journal." In *Coastal Encounters: The Transformation of the Gulf South in the Eighteenth Century*, edited by Richmond Brown, 31–58. Lincoln: University of Nebraska Press, 2007.

Gikandi, Simon. "Rethinking the Archive of Enslavement." *Early American Literature* 50, no. 1 (2015): 81–102.

Landers, Jane. *Black Society in Spanish Florida*. Champaign: University of Illinois Press, 1999.

Strong, Pauline Turner. "Captive Ethnographers, 1699–1736." In *Captive Selves, Captivating Others: The Politics and Poetics of Colonial American Captivity Narratives*, 151–76. Boulder, CO: Westview, 1999.

CHAPTER THREE

Execution of Joseph Hanno, a "Miserable African," 1721

Introduction

The "miserable African" referenced in the title of this Puritan sermon was Joseph Hanno, who arrived in New England as a servant in the latter half of the seventeenth century. His owners taught him to read, a skill he employed to master and then publicly pronounce biblical scripture. At some point he was freed and married a free black African woman named Nanny Negro. By Hanno's account, the two endured a tumultuous marriage that ended in early 1721 when Hanno murdered her. After beating her with an axe handle, he cut her throat with a razor. Hanno initially claimed that his wife committed suicide but later confessed to the gruesome deed. He was convicted and sentenced to death by hanging, which was carried out on 25 May 1721. Executions in colonial New England—as elsewhere—were public spectacles, and Puritan ministers often preached "execution" sermons in anticipation of the event. The sermons were delivered as spiritual warnings to listeners and upheld the convicts as moral cautionary tales. The sermons also exhorted those convicted to repent and express remorse for their crimes. Cotton Mather delivered the execution sermon for Hanno; he also conversed with Hanno in jail one day earlier. He added the content of their conversation as an appendix to the sermon and published both in Boston just after the execution. Their conversation, included in its entirety below, is an interesting display of mediation and collaborative tension. Mather endeavors to extract contrition from Hanno. Hanno vacillates between defending his actions—as the deed of a frustrated husband fending off a *nagging* wife—and mimicking religious rhetoric. Mather's efforts to advocate for the spiritual salvation of black Africans in the colony complicate his interest in Hanno's repentance. In 1706, Mather published a treatise, "The Negro Christianized," urging enslavers to baptize those they enslaved. In it, he refutes the idea, popular among white colonists, that black Africans did not have souls and could not be saved. He promotes a kind of universal salvation—or the idea that the elect could appear in any human group. Hanno's lack of contrition undermines Mather's efforts; Mather's contemporaries could all too easily stereotype Hanno's perceived reprobate attitude as a general feature of a depraved nature in black Africans. To counter that kind of reading, Mather represents Hanno's actions and attitude as exceptionally cruel and sets him against the general population of black Africans.

Text

From Cotton Mather, *Tremenda. The dreadful sound with which the wicked are to be thunderstruck*. Boston, 1721, Evans: Early American Imprints, accessed May 18, 2009, http://infoweb.newsbank.com/.

The Sum of a Conference Between a Minister and the Prisoner, the Day Before His Execution

> MIN: THE Report of your sad Condition, *Joseph*, has brought me to Visit you, and Advise you. I know not how better to Express an Obedience and Conformity to the Glorious CHRIST, who came down *to Seek and to Save that which was Lost*, and who had a wonderful Compassion on us, when we were *Shut up* in Sin, *and Unbelief*. That which yet more Encourages me, is the Encouragement which I have to bring unto *you*; That is, That this Glorious CHRIST is a SAVIOUR, whom *Negro*'s themselves, yea, the *worst of Sinners* among those poor *Black Outcasts*, may be welcome to. *Ethiopians* will be found by His Grace, in His fulfilling that word; *He shall Sprinkle many Nations*.
>
> JOSEPH HANNO: *I thank you, Sir, I'm glad to see you, Sir.*
>
> MIN: In a very singular manner may I now tell you; not only, *That your Days are determined*, but also, That you now do your self Know, which is *determined* for the *Last of your Days*; yea, and how many *Hours* you have now to Live; and how few times the Clock is to Strike, before your *Lamp is to be put out*, and you must appear before *GOD the Judge of all*, and [*Except a Sincere and Serious Repentance prevent it!*] you will *fall into Hands which it is a fearful thing to fall into*.
>
> JOS: *I cast my self on the Mercies of GOD.*
>
> MIN: My Endeavours must be, that you may do it *Hopefully*, and not Perish in the Errors and Follies of a *Deceived Heart*, but have an *Hope which will not make ashamed*. You have been many Months in the Prison; I pray, how have you spent your Time hitherto? I hope, they have not all been *Months of Vanity*.
>
> JOS: *In Reading and Praying, Sir.*

MIN: In *Reading*!—Of what, I pray? I know that within these few Dayes, a Gentleman, who heard you had no *Bible* with you, sent a *Bible* to you. You lived many Months without Reading a word in that most Necessary Book, *The Bible*. It has, I must plainly tell you, a very uncomfortable Aspect on you; it looks very strangely, very oddly, how you could Live quietly so long, and have no *Bible* with you.

JOS: *I had no Bible; and I knew not where to get one.*

MIN: *Not where to get one*! There are more than twice five hundred Christians in the Town; that would have helped you to a *Bible*, if you had asked for it.

KEEPER: And, *Joseph*, I would have helped you to one at the first word, if you had asked for it.

MIN: Your Neglect of the *Holy Scriptures* at such a Time; and this after you have been a Great pretender to the *Reading* of them, and were always vain gloriously *Quoting* of Sentences from them wherever you came,—It looks very Suspiciously. It confirms my Fear of a Reigning *Hypocrisy*, under all the Noisy Profession of Religion you have made among us. I am also afraid, That you have spent your Time ill; under the Delusions of some wicked People, who did perswade you, that you would never be convicted of the *Murder* you are now to dy for; because, forsooth, there were no *Eye-Witnesses* of your doing it. For these causes, I must now, be the more Earnest and Thorough with you. Give me your best Attention, as One within a Few Hours of an awful Eternity!

JOS: *Yes, Sir.*

MIN: You are now to Dy; the Land where you now Live, would be polluted, if you should be spared from *Death*;— for an horrible *Murder*. The *Murder* of any Person, is a Crime, which forfeits the Life of him that commits it. And, you know very well, That *no Murderer has Eternal Life*. But the *Murder* that you have been guilty of, is a very *Uncommon* One; One so *Barbarous* as rarely to be Known among the Children of Men. To *Murder* ones *Wife*! How Inhumane! How Hideous! How Monstrous the Wickedness! To *Murder*, where the *greatest Love*, that is possible, is called for!— I know, you have gone to Extenuate your Crime, with grievous Accounts, of the Base Humour and Vile Carriage' in her that should have been a *Wife* unto you. And I do believe, She was a very *Insupportable Wretch*. But GOD call'd you to Patience, and Meekness, and Goodness; and all possible Trials to *overcome Evil with Good*,—Not, to Knock her o' th' Head!

JOS: *Truly, Sir, I have a great deal to say of That; But I have done with it. I shall say no more. The Sixth Commandment is,* Thou shalt not Kill. *And I have* [wringing his hands;] *broken this Commandment of GOD.*

MIN: How did you proceed in it? How long was you purposing and projecting of it?

JOS: *Never till she told me, that she had as liev talk with the Devil, as talk with any of GODS Ministers. This was, but a little before I did the Fact. At last the Devil putting it into my Heart, in the Night, I took my Ax, and with the Head of it, I knock'd her down; and that she might not recover, I gave her the second Blow. After this, I put her to Bed, and hackled her Throat with a Razour: So I left her, and went and call'd the Neighbours; and told them, I was afraid of my Wifes making away with her self. But GOD has now brought me out.*

MIN: 'Tis time for you, not only to be sensible of this horrid Crime, and the *Cry of Blood* in the Ears of Heaven against you: But also to come into some Sense of all your other Sins. You have broken all the *Commandments* of GOD. You must now Examine your self by what your *Catechism* tells you, is *Forbiden* and *Required* in the *Commandments*. And *Judge* and *Loath* your self, in the view of what you have done; so many Thousands of Times, *Denying the GOD that is Above*, and *Henrkening* to the *Devil* more than to GOD, and Exposing your self to all the *Evil* that *Pursueth Sinners*. Yea, procuring of *Plagues* upon all about you. But then, be sure to lay to Heart, the *Fountain of all Sin* in the *Heart* that you brought into the World with you; an *Heart* that is *desperately Wicked*, and the *Mother of Abominations*. What must you think, that you deserve at the Hands of the Glorious GOD, whom you have so affronted and offended?

JOS: *Be sure, I deserve to dy. I deserve all that the Word of GOD has told me, is the Wages of Sin.*

MIN: Are you sensible of this; That unless you Turn and Live to GOD, it had been *Good for you that you had never been born*?

JOS: *Yes, I am, Sir.*

MIN: But can you of *Your self* Turn & Live unto GOD?

JOS: *I will do my Endeavour.*

MIN: But except there be more than your own *Endeavour* for it, it will not be done. Except GOD give you the Help of His Grace; and *Quicken* you, it will never be done.

JOS: *I say so, Sir.*

MIN: But are you not *Unworthy* that GOD should *Quicken* you?

JOS: *I cast my self on His Mercy.*

MIN: But you must see, That He may *Justly* withold the *Help* of His *Grace* from you. Tho' if you seek to Him for it; there is *Hope*, and it is a *Sign*, that He will grant it.

JOS: *Yes, Sir, I know it.*

MIN: But the first thing you have now to look after is, That your *Sin* may be all pardoned; and that GOD may be Reconciled unto you. Look you; *Sin* must be punished. You have *Sinn'd*, and the *Punishment* of your Sin is unavoidable. The *Law* of GOD has assigned a *Punishment* for it, which there is no avoiding of. The *Punishment* has those Miseries in it, which cannot without Horror be thought upon. You must either undergo this *Punishment* your self, and the *Smoke of your Torment* under it *ascending for ever and ever*: Or else you must find One to undergo the *Punishment* for you; One to be such a *Sacrifice* for you, as GOD shall be *well-pleased* withal; the Infinite *Justice* of GOD Satisfied withal. Can you tell where to find such an One?

JOS: *I fly to the Mercy of GOD.*

MIN: But I tell you, the Infinite *Justice* of GOD must be Satisfied; or else, *He that made you will not have Mercy on you*. Are you willing Your self to suffer the *Punishment* of your *Sin*?

JOS: *I am willing to Dy.*

MIN: What? The *Second Death*! Willing to be Banished from GOD, United with Devils, Tortured with all the Rage of a Guilty Conscience; Thrown down into a *Devouring [F]ire and Everlasting Burnings! Can thy Heart Endure, when I shall deal with thee, saith the Lord?*

JOS: *I fly to the Lord JESUS CHRIST.*

MIN: Ay, Now you say Something. This is the *Only Flight* for a Perishing Soul Fall down before the Blessed GOD; and Humbly tell Him, *That you beg to have your Sins all Pardoned, because a Glorious CHRIST has been Punished for the Sins of all His People.* The Sacrifice Offered by a Glorious CHRIST, unto the *Justice* of GOD, when GOD *laid on Him the Iniquity of us all*, has been of more Account unto Him, than if a Thousand Worlds had been made an Entire *Burnt-Offering*. He is GOD as well as Man, who has been the *Sacrifice* for our Sin, and Suffered in our Stead. And GOD allows the Benefit of the *Sacrifice*, to the Sinner, that comes, and pleads it, and admires it, and values it, and relies upon it.

JOS: *Lord, Pardon me, for the sake of Jesus Christ.*

MIN: But it is not enough, that you be *Pardoned*; You must be *Righteous* too. Else you cannot Look for the *Blessedness of the Righteous*. Now you have no *Righteousness* of your own. You have broke the Law of GOD numberless times. Nor can you now keep it. The Best of your Devotions and Services, will be defective Things; Blemished Things: There will be *Iniquities* in your most *Holy Things*: Your very *Tears*, whereof you have so many, want Washing. In your best *Repentance*, there will be that which will be to be Repented of. But now, a Glorious CHRIST coming as the *Head* of His People, He did for them *Fulfil all Righteousness*; He had a most *Holy Heart*; He led a most *Holy Life*. Such was His *Righteousness*, that the *Pure Eyes* of the Infinite GOD, could never tax any thing *amiss* in it; could never see any elsewhere that *Equall'd* it. Now, you must Renounce all Dependence on any *Righteousness* of your own; and Entreat of GOD, that He will deal with you as *Righteous*, because of what His JESUS has been and has done, on the behalf of His People. Yea, Entertain a *Comfortable Perswasion*, that He will do so. Do you understand what I say to you?

JOS: *Yes, Sir, I have a Great deal of Knowledge. No body of my Colour, in Old England or New, has so much.*

MIN: I wish you were less *Puffed up* with it. But the more you *Know*, the more your Sins are aggravated. The Sins of your more Ignorant Country-men, have not such Aggravations as yours.—But the Point I have been upon, must be further prosecuted. The *Sacrifice* and *Righteousness* of your SAVIOUR; you will hope for the Benefit of it. But, how dare such a *Sinner* as you are, One so horribly Criminal, hope for such a Thing? What have you to Embolden your *Hope*?

JOS: *I find my self to be more as GOD would have me to be; my Heart is broken.*

MIN: Now, This is to Spoil all! *Sinse, Man*, Thou must come and hope for the Benefit of the *Sacrifice* and *Righteousness* provide for thee in thy SAVIOUR, under no Recommendation but This; *Lord, I am a Perishing Sinner. I want a CHRIST, and I am undone if the Sacrifice and Righteousness of a CHRIST be not allow'd unto me.* Emboldned by nothing but the Grace of GOD, which makes the Tender to thee; Qualified with nothing but most wretched Circumstances. Come, as a Filthy Sinner, adoring the *Free-Grace*, the *Rich Grace*, which will make this Allowance unto the *Chief of Sinners*.

JOS: *I am a Sinner. And I deserve to Dy.*

MIN: But now, if your *Faith* in the *Sacrifice* and the *Righteousness* of your SAVIOUR, be not the *Hope of the Hypocrite*, you will find this precious Effect of it. The *Blood* of your SAVIOUR being *Sprinkled* on your Soul, will run warm in the Veins of your Soul, and make you Wish, and Long, and Groan to be *Like Him*, and be *all that He would have you to be*. You will Detest the Sins, which are *Forgiven* you; and abhor to *Repeat* them. You will study to be *Holy in all manner of Conversation*. You will be filled with the *Love* of GOD; and aim at Serving and Pleasing of GOD as the *Chief End* of all; and you will have your *Will* to be Swallowed up in the Will of GOD; and give up your *All* unto Him.

JOS: *I desire your Prayers for me.*

MIN: But, what may be the more *Special sins*, which you may apprehend, have provoked the Holy One, to leave you unto what you are now come unto?

JOS: *I can't say. For all my Sins.*

MIN: But you are now *Troubled* for your Sins. Which of all your Sins, gives *most of Trouble* to you?

JOS: *All my Sins.*

MIN: I wish you had Glorified GOD, by being more *Particular* in confessing what might be for His Glory—. But, Is there any more that I may do for you?

JOS: *No, Sir; I can desire no more.*

FINIS

Suggested Reading

Schorb, Jodi. *Reading Prisoners: Literature, Literacy, and the Transformation of American Punishment, 1700–1845*. New Brunswick, NJ: Rutgers University Press, 2014.

Slotkin, Richard. "Narratives of Negro Crime in New England, 1675–1800." *American Quarterly* 25, no. 1 (March 1973): 3–31.

Tarter, Michele Lise, and Richard Bell, eds. *Buried Lives: Incarcerated in Early America*. Athens: University of Georgia Press, 2012.

Weiner, Mark S. "Let Us Make a Tryal." In *Black Trials: Citizenship from the Beginnings of Slavery to the End of Caste*, 33–50. New York: Knopf, 2007.

CHAPTER FOUR

A Letter from Black Enslaved Christians on a Virginia Plantation, 1723

Introduction

In 1723, on behalf of a community of mixed-race colonists enslaved in Virginia, an anonymous black African writer penned a letter to Bishop Edmund Gibson of the Anglican Church in England. In the letter, the enslaved colonists petition the bishop to help them secure their freedom. Describing themselves as "a Sort of people that is calld molatters which are Baptised and brouaht up in the way of the Christian faith," they contest their enslavement on the basis that they have been Christianized and that they are the children of white, English colonists. They eschew the concept that would become known later as the "one drop rule," which mandated that a person was racially Black if they had any trace of Black ancestry—through a parent, grandparent, great-grandparent, and so on. In their letter, the Virginia petitioners align themselves with the white relatives who hold them captive. They aim ultimately to live and worship as free men and women and to secure an education for their children. There is a lot we do not know about this letter. Who, for example, wrote it? The writer purposely withheld the name. We do not know how the petitioners planned to get the letter to the bishop. We know nothing about what became of the letter and the community's appeal. Despite the unknowns, this letter is a valuable archival document that presents a Black-centric view on enslavement, a view presumably unfiltered by a white editor or amanuensis. The petitioners do not, notably, condemn slavery, only the law that designates them as slaves. It is one of the earliest illustrations to date of black Africans employing their own literacy skills to advocate for freedom.

Furthermore, the letter expands the generic bounds of what we typically consider to be Black life writing. The letter does not present a narrative detailing incidents in the lives of early black Americans. It is more lyrical in structure and style, which is to say that the text is not beholden to narrative time but to emotion. It expresses the petitioners' dismay, their bemusement about their legal status, their desperation to secure a better future for their children. It meditates on freedom, race, worship. Through this lyrical mode, the letter offers valuable information about the lives of those Virginia petitioners, who ultimately use the letter form to self-construct as pious Christians with a racial status that they believe belies their enslavement.

Text

From Thomas N. Ingersoll, "'Releese us out of this Cruell Bondegg': An Appeal from Virginia in 1723." *William and Mary Quarterly* 51, no. 4 (October 1994): 777–82.[1]

A Letter from Black Enslaved Christians in Virginia to Bishop Edmund Gibson in London (1723)

> August the forth 1723
> The Right Raverrand father in god my Lord arch Bishop of Lonnd this coms to sattesfie your honour that there is in this Land of verJennia a Sort of people that is Calld molatters which are Baptised and brouaht up in the way of the Christan faith and followes the wayes and Rulles of the Chrch of England and sum of them has white fathars and sum white mothers and there is in this Land a Law or act which keeps and makes them and there seed SLaves forever—and most honoured sir a mongst the Rest of your Charitabell acts and deed wee your humbell and poore partisshinners doo begg Sir your aid and assisttancce in this one thing which Lise as I doo understand in your LordShips brest which is that your honour will by the help of our Sufvering [i.e., sovereign] Lord King George and the Rest of the Rullers will Releese us out of this Cruell Bondegg and this wee beg for Jesus Christs his Sake who has commaded us to seeke first the kingdom of god and all things shall be addid un to us and here it is to bee notd that one brother is a SLave to another and one Sister to an othe which is quite out of the way and as for mee [cancellation] my selfe I am my brothers SLave but my name is Secrett and here it is to bee notd againe that wee are commandded to keep holey the Sabbath day and wee doo hardly know when it comes for our [cancellation] task mastrs are has hard with us as the Egypttions was with the Chilldann of Issarall god be marcifll unto us here follows our Sevarity and Sorrowfull Sarvice we are hard used up on Every account in the first place wee are in Ignorance of our Salvation and in the next place wee are kept out of the Church and matrimony is deenied us and to be plain they doo Look no more up on us then if wee ware dogs which I hope when these

Strange Lines comes to your Lord Ships hands will be Looket in to and here wee beg for Jesus Christ his Sake that as your honour do hope for the marcy of god att the day of death and the Redemtion of our Savour Christ that when this comes to your Lord Ships hands your honour wll Take Sum pitty of us who is your humble butt Sorrowfull portitinors and Sir wee your humble perticners do humblly beg the favour of your Lord Ship that your honour will grant and Settell one thing upon us which is that our childarn may be broatt up in the way of the Christtian faith and our desire is that they may be Larnd the Lords prayer the creed and the ten commandements and that they may appeare Every Lord's day att Church before the Curatt to bee Exammond for our desire is that godllines Shoulld abbound amongs us and wee desire that our Childarn be putt to Scool and and Larnd to Reed through the Bybell which is all att prasant with our prayers to god for itts good Success before your honour these from your humbell Servants in the Lord my Riting is vary bad I whope yr honour will take the will for the deede I am but a poore SLave that writt itt and has no other time butt Sunday and hardly that att Sumtimes

September the 8th 1723

To the Right Reverrand father in god

my Lord arch bishup of J London

these with care wee dare nott Subscribe any mans name to this for feare of our masters for if they knew that wee have Sent home to your honour wee Should goo neare to Swing upon the gallass tree

Suggested Reading

Goetz, Rebecca Anne. "The Children of Israel." In *The Baptism of Early Virginia: How Christianity Created Race*, 138–67. Baltimore: Johns Hopkins University Press, 2012.

May, Cedrick. *Evangelism and Resistance in the Black Atlantic, 1760–1835*. Athens: University of Georgia Press, 2008.

Vaughan, Alden T. "Blacks in Virginia: A Note on the First Decade." *William and Mary Quarterly* 29, no. 3 (July 1972): 469–78.

Wilkinson, A. B. "Mixed-Heritage Identities in the Eighteenth Century." In *Blurring the Lines of Race and Freedom: Mulattoes and Mixed Bloods in English Colonial America*, 128–62. Chapel Hill: University of North Carolina Press, 2020.

CHAPTER FIVE

The Confession of Flora Negro, 1748

Introduction

In 1748, a young enslaved woman named Flora offered an apology for some unknown transgression to the Congregational Church of Chebacco in Ipswich, Massachusetts. Of the congregation's first twenty-two members, four—including Flora—were enslaved black Africans. The Fourth Church, as it was later known, staunchly supported the evangelical movement now known as the First Great Awakening, and in addition to the preaching of John Cleaveland, who recorded her confession, Flora would have listened regularly to sermons preached by itinerant ministers, including George Whitefield, who visited several times. Her confession, which concludes with a warning against sin, was read aloud twice at a special Tuesday meeting convened specifically so that Flora could share this pledge of repentance, and the narrative occasionally slips into a sermonic voice, demonstrating her authority.

Several passages offer perspective on the ways in which Flora's experience of religion and of God was shaped by her racial identity. Twice, she paraphrases Isaiah, speaking of her sin as a crimson or scarlet dye that must be purged by God so that she might be left blameless: "Come now, and let us reason together, saith the Lord: though your sins be as scarlet, they shall be as white as snow; though they be red like crimson, they shall be as wool" (Isaiah 1:18). The book of Isaiah was frequently cited by later evangelicals and writers of African descent. Flora embraces the color logic of Isaiah in the Bible but rejects the notion that salvation is only accessible through whiteness. At the hinge point of her narrative of repentance, as she describes a feeling that her penitence has been accepted by God, Flora expresses the joy of her justification in scriptural language: "the Lord heard, to my Surprize & Astonishment, he ran to my Relief, he kissed me with the Kisses of his mouth and I found his Love to be better than wine." The erotic relationship Flora enjoys with her God draws from the biblical Song of Solomon, which recounts an interracial love affair. Its female protagonist declares, "I am black, but comely, O ye daughters of Jerusalem, as the tents of Kedar, as the curtains of Solomon" (Song of Solomon 1:5). In the Bible, Flora found textual models for her own experience of the divine, and her confession to the Chebacco church is also a celebration of the ecstatic divinity experienced by black African worshippers in colonial North America.

Text

From Erik R. Seeman, "'Justise Must Take Plase': Three African Americans Speak of Religion in Eighteenth-Century New England." *William and Mary Quarterly* 56, no. 2 (April 1999): 393–414.[1]

The Confession of Flora Negro
To the New-Gathered Congregational Chh in Chebacco—
Rev'd Hon'd and Beloveds

> I freely Confess and acknowledge unto you as in the Presence of the great God and his Elect Angels, as also what I expect to answer to, before the Judge of the quick and Dead, at the Tribunal Seat of Jesus Christ; that I have been made truly sensible, that my conduct of late has been such as Justly to cool your charity for, and be matter of just offence against me—I have sinned against Heaven and in your sight and am not worthy to be reckoned among the Sons and Daughters of God; As to my Sin it is not hid from you, God has bro't it to light by his providence[,] Oh the great God is my witness how I have seen it to be of a Crimson Colour & of a Scarlet Die attended with grievous aggrevations indeeds[,] I do therefore beg leave for your Satisfaction my own Humiliation & Abasement & the warning of others: to Confess and Lay open before you, what were the provocations I gave the Lord to leave me to fall into Temptation and Sin, what apprehensions I have had and Tryals respecting my Fall, and the Satisfaction I have received that the Lord hath covered my sin with a mantle of his pardoning Love.
>
> As to my provocations they were indeed great for God does not afflict willingly, nor leave his pardoned ones without a Just Cause, the Provocations, I gave, that have Especially been made plain to my view; [were?] spirituall Pride, Ingratitude, Unwatchfulness and Levity or Lightness; spiritual [illeg.] rise up after manifestations of God's smiles, & great Freedom to utter [the] same before men, & also after freedom in persuading sinners to repent [sins?] and live, Ingratitude, also that Beastlike Satanical & God provoking Sin to be Unmindful of the God that made me, and lightly to esteem the Rock of my salvation would

frequently creep in upon me—and Unwatchfulness and Levity also, especially when I did not feel much bowed down by the Majesty of Heaven, & hereby a wide Door was hath been opened, I have seen for Satan to spread his Temptations and Snares to beguile souls and stir them up to wantonness and concupiscence; Yea! To provoke God to leave them as it were to Satan and their own Lusts [illeg.]: And what can poor souls do? when God is thus provoked? Thus I provoked God; oh, pray for & take learning by such an Instance as I am.

As to the apprehensions I have had & tryals respecting my Fall they are many, I have had Temptations to seek ways, to hide my Iniquity from Men, but the Lord in Mercy frustrated them all, and gave me to see that it was against him I had sinned, and done wickedly in his sight, And also gave me to Behold my sin in some measure in a true Light; as it was attended with most heinous Aggrevations indeed; as being against a pardoning God,—after pardon received—and wonderful endearing Manifestations of his Love and Favour to me, Tending not only, to make such settle down in their opposition (as being in the right) that have all along appeared against the work of God: but also to Occasion the holy name of God, to be blasphemed, especially by such as I have heretofore endeavoured to persuade and beseech to Embrace a precious Christ—but Time and your Patience would fail me to relate particularly, what Darkness has been spread over my Mind and cast in my way, by reason of this my Fall. What shame has covered me before Men and Confusion of Face before God; how God frown'd upon me and hid his Face from me, how Just it appeared to me, for God to cast me below [p. 2] Sodomites, yea, below Devils in Torment—now my soul sunk down into the Deep Mire where there was no standing; and now the bellows [?] and floods overflowd me. But while I was in this Condition God gave me a Spirit of Prayer, out of the Deep I cry'd to him [illeg.] God, out of the Depths of Confusion Shame Sin Impotency and Unworthiness, and the Lord heard, to my Surprize & Astonishment, he ran to my Relief, he kissed me with the Kisses of his mouth and I found his Love to be better than wine.

The way that God Took with me, to pluck my Feet out of the Miery Clay and horrible Pitt, was by bringing home to my soul some Texts of holy Scripture. The first were those blessed words of our Saviour, John 7.37—that great Day of the Feast Jesus stood and Cryed, if any man Thirst Let him come unto me and Drink; at first I was not sensible of much Spiritual Thirsting, but soon after they were bro't with power to my mind, I found some thirsting, but Unbelief immediatly step'd in, and argued, that the Call could not be to me, my sin was so great: which caused me to Question whither it was bro't to my Mind by the holy Ghost, but These workings were soon silenced by those words in Isai: 63.1—It is I that speak in Righteousness, mighty to save: Which came with such Evidence & Demonstration that I was not only satisfyed that Christ called me before to Drink of his pardoning and healing Love but also that altho' my Sin was of a Crimson Colour and Scarlet Die attended with greivous aggrevations; yet there was enough in Christ to pardon—O them words: *mighty to Save* silenced unbelief & reviv'd my shattered and disconsolate Soul[,] now the pardoning Love of God again flowed into my Soul & caused my Heart to melt & flow with penetential streams; I could then have wished my head a Fountain & my Eyes Rivers of water to weep over my Sins; never did I before, find my heart so Resolved, never to harbour Sin or to be reconciled again to it as now I found it. No Tongue of Men or Angels can fully Express (it seems) what an Indignation & Revenge boiled in my Heart against myself, and *the* Sin that I had been besett with & overtaken by: O I beg your Prayers for me that I may bring forth much Fruit, meet of Repentance and be made to Discover to all in my futer Life Conversation Conduct and Behaviour, the Truth of what I have now been Declaring unto you. I beg your Forgiveness. I pray you to Restore me to your Charity and Fellowship and the Privileges that I have forfitted, by my Fall, I beg Desire your Prayers for me, that in Every Relation I might walk becoming one professing Godliness, & adorn the Doctrine of God my Saviour in all Things[,] yea that I may be made more circumspect than ever heretofore in my Walk, so as to declare God's Glory abroad; And Let all that have named the Name of Christ, take warning by me, not to let down your Watch for such will Certainly fall into Temptation as I Do.

Your's &c,
Flora Negro
Her F Mark

Suggested Reading

Brooks, Joanna. *American Lazarus: Religion and the Rise of African-American and Native American Literatures*. New York: Oxford University Press, 2003.

Glaude, Eddie S. *Exodus! Religion, Race, and Nation in Early Nineteenth-Century Black America*. Chicago: University of Chicago Press, 2000.

Lambert, Frank. "'I Saw the Book Talk': Slave Readings of the First Great Awakening." *Journal of African American History* 87 (Winter 2002): 12–25.

May, Cedrick. "John Marrant and the Narrative Construction of an Early Black Methodist Evangelical." *African American Review* 38 (Winter 2004): 553–70.

Moody, Joycelyn. *Sentimental Confessions: Spiritual Narratives of Nineteenth-Century African American Women*. Athens: University of Georgia Press, 2000.

CHAPTER SIX

The Antislavery Argument of Negro Greenwich, 1754

Introduction

Whether the "Negro Grinnig [Greenwich]" wrote the following antislavery document himself or narrated it to an amanuensis, the document illustrates the means by which this enslaved black African in early America employed technologies of literacy to speak out against slavery.

Greenwich was born and enslaved in 1725 in Canterbury, Connecticut. As a young adult, he joined the Canterbury Separate Church, a congregationalist splinter group of reform-minded New Lights organized amid the First Great Awakening. Greenwich begins his antislavery document with the claim that God has commanded he speak. He dons the voice of a biblical exegete, pointing to scripture to expose the sins of slavery. Importantly, he does not challenge slavery in theory. Instead, he points to examples of slavery in the Old Testament to argue that slavery is permissible only under certain conditions, such as warfare. To take and enslave a person with whom you are not at war, Greenwich argues, amounts to man-stealing. He does not voice a novel distinction here; slavery advocates and critics had been debating that distinction since slavery was introduced to colonial New England in the 1630s. For example, colonial Massachusetts's 1641 Body of Liberties accepted slavery in the colony that resulted from justified warfare and deemed other means of procuring slaves man-stealing. The slavery debate between Massachusetts jurists Samuel Sewall and John Saffin in 1700 and 1701 turned, in part, on the question of whether enslavement was ever justified. Greenwich's document ends midsentence, but enough of the record survives to give readers a clear sense of Greenwich's knowledge of the Bible and his grasp of the discourse surrounding slavery in colonial New England.

Greenwich's document anticipates the spiritual rationality of later black African writers like Phillis Wheatley Peters, who in her poem "On Being Brought from Africa to America" subtly reminds her white readers that black African and white Christians belong to one spiritual body. Greenwich's document, published in 1754, did not result in Greenwich's immediate emancipation. He and his wife remained enslaved until 1776 when they purchased their freedom.

Text

From Erik R. Seeman, "'Justise Must Take Plase': Three African Americans Speak of Religion in Eighteenth-Century New England." *William and Mary Quarterly* 56, no. 2 (April 1999): 393–414.[1]

"Negrow Grinnig [Greenwich] of Canterbury"

this the 29 day of March 1754
As I have ben Instructed by the Lord so I think it is Nesseary to Indite fue things which I have brought Into the church[,] brotherin some say that we are the seed of Canaan and some say that we are the Tribe of Ham but Let that be as it will Justise must Take Plase therefore I will I shou you how Abraham came by his servents in the 15 Chapt of Geneseis 18 wher the Lord Covenant with Abraham saying unto thy seed have I given this Land from the river eupherates and the kenites and the kenizites and the kadmonites and also in the 17 Chap of Genesies and 8 vers and I will give unto the[e] and to thy seed after the Land wherein thou art a stranger all the Land of Canaan for an everlasting possession and I will be the[i]r God and In the 12 vers and he that is eight days old shall be circumsized among you every man child In your Generation he that Is born In thy house or bought with mony of any strangers which Is not of thy seed and now bretherin thes strangers that Abraham bought with mony were of kanites now bretherin cast your eyes upon the fase of the earth how god hath set the bounds to the nation and that non [e] shold impose upon another nation 10 Chapter of Genesis 20 vers these are the sons of ham after there families after there Tongues In their Contries and in their nation and now bretherin suppose any nation shold have a continual war amongst themselves and any of you should supply them of ammonition and when you have don this you will steel as many of them and bring them over Into your Contry to make slaves of them their soul and body as much as in thereby [?] 3 Chap of proverbs and 30 vers strive not with a man without Cause if he hath don the[e] no harm and now in the 21 first Chapter of Exodus and 16 vers and he that steel A man and seleth him or if he be found in his hands he shall surely be put to death the first of kings and 9 Chapter 16 verse and 20 vers their you will se[e] how pharaoh king of Egypt had gon yup [i.e., up] and taken gezer and given as a present unto his dafter Solomon wife theis were of

Cannaan and so to the 21 vers and their Children that were left after them in their Land whome the Children of Israel were not able utterly to destroy upon thoes did Solomon levy a tribute of bonds service unto this day and they were Cannanits Jeremiah 34 Chapter and 14 verse at the end of seventh year let you go every man his brother in hebrew which hath ben sold unto the[e] and when he hath served the six year thou shall let him go free from the[e] and now bretherin you may se[e] for your selves th[r]ou[gh]out the Scriptures that every nation that is taken by conquest you may make slaves

Suggested Reading

Bailey, Richard A. *Race and Redemption in Puritan New England*. New York: Oxford University Press, 2011.

Frey, Sylvia R., and Betty Wood. *Come Shouting to Zion: African American Protestantism in the American South and British Caribbean to 1830*. Chapel Hill: University of North Carolina Press, 1998.

Saillant, John. "Slavery and Divine Providence in New England Calvinism: The New Divinity and a Black Protest, 1775–1805." *New England Quarterly* 68, no. 4 (December 1995): 584–608.

Thomas, Rhondda Robinson. *Claiming Exodus: A Cultural History of Afro-Atlantic Identity, 1774–1903*. Waco, TX: Baylor University Press, 2013.

Part II
In the Legal Records

The enslavers who purchased captive black Africans and transported their bodies to colonial North America did so with the sanction of international law. Jurists such as John Locke and Samuel Sewall argued that prisoners taken in a just war might rightfully be enslaved, and enslavers invoked that doctrine as a justification for their participation in human trafficking. Once in the colonies, black Africans found that slave codes restricted their movements, worship, education, and speech, stripping them of humanity and identifying them as property. Even freed persons, whose liberty was always provisional because of the ease with which unscrupulous white colonists could kidnap and reenslave black Africans, were often subjected to such codes. Because these discriminatory legal systems deprived black Africans of basic human rights, both freed persons and enslaved persons frequently found themselves in court, where their testimony would be transcribed or summarized.

White colonists rarely recorded the words or described in detail the actions of black Africans unless they had violated some tenet of the legal systems justifying their dehumanization. As a result, the surviving records of black African speech from this period disproportionately feature the voices of men and women accused of criminal behavior, ranging from petty theft to acts of war. This part of *The Earliest African American Literatures* is, accordingly, twice the length of any other part in this volume—not because black Africans living in colonial North America were inherently antisocial but because the white writers whose works fill the archive from this period seldom regarded the family life or the emotional state or the personal triumphs of black Africans as worthy of notice. The kindnesses, curiosities, and social contributions of these individuals have largely been lost to history, but white writers took care to preserve a record of their transgressions and rebellions.

Many of the men and women whose thoughts and lives have been preserved in this part were accused of crimes. Some served as witnesses and offered testimony about the alleged crimes of others. A select few were able to work through the legal system to secure rights taken for granted by white colonists, such as the right to divorce or the right to bequeath property in a will. Whatever their standing, black Africans repeatedly discovered that the laws of colonial North America worked to dehumanize them and criminalize their desire for self-determination. Black African lives and viewpoints are stigmatized in the texts that follow, but these legal documents are a record of their resistance to the systems and institutions that legitimized their status as human chattels.

CHAPTER SEVEN

Anthony Johnson and the Casor Suit, 1655

Introduction

As one of the earliest illustrations of a freedom suit, the case of John Casor (and the counterclaim of his Black owner Anthony, or Antonio, Johnson) provides alternative perspectives on the Black experience. In March of 1655 in Northampton County, Virginia, Casor petitioned Johnson for his freedom. Casor claimed that he arrived in Virginia as an indentured servant, contracted to work for seven to eight years; he had served Johnson twice that long. Although Casor could not produce the written indenture contract, which was said to have been drawn up by a neighbor in another county, Johnson conceded the claim based on the counsel of family members and the threats of a white neighbor, Robert Parker, who advocated on Casor's behalf. Subsequently, Casor secured employment with Parker. In June of that year, Johnson shifted course. He sued Parker in county court, insisting that Parker had wrongfully deprived him of his property (Casor). The court agreed with Johnson and declared that Casor was Johnson's servant for life.

From Casor's perspective, the textual record gives voice to one black African man's efforts to confront the social and economic confines of colonial Virginia. The ultimate outcome, however, illustrates a precarious link between Blackness and captivity. Nothing in the final court ruling explicitly linked Casor's servant status to his race, but the sentence of perpetual servitude—absent a conviction for criminal behavior—was a punishment unique to black Africans in the colony, laying the groundwork for race-based slavery as a legal institution.

From Johnson's perspective, the freedom suit tells a story that does not emphasize racial difference but elides it. Johnson, a tobacco farmer, was able to participate in the legal and economic systems of colonial Virginia much like his white neighbors. When necessary, he could mobilize the resources of those systems to protect his self-interest. He exhibited a certain cultural literacy, illustrated in his decision to sue Parker rather than further engage with Casor. Johnson challenged Parker on legal and moral grounds, accusing him of violating the sanctity of property ownership. More importantly, by deeming Casor his property, Johnson excised the servant as an active, human participant in the legal controversy.

Both Casor and Johnson leave behind written records—even if not produced by their own pens—that result in narratives of agency and self-preservation. The two excerpts below come from the court proceedings. One is the deposition of a neighbor; the other is the final court ruling issued in June 1655.

Text

From Warren M. Billings, *The Old Dominion in the Seventeenth Century: A Documentary History of Virginia, 1606–1689*. Chapel Hill: University of North Carolina Press, 1975.[1]

Deposition

> The deposition of Captain Samuel Goldsmith taken (in open court) 8th of March Sayth, That beinge at the howse of Anthony Johnson Negro (about the beginninge of November last to receive a hogshead of tobacco) a Negro called John Casar came to this Deponent, and told him that hee came into Virginia for seaven or Eight yeares (per Indenture) And that hee had demanded his freedome of his master Anthony Johnson; And further said that Johnson had kept him his servant seaven yeares longer than hee ought, And desired that this deponent would see that hee might have noe wronge, whereupon your Deponent demanded of Anthony Johnson his Indenture, hee answered, hee never sawe any; The said Negro (John Casor) replyed, hee came for a certayne tyme and had an Indenture Anthony Johnson said hee never did see any But that hee had him for his life; Further this deponent saith That mr. Robert Parker and George Parker they knew that the said Negro had an Indenture (in on Mr. Carre hundred on the other side of the Baye) And the said Anthony Johnson did not tell the negro goe free The said John Casor would recover most of his Cowes of him; Then Anthony Johnson (as this deponent did suppose) was in a feare. Upon this his Sonne in lawe, his wife and his 2 sonnes perswaded the said Anthony Johnson to sett the said John Casor free. more saith not.
>
> Samuel Goldsmith

Court Ruling

> This daye Anthony Johnson Negro made his complaint to the Court against mr. Robert Parker and declared that hee deteyneth his servant

John Casor negro (under pretence that the said Negro is a free man.) The Court seriously consideringe and maturely weighinge the premisses, doe fynde that the said Mr. Robert Parker most unjustly keepeth the said Negro from Anthony Johnson his master as appeareth by the deposition of Captain Samuel Goldsmith and many probable circumstances. It is therefore the Judgment of the Court and ordered That the said John Casor Negro forthwith returne unto the service of his said master Anthony Johnson, And that mr. Robert Parker make payment of all charge in the suit.

Suggested Reading

Brewer, James H. "Negro Property Owners in Seventeenth-Century Virginia." *William and Mary Quarterly* 12, no. 4 (1955): 575–80.

Fuente, Alejandro de la, and Ariela J. Gross. *Becoming Free, Becoming Black: Race, Freedom, and Law in Cuba, Virginia, and Louisiana*. Cambridge: Cambridge University Press, 2020.

Halliburton, R., Jr. "Free Black Owners of Slaves: A Reappraisal of the Woodson Thesis." *South Carolina Historical Magazine* 76, no. 3 (1975): 129–42.

Vaughan, Alden T. "The Origins Debate: Slavery and Racism in Seventeenth-Century Virginia." *Virginia Magazine of History and Biography* 97, no. 3 (1989): 311–54.

Wood, William J. "The Illegal Beginning of American Negro Slavery." *American Bar Association Journal* 56, no. 1 (1970): 45–49.

CHAPTER EIGHT

The Case of Elizabeth Key Grinstead, 1656

Introduction

Elizabeth Key, born in Warwick County, Virginia, in 1630, was the illegitimate daughter of a white, English planter and an enslaved black African woman. In 1636 Key's father, after reluctantly acknowledging paternity, negotiated a nine-year indenture contract for his young daughter to be apprenticed with a neighboring family. After several years, during which time her father died, Key's indenture was transferred to another Virginia planter named John Mottram. Mottram did not free Key on her fifteenth birthday. Instead, she remained his servant until he died in 1655. The executors of Mottram's estate classified Key, who by that time had become a mother, as property. They also determined that her young son was enslaved. Key sued Mottram's estate for her freedom and for her son's, on the basis that they were the children of free-born Englishmen. She evoked English common law that dictated a child assumed the legal status of the father. Furthermore, she argued that she was an indentured servant who had worked well past her contracted time. With the corroborating testimonies of those who knew details about Key's childhood, the Virginia courts ultimately ruled in her favor. Not incidentally, in the aftermath of Key's case, Virginia passed a law in 1662 mandating that the status of a child followed that of the mother, not the father.

Key's legal efforts represent an early form of what would become known as freedom suits, one of the earliest strategies that black Africans employed to secure or protect their freedom in British America. These lawsuits allowed enslaved black Africans to pursue legal means to challenge the legitimacy of their enslavement. Importantly, Key's freedom suit provides basic information about her birth and parentage. We are afforded details about her upbringing and key events that mark her transition into womanhood, such as becoming a mother and working to preserve her child's freedom alongside her own. Hers is the earliest record we have of a black African woman employing the courts to challenge her unfree status in British America. Her strategy employed contractual, religious, and genealogical rationales. Notably, others provide the details of Key's life. There is no direct testimony from Key herself, but this should not be interpreted as silence, definitely not invisibility. Key's guiding hand mobilized a cadre of witnesses to affirm her claims, a move that produced a textual record and a proclamation of self-possession.

Text

From Warren Billings, "Bound Labor: Slavery." In *The Old Dominion in the Seventeenth Century: A Documentary History of Virginia, 1606–1689*, 195–99. Chapel Hill: University of North Carolina Press, 1975.[1]

> ELIZABETH KEY, 1655/56 Northumberland County Record Books, 1652–1658, fols. 66–67, 85, 1658–1660, fol. 28; Northumberland County Order Book, 1652–1665, fols. 40, 46, 49.
>
> The Court doth order that Col. Thomas Speke one of the overseers of the Estate of Col. John Mottrom deceased shall have an Appeale to the Quarter Court next att James City in a Cause depending betweene the said overseers and Elizabeth a Moletto hee the said Col. Speke giving such caution as to Law doth belong. Wee whose names are underwritten being impannelled upon a Jury to try a difference between Elizabeth pretended Slave to the Estate of Col. John Mottrom deceased and the overseers of the said Estate doe finde that the said Elizabeth ought to be free as by severall oathes might appeare which we desire might be Recorded and that the charges of Court be paid out of the said Estate. [names of the jury omitted]
>
>   Memorandum it is Conditioned and agreed by and betwixt Thomas Key on the one part and Humphrey Higginson on the other part [word missing] that the said Thomas Key hath put unto the said Humphrey one Negro Girle by name Elizabeth for and during the [term?] of nine yeares after the date hereof provided that the [said?] Humphrey doe find and allow the said Eliza- beth meate drinke [and?] apparrell during the said tearme And allsoe the said Thomas Key that if the said Humphrey doe dye before the end of the said time abovespecified that then the said Girl be free from the said Humphrey Higginson and his assignes Allsoe if the said Humphrey Higginson doe goe for England with an Intention to live and remaine there that then hee shall carry [the?] said Girle with him and to pay for her passage and likewise that he put not of[f] the said Girle to any man but to keepe her himselfe In witness whereof I the said Humphrey Higginson. Sealed and delivered in the presence of us Robert Booth Francis Miryman. 20th January 1655 this writing was Recorded.

Mr. Nicholas Jurnew aged 53 yeares or thereabouts sworne and Examined Sayth That about 16 or 17 yeares past this deponent heard a flying report at Yorke that Elizabeth a Negro Servant to the Estate of Col. John Mottrom deceased was the Childe of Mr. Kaye but the said Mr. Kaye said that a Turke of Capt. Mathewes was Father to the Girle and further this deponent sayth not signed Nicholas Jurnew

20th January 1655 Jurat in Curia ["sworn in court"]

Anthony Lenton aged 41 yeares or thereabouts sworne and Examined Sayth that about 19 yeares past this deponent was a servant to Mr. Humphrey Higginson and at that time one Elizabeth a Molletto nowe servant to the Estate of Col. John Mottrom deceased was then a servant to the said mr. Higginson and as the Neighbours reported was bought of mr Higginson with the said servant both himself and his Wife intended a voyage for England and at the nine yeares end (as the Neighbours reported) the said Mr Higginson was bound to carry the said servant for England unto the said mr. Kaye, but before the said mr Kaye went his Voyage hee Dyed about Kecotan, and as the Neighbours reported the said mr. Higginson said that at the nine yeares end hee would carry the said Molletto for England and give her a portion and lett her shift for her selfe And it was a Common report amongst the Neighbours that the said Molletto was mr Kays Child begott by him and further this deponent sayth not the marke of Anthony Lenton 20th January 1655 Jurat in Curia

Mrs. Elizabeth Newman aged 80 yeares or thereabouts sworne and exam- ined Sayth that it was a common Fame in Virginia that Elizabeth a Molletto nowe servant to the Estate of Col. John Mottrom deceased was the Daughter of mr. Kay; and the said Kaye was brought to Bluntpoint Court [Warwick County court] and there fined for getting his Negro woman with Childe which said Negroe was the Mother of the said Molletto and the said fine was for getting the Negro with Childe which Childe was the said Elizabeth and further this deponent sayth not the marke of Elizabeth Newman 20th January 1655 Jurat in Curia

John Bayles aged 33 yeares or thereabouts sworne and Examined Sayth That at the House of Col. John Mottrom Black Besse was tearmed to be mr Kayes Bastard and John Keye calling her Black Bess mrs. Speke Checked him and said Sirra you must call her Sister for shee is your Sister and the said John Keye did call her Sister and further this deponent Sayth not the marke of John Bayles 20th January 1655 Jurat in Curia

The deposition of Alice Larrett aged 38 yeares or thereabouts Sworne and Examined Sayth that Elizabeth which is at Col. Mottroms is twenty five yeares of age or thereabouts and that I saw her mother goe to bed to her Master many times and that I heard her mother Say that shee was mr. Keyes daughter and further Sayth not the marke of Alice Larrett Sworne before mr. Nicholas Morris 19th Jan. 1655. 20th January this deposition was Recorded

Anne Clark aged 39 or thereabouts Sworne and Examined Sayth that shee this deponent was present when a Condition was made betweene mr. Humphrey Higginson and mr. Kaye for a servant called Besse a Molletto and this depo- nents Husband William Reynolds nowe deceased was a witness but whether the said Besse after the Expiration of her time from mr Higginson was to be free from mr Kaye this deponent cannot tell and mr Higginson promised to use her as well as if shee were his own Child and further this deponent Sayth not Signum Ann Clark 20th January 1655 Jurat in Curia

Elizabeth Newman aged 80 yeares or thereabouts Sworne and Examined Sayth that shee this deponent brought Elizabeth a Molletto, Servant to the Estate of Col. John Mottrom deceased to bed of two Children and shee layd them both to William Grinsted and further this Deponent Sayth not Elizabeth Newman her marke 20th January 1655 Jurat in Curia

A Report of a Comittee from an Assembly Concerning the freedome of Elizabeth Key

It appeareth to us that shee is the daughter of Thomas Key by severall Evidences and by a fine imposed upon the said Thomas for getting her mother with Child of the said Thomas That she hath bin by verdict of a Jury impannelled 20th January 1655 in the County of Northumberland found to be free by severall oathes which the Jury desired might be Recorded That by the Comon Law the Child of a Woman slave begott by a freeman ought to bee free That shee hath bin long since Christened Col. Higginson being her God father and that by report shee is able to give a very good account of her fayth That Thomas Key sould her onely for nine yeares to Col. Higginson with severall conditions to use her more Respectfully then a Comon servant or slave That in case Col. Higginson had gone for England within nine yeares hee Was bound to carry her with him and pay her passage and not to dispose of her to any other. For theise Reasons wee conceive the said Elizabeth ought to bee free and that her last Master should give her Corne and Cloathes and give her satisfaction for the time shee hath served longer then Shee ought to have done. But forasmuch as noe man appeared against the said Elizabeths petition wee thinke not fitt a determinative judgement should passe but that the County or Quarter Court where it shall be next tried to take notice of this to be the sence of the Burgesses of this present Assembly and that unless [original torn] shall appear to be executed and reasons [original torn] opposite part Judgement by the said Court be given [accordingly?]

        Charles Norwood Clerk Assembly James Gaylord hath deposed that this is a true coppy

        James Gaylord

21th July 1656 Jurat in Curia
21th July 1656 This writeing was recorded

Att a Grand Assembly held at James Citty 20th of March 1655 Ordered that the whole business of Elizabeth Key [and?] the report of the Comittee thereupon be returned [to the?] County Court where the said Elizabeth Key liveth

   This is a true copy from the book of Records of the Order granted the last Assembly

Teste Robert Booth

21th July 1656 This Order of Assembly was Recorded

Upon the petition of George Colclough one of the overseers of Col. Mottrom his Estate that the cause concerning a Negro wench named Black Besse should be heard before the Governor and Councell Whereof in regard of the Order of the late Assembly referring the said caise to the Governor and Councell at least upon Appeale made to them These are therefore in his Highness the Lord Protector his name to will and require the Commissioners of the County of Northumberland to Surcease from any further proceedings on the said Cause and to give notice to the parties interested therein to appear before the Governor at the next Quarter Court on the fourth day for a determination thereof. Given under my hand this 7th of June 1656. Edward Digges 21th *1656* This Writeing was Recorded.

Whereas mr. George Colclough and mr. William Presly overseers of the Estate of Colonell John Mottrom deceased were Summoned to theis Court at the suite of Elizabeth Kaye both Plaintiffe and Defendant being present and noe cause of action at present appearing The Court doth therefore order that the said Elizabeth Kaye shall be non-suited and that William Grinsted Atturney of the said Elizabeth shall by the tenth of November next pay fifty pounds of tobacco to the said overseers for an non-suite with Court charges else Execution. Whereas the whole business concerning Elizabeth Key by Order of Assembly was Referred to this County Court. According to the Report of a Comittee at an Assembly held at the same time which upon the Records of this County appears, It is the judgment of this Court that the Said Elizabeth Key ought to be free and forthwith to have Corne Clothes and Satisfaction according to the said Report of the Comittee. Mr. William Thomas dissents from this judgment.

. . .

I Capt. Richard Wright administrator of the Estate of Col. John Mottrom deceased doe assigne and transfer unto William Greensted a maid servant formerly belonging unto the Estate of the said Col. Mottrom commonly called Elizabeth Key being nowe Wife unto the said Greensted and doe warrant the said Elizabeth and doe bind my Selfe to save here [her] and the said Greensted from any molestation or trouble that shall or futurely arise from or by any person or persons that shall pretend or claime any title or interest to any manor of service [original torn] from the said Elizabeth witness [my ha]nd this 21th of July 1659

        Test William Th[omas] Richard Wright James Aust[en]

Suggested Reading

Banks, Taunya Lovell. "Dangerous Woman: Elizabeth Key's Freedom Suit - Subjecthood and Racialized Identity in Seventheenth Century Colonial Virginia." *Akron Law Review* 41 (2008): 799–837.

Billings, Warren M. "The Cases of Fernando and Elizabeth Key: A Note on the Status of Blacks in Seventeenth-Century Virginia." *William and Mary Quarterly* 30, no. 3 (1973): 467–74.

Coombs, John C. "Beyond the 'Origins Debate': Rethinking the Rise of Virginia Slavery." In *Early Modern Virginia: Reconsidering the Old Dominion*, edited by Douglas Bradburn and John C. Coombs, 239–78. Charlottesville: University of Virginia Press, 2011.

Irons, Charles F. *The Origins of Proslavery Christianity: White and Black Evangelicals in Colonial and Antebellum Virginia*. Chapel Hill: University of North Carolina Press, 2008.

CHAPTER NINE

The Salem Witch Trials, the Testimony of Candy and Mary Black, 1692

Introduction

Most historical and literary studies of the 1692 Salem witch trials ignore the presence and testimony of Candy and Mary Black, two black African women who were accused of being witches. Even less is known about Old Pharaoh, a black African man who was also accused. Neither of these two women was as prominent as the first woman of color accused during the trials—Tituba. We know precious little about the women's lives. Candy, a Barbados native and transplant to Salem, was the servant of Margaret Hawkes. In her testimony, a brief paragraph in court records, she confessed to practicing witchcraft but claimed that she did so at the command of her mistress Hawkes. She, herself, was not a witch, she insisted. Mary Black was a servant in the household of Nathaniel Putnam. In answer to the accusations about being a witch, Black never explicitly denied the charges. Instead, she offered the ambiguous response, "I cannot tell." She did deny causing bodily harm to her neighbors. Candy was found not guilty during an indictment hearing, and Mary Black was cleared of charges by proclamation.

Despite the brevity of their testimonies, provided below, these snippets of black African life in colonial Massachusetts stand out as rare instances of recorded speech. One could debate the accuracy and reliability of the transcriptions, as the transcribers made certain rhetorical choices when rendering their speech acts. In Candy's case, for example, the transcriber renders her words in a pidgin English, his effort to capture faithfully what he heard or what he *expected* to hear. The testimony of Mary Black (and Tituba) is rendered in a more standard English. It might be tempting to dismiss these mediated archival moments as figments of a white, colonial imagination. To do so, however, misses the point that both Candy and Mary Black provide the source material for the transcripts. The recorded speech acts are not merely events filtered through a colonial perspective but events also filtered through the perspective of these two black African women.

Text

From Paul Boyer and Stephen Nissenbaum, eds., *The Salem Witchcraft Papers: Verbatim Transcriptions of the Court Records in Three Volumes*. New York: Da Capo, 1977, The University of Virginia, 2018, accessed April 13, 2020, http://salem.lib.virginia.edu/n23.html.

Examination of Candy

[July 4, 1692]

SALEM, Monday, July 4, 1692. The examination of Candy, a negro woman, before Bartholomew Gedney and John Hawthorne Esqrs. Mr. Nicholas Noyes also present.

Q. Candy! are you a witch? A. Candy no witch in her country. Candy's mother no witch. Candy no witch, Barbados. This country, mistress give Candy witch. Q. Did your mistress make you a witch in this country? A. Yes, in this country mistress give Candy witch. Q. What did your mistress do to make you a witch? A. Mistress bring book and pen and ink, make Candy write in it. Q. What did you write in it?—She took a pen and ink and upon a book or paper made a mark. Q. How did you afflict or hurt these folks, where are the puppets you did it with?—She asked to go out of the room and she would shew or tell; upon which she had liberty, one going with her, and she presently brought in two clouts, one with two knots tied in it, the other one; which being seen by Mary Warren, Deliverance Hobbs and Abigail Hobbs, they were greatly affrighted and fell into violent fits, and all of them said that the black man and Mrs. Hawkes and the negro stood by the puppets or rags and pinched them, and then they were afflicted, and when the knots were untied yet they continued as aforesaid. A bit of one of the rags being set on fire, the afflicted all said they were burned, and cried out dreadfully. The rags being put into water, two of the aforenamed persons were in dreadful fits almost choaked, and the other was violently running down to the river, but was stopped. Attest. John Hawthorne, Just. Peace.

(Thomas Hutchinson, History of Massachusetts-Bay. Cambridge, MA: 1936.II, 26.)

* * *

Examination of Mary Black and Clearance by Proclamation (SWP No. 015)

[April 22, 1692]

The examination of Mary Black (a Negroe) at a Court held at Salem Village 22. Apr. 1692 By the Magistrates of Salem

Q: Mary, you are accused of sundry acts of witchcraft: Tell me be you a Witch?
— Silent.
Q: How long have you been a witch?
A: I cannot tell.
Q: But have you been a witch?
A: I cannot tell you.
Q: Why do you hurt these folks
A: I hurt no body
Q: Who doth?
A: I do not know.

[Benj'a Putnam] Her Master saith a man sat down upon the farm with her about a twelve month agoe.

Q: What did the man say to you?
A: He said nothing.
Q: Doth this Negroe hurt you?

[Directed at afflicted-accusers sitting in the gallery]
Severall of them said yes.

Q: Why do you hurt them?
A: I did not hurt them.
Q: Do you prick sticks?
A: No I pin my Neck cloth
Q: Well take out a pin, & pin it again.

She did so, & severall of the afflicted cryed out they were prick't. Mary Walcott was prick't in the arm till the blood came, Abigail Williams was prick't in the stomach & Mercy Lewis was prick't in the foot.

Mr Samuel parris being desired to take in wrighting the Examination of Mary Black, a Negro Woman delivered itt as aforesaid And upon heareing the same and seeing what wee did then see togather with the Charge of the afflicted persons then present Wee Committed s'd Mary black.

Per us *John Hathorne
*Jonathan. Corwin {Assis'ts

(Reverse) The Examination of (9) Mary Black 22. Apr. 1692
Cleerd by proclamacon
Jan'ry. 11. 1692 Mr Nathaniell Putnam of Salem Village his negro

Suggested Reading

McMillan, Timothy J. "Black Magic: Witchcraft, Race, and Resistance in Colonial New England." *Journal of Black Studies* 25, no. 1 (1994): 99–117.

Norton, Mary Beth. *In the Devil's Snare: The Salem Witchcraft Crisis of 1692*. New York: Vintage Books, 2002.

Rissanen, Matti. "'Candy No Witch, Barbados': Salem Witchcraft Trials as Evidence of Early American English." In *Language in Time and Space: Studies in Honour of Wolfgang Viereck on the Occasion of His Sixtieth Birthday*, edited by Heinrich Ramisch and Kenneth Wynne, 183–93. Stuttgart: Franz Steiner, 1997.

Smith, Cassander L. "'Candy No Witch in Her Country': What One Enslaved Woman's Testimony during the Salem Witch Trials Can Tell Us about Early American Literature." In *Early Modern Black Diaspora Studies: A Critical Anthology*, edited by Cassander L. Smith, Nicholas R. Jones, and Miles P. Grier, 107–34. New York: Palgrave Macmillan, 2018.

Tucker, Veta Smith. "Purloined Identity: The Racial Metamorphosis of Tituba of Salem Village." *Journal of Black Studies* 30, no. 4 (2000): 624–34.

CHAPTER TEN

Adam Negro's Tryal, 1701

Introduction

Adam Negro's Tryal centers on the freedom suit of a black African man, named Adam, living in colonial Massachusetts. At various times Adam was enslaved or indentured to a Massachusetts judge and merchant named John Saffin. In 1700, Adam sued Saffin to enforce the terms of an indenture contract. Saffin revoked the contract on the grounds that Adam did not comport himself properly during the term of his indenture. Through a series of court petitions and depositions, Saffin described Adam as violent and surly, a menace to society. Adam constructed a counterimage, one that rendered him compliant with the legal and social status quo. Securing the assistance of two attorneys through whom he filed legal documents and appeared in court, Adam insisted that he complied with the primary—indeed the only—condition of the contract, that he serve for seven years. The way he served, he argued through his attorneys, was irrelevant. The court battle stretched out for some three years; during that time, twice the courts found in Adam's favor, then reversed their decisions, before ultimately granting him his freedom in 1703. Historians and literary scholars alike read Adam's legal battle as an early example of the textual self-fashioning that characterizes the African American tradition of life writing and autobiography.

Adam's efforts are significant in another regard. In 1701, amid the legal controversy, Saffin wrote a pamphlet in defense of slavery titled "A Brief and Candid Answer to a late Printed Sheet Entitled, The Selling of Joseph." Most often, literary scholars discuss this pamphlet as a response to the antislavery tract of another Massachusetts judge named Samuel Sewall, who a year earlier published "The Selling of Joseph," in which he argued that slavery was wrong because black Africans, like whites, were children of God. Saffin not only responds to Sewall with his pamphlet. He also responds to Adam, as evident by a narrative he appends to the pamphlet and references on the title page. In that appended narrative, Saffin includes a timeline to explain how and why he initiated the indenture contract and the various means by which he and Adam sought arbitration. While Adam did not pick up a pen himself, his actions circumscribed Saffin's writing project. "A Brief and Candid Answer," then, is not simply the ideological response of a proslavery jurist defending colonial Massachusetts's economic system against an opposing ideological perspective. It also answers the challenge of an enslaved black African man pursuing his freedom.

Text

From Abner Goodell, "John Saffin and His Slave Adam." *Publications of the Colonial Society of Massachusetts* 1:85–112. Boston, 1895, *GoogleBooks*, accessed June 10, 2021, https://www.google.com/books/.

The Indenture Contract

> Bee it known unto all men by these presents That I John Saffin of Bristol in the Province of the Massachusetts Bay in New England out of meer kindness to and for the Encouragemt of my negro man Adam to go on chearfully in his Business & Imploymt by me now putt into, the Custody Service and command of Thomas Shepherd my Tenant on boundfield Farm in Bristol aforesd for and During the Terme of Seaven years from the Twenty fifth day of March last past 1694—fully to be compleat and Ended or as I may otherwise See cause to Imploy him. I say I doe by these presents of my own free & Voluntary Will & pleasure from and after the full end & Expiration of Seven years beginning on the Twenty fifth day of March last past and from thenceforth fully to be compleat and Ended, Enfranchise clear and make free my sd negro man named Adam to be fully at his own Dispose and Liberty as other free men are or ought to be according to all true Intents & purposes whatsoever. Allways provided that the sd Adam my Servant do in the mean time go on chearfully quietly and Industriously in the Lawfull Business that either my Self or my Assigns shall from time to time reasonably Sett him about or imploy him in and doe behave and abear himself as an Honest true and faith full Servant ought to doe during the Tearm of Seven years as aforesaid In Witness whereof I the sd John Saffin have hereunto sett my hand and Seal this Twenty Sixth day of June 1694–In the Sixth year of their Majesty Reign
>
> Signed Sealed & Delivd in the prsence of
> RACHEL BROWNE ∞ her marke.
> RICHARD SMITH
> SAMUEL GALLOP
> John SAFFIN (Seal)

Saffin Petition (1703)

Whereas John Saffin Esq: by his Petition to the Great and General Court or Assembly for Her Majesty Province of the Massachusetts Bay held at Boston upon the Twenty sixth day of May last, did Insinuate that a certain negro man named Adam is withheld or taken from him &c°ſ upon which he obtained an order of the said Great & General Court that the matter be heard before the next Court of General Sessions of the Peace for the County of Suffolk—In Pursuance whereof the said John Saffin & the said Adam negro now appeared, and the said Adam by Thomas Newton his attorney pleaded that he oweth the said John Saffin no service butt is free by virtue of an Instrument under the hand and seal of the said John Saffin; and the allegations of both partyes being fully heard the matter was committed to the Jury who were sworn to try the same and returned their verdict therein upon oath, That is to say—they find that the said Adam negro hath not performed the condition for which he was to be Enfranchized & therefore is to continue a servant to his said Master. It's therefore considered by the court That the said Adam negro hath not performed the condition for which he was to be Enfranchized and therefore is to continue a servant to his said Master; The said Adam by his aforesaid Attorney appealed from this Judgment or sentance unto the next Court of Assize and General Goal delivery to be holden for this county and Entred into Recognizance with sufficient suretyes for his appearance and prosecuting his Appeal there with Effect and for the abiding and performing the order or sentance of the said court; and for his good behaviour in the meantime

Adam's Appeal filed October 1703

Suffolk ss [scilicet] The Reasons of appeale of Adam negro appelled against John Saffin of Bristoll in the County of Bristol Esq: Defendſ from the Judgment or Sentence of her Majesty Justices of her Majesty Court of generall Sessions of the peace held at Boston for the County of Suffolk on the first Tuesday of August 1703, by adjournment from the first Tuesday of July foregoing. To the honble Justices of her Majesty Court of Assize and generall Gaol Delivery to be held at Boston for the said County of Suffolk on the first Tuesday of November 1703. That whereas at the said Court of generall Sessions of the peace, the sd appellant had a tryall for his freedom & Claimed the same by vertue of an Instrument under the hand & seal of the Defendant bearing date the 26* day of June 1694. Yet sentence was given against him, which is wrong & erronious and ought to be reversed for the reasons following, viz: 1 * That whereas at the sd Court of generall Sessions of the peace sentence was given for the Defendant against the appellant when by Law the same ought to have been rendred for the appell against the Defendant 2 That it is evident, that the appellant served the Defendant faithfully & honestly during the Term of seven years from the 25" day of March 1694. and ought to have his freedom & liberty pursuant to the Instrument abovementioned. 3. That there is no penalty in the sd Instrument if the appellant did not serve the Defend faithfully during the abovesd Term of seven years, nor doth he thereby forfeit his freedom or liberty given him for that there is no provisoe or Condition in the sd Instrument that if the sd appellant did not faithfully serve the Defendt & his assignes during the sd Term, then he should forfeit the freedom or liberty thereby intended and the word provided mentioned in the sd Instrument is a consideracon and not a Condition, and the Enffranchisement is positive & not conditionall and liberty being a priviledge the greatest that can be given to any man save his life, it ought not to be forfeited upon trivial and frivolous matters as is pretended by the Defendant all which matters & things (with what further may be alledged by the Defendant) being duely weighed & considered by the honoble Court and the Genth of the Jury, the appellant hopes they will see good reason to Reverse the former sentence and give him his freedom.

—THO: Newton attorney for the appell'

Court's Final Ruling (November 1703)

Suffolk ss.[scilicet] Anno Regni Reginae Annae nunc Angliae &c Secundo–s. At her Majesty's Superiour Court of Judicature, Court of Assize & General Goal Delivery, Begun & held at Boston, within & for the County of Suffolk on Tuesday the second of November. 1703—.

By the Honorable Samuell Sewall Esqr
John Hawthorne Esqr
John Walley. Esqr
John Leverett Esqr

Adam negro Appellt us John Saffin Esq. Appellee. from a Judgment or sentence of a Court of General Sessions of the Peace held at Boston by adjournment on the Third day of August 1703. for that whereas the said John Saffin by his Petition to the Great and General Court or Assembly for Her Majesty's Province of the Massachusetts Bay held at Boston upon the 26th day of May last did Insinuate that the said Adam is withheld or taken from him &c. Upon which he obtained an Order of said Court that the matter should be heard before the Court of General Sessions of the Peace for the County of Suffolk. At which said Court Judgment was rendered that the said Adam negro had not performed the Condition for which he was to be Enfranchised & therefore to Continue a servant to his said master. Both Parties now appearing. The Judgment of said Court Reasons of appeal & all things touching the same being fully heard the whole was Committed to the Jury, who were sworne to try the same & Returned their verdict therein upon Oath That is to say They find for the appellt Revertion of the former Judgment & Cost of suits. Its therefore Considered by the Court That the said Adam & his heirs be at peace & quiet & free with all their Chattles from the said John Saffin Esq., & his heirs for Ever.

From Saffin's Narrative (excerpts)

"A true and particular Narrative by way of Vindication of the Authors dealing with, and prosecution of his Negro Man servant, for his vile and exorbitant Behaviour towards his Master,
    and his Tenant, Thomas Shepard, &c."

WHereas there hath been divers false Reports raised, which hath occasioned misunderstandings among good people concerning a Negro man, that goes by the name of Adam, Servant to me John Saffin; whereby some evil affected and prejudiced persons have taken occasion by false suggestions to blast my Name; and render me infamous in reference unto the said Negro, intimating that I having promised the said Negro to give him his freedom after the expiration of such a term of years, and that in order thereunto I had given it under my hand and seal. But after the expiration of the said term, I had violated my promise, and without cause, endeavoured unjustly to continue the said Negro a Bond man still, &c. These things being falsely suggested Doeg-like, partly true, and partly false (per verting the truth, and turning it into a lye) I have been advised by some Christian friends (agreeable to my own inclination) to set forth the truth of the matter, which for the most part is founded upon, and proved by Evidence upon Oath, and the Records of Courts, and not by my own bare assertion, which I doubt not, but that all unbiassed per sons will take notice of it for the clearing of my innocence therein, and the vindication of my Reputation, which at all times I valued above my Estate, which through the goodness of God (though not great, yet hath been competent).

DEPOSITIONS FROM NEIGHBORS

Joshua Finney (1701)

Joshua Finney of lawful age Testifieth & saith, That I this Deponent dwelling not far from Mr. Saffin's Farme at Bristol gate where Thomas Shepard was several years Tenant, with whom a Negro man named Adam that was said to be Mr. Saffins Negro dwelt, who came from the Mill as I understood for Thomas Shepard, asked him whether he had ground or had Meal, he said no; why then said Shepard did you not come sooner, upon which said Negro came up with his hand to Shepards face as if he would have struck him and Jabbar'd, but I could not tell what he said, but it seem'd to me as if he challenged said Shepard or threatned him, this he did two or three times that evening in my sight about two years agoe, and further saith not. Bristol April the 9th. 1701. Then the above said Joshua Finney took his Oath to the truth of the abovesaid, the Negro not being present. Coram John Brown Justice. Bristol Septemb. 11th. 1701. Sworn to in the Superiour Court of Judicature. A true Copy of that on file, Examined by Elisha Cooke Clerk.

Thomas and Hannah Shepard (1701)

Bristol March 24th 1701. Thomas Shepard and Hannah his Wife both of lawful Age, doth Testify and say, That we sometime about the year 1693. hired a Farm in Bristol of the Honoured Mr. Saffin, and a stock of Cattle and Sheep, and also one Negro man named Adam, which we were to have and to hold for the term of Seven years, but the aforesaid Negro man carried and behaved himself so basely, disobediently and outragiously, both in words and in actions, that so in some of his mad fits (which were many) I was in fear of some bodily mischief from him; for one night according to my best apprehension, he drew his Knife at me, so that I was glad to deliver him up to his former Master again, the

Honoured Mr. Saffin before the time was out. The said Hannah Testifies, That she see the said Knife in the said Negros hand, and see him take up an Ax, speaking to her Husband to Cut off his head. Sworn before me Nath. Paine one of His Majesties Justices of the Peace for the County of Bristol, the day and year above written Nath. Paine. Bristol Sept. 11th. 1701. Sworn to in the Superiour Court of Judicature by Thomas Shepard. A true Copy of that on file, Examined by Elisha Cooke Clerk.

John Griffin on Castle Island (1701)

Castle Island, Octob. 9th. 1701. John Griffin of full Age testifieth and saith, That on Tuesday the 7th Instant, Adam a Negro man being then a Labourer at the Castle, was removing some Earth, but did it not to Captain Clark's mind, who ordered him to do it otherwise, but the said Negro refused to do it according to his Order; at which Captain Clark said you Rascal, why don't you do it as I order you; the said Negro said he was no Rogue, no Rascal, no Thief; at which Captain Clark with a Stick broke his pipe, and said, you Rogue you shall do as I bid you, and gave him a push, at which said Negro gave him a push, and said, that if he struck him, he would strike him again; Captain Clark gave him a stroke or two with his stick; the Negro took hold of the Stick and brake it, and took up his Shovel and struck at Captain Clark, and had like to have spoilt him; but the other Labourers came to Captain Clarks assistance, and rescued him until some of the Garrison Souldiers came to help, and carried the said Negro to the Dungeon. And further, that in rescuing Captain Clark, the Negro got one of the Labourers hands in his mouth, and had like to have bit it off, but with help got it clear without much damage.

Suggested Reading

Foster, Frances Smith. *Witnessing Slavery: The Development of Ante-Bellum Slave Narratives.* 2nd ed. Madison: University of Wisconsin Press, 1994.

Peterson, Mark A. "The Selling of Joseph: Bostonians, Antislavery, and the Protestant International, 1689–1733." *Massachusetts Historical Review* 4 (2002): 1–22.

Towner, Lawrence W. "The Sewall-Saffin Dialogue on Slavery." *William and Mary Quarterly* 21, no. 1 (1964): 40–52.

Von Frank, Albert J. "John Saffin: Slavery and Racism in Colonial Massachusetts." *Early American Literature* 29, no. 3 (1994): 254–72.

CHAPTER ELEVEN

The Deposition of Lydia Draper in Dedham, MA, 1723

Introduction

The deposition of a white colonist in Massachusetts Bay named Lydia Draper, which was recorded in 1723, provided evidence for an investigation into the disappearance of twenty-seven pounds in bills of credit. While her account implicates two enslaved Native men, James and Titus, as the guilty parties in this alleged act of theft, it also describes the involvement of an enslaved black African man, Primus. Primus is a tangential presence in Draper's testimony, but her relation both preserves his speech and provides an important perspective on a system of bondage in which Native persons and black Africans were held together as chattels.

When the Drapers discovered that the bills of credit were missing, they questioned "our said Indian James," who confessed that he had given the money to Titus, a servant to the prominent sea captain John Foye. Titus denied these allegations, admitting only that he had accepted a parcel of tobacco from James. In an attempt to sway Foye, Draper introduced the secondhand testimony of Primus—who had witnessed the exchange between James and Titus. Primus testified that he saw James give Titus money and that he knew it was money, rather than paper, because of the marks on the bills. Because his testimony implicated Titus, Foye treated Primus contemptuously and suggested that Primus was actually responsible for the theft, illustrating the dangers of legal entanglement for enslaved black Africans. Primus was unlikely to realize any benefit by testifying in this case and endured unfounded accusations as a result of his participation; he could neither testify nor refuse to testify safely in a legal system with no regard for his rights.

Draper's testimony also documents the ways in which racism divided individuals whose shared bondage might otherwise have united them in a common cause. James's refusal to "have any intimacy with negros" reflects an unexplained and unexplainable racial animus. Primus had to contend not only with the prejudice of white men in power, such as Foye, but also with the racism of other enslaved individuals from whom he likely hoped for kindness.

Text

From "Deposition of Lydia Draper." *Depositions*, 251–53. Massachusetts State Archives. Microfilm.

> Lydia Draper, of full age, testifieth and saith that her husband had an Indian man named James who lived in our family many years, and now with Mr. John Fisher of Dedham, this said indian was observed not to have any intimacy with negros, but with Spanish indians that were his own Country men. And of late years an indian man named titus belonging to captain John Foy of Charlestown who was very intimate with our James, coming often to visit him, always calling him brother (though they were no relation) and said Draper man being employed about tobacco in a front Cellar with the Doors usually open to the street, said titus often come there under pretense to see his brother. But as James since looked was that Titus often advised him to steal money and give it to him the said Titus to keep for him; was missed twenty-seven pounds of province bills of credit on Monday the 30th of July Last at Even, which we know was in the house the Day before. And no one being in the house but said James, we were certain he must know of it, but before we spake to him we searched the house, and found only nine pounds of it in an old Drawer under some things of titus . . . and having Examined our said Indian James, he first made some pretense of giving it to an Indian who as he said went to the Eastward the week before the money was lost, then said James being told if he would confess the truth, he should escape punishment, upon which he said he gave the money to Captain Foy's Indian man titus, who had been in our cellar unknown to us, and also a half pound paper of our best tobacco, and the same afternoon before we missed the money, our James asked leave to go to Charlestown to see said Titus, who as our Indian has since owned to me had promised to make a pail of punch, when said James came to Charlestown. But captain Foy seeing him before his man saw him prevented their coming together at that time. I asked our Indian why he first said that he gave the money to another? He answered me he was not willing to bring out Titus. I then went to captain Foy's at Charlestown and asked that titus's chest might be searched. titus was caused he owned he was in our cellar, at the same time, but his brother gave him nothing but some letter. Then captain Foy and his wife and my self searched his chest, and found the

paper of tobacco in his chest, which I know by print on the paper. Titus said that our Indian gave him that and if he gave it him he must take it. Captain Foy said in the hearing of his man Titus that was not counted stealing, so captain Foy took said paper of tobacco into his custody, Saying he would pay for it. I asked leave of captain Foy for Titus to come to boston to have the two indians face to face but he denied me saying we might bring our Indian to Charlestown. I spake to captain Foy of having them Examined before a Justice of the peace but captain Foy answered he was a Justice himself. When said Draper's Indian understood that said Foy's Indian would not own that he had the money, our Indian said that primus a negro of mr Davidsons was at the cellar stair head and saw him give titus the money, so our Indian James and primus as a witness went to Charlestown to be Examined which was as follows. Captain Foy asked our Indian James if he stole money from his master? he answered yes, and that he gave it to said Foy's man titus, then captain Foy asked his man whether he had the money? who answered no. Captain foy Looking on primus who was the witness with an angry countenance saying what have you to say? said primus answered I see James give titus a bundle of money, captain Foy said how do you know it was money? primus answered I know it was money by the marks on the back side of the bills, as James was wrapping a paper about it and I saw James give it to titus, bidding him take care he did not lose it. titus answered no no, then putting the money under his arm and hasted away. And captain Foy said, he supposed it was the paper of tobacco that primus saw. primus said it was money that he saw James give to titus, and that he saw no tobacco, to which captain Foy replied you are a lying black dog, had not you the money? I suppose you had it. I then Desired that James and titus might go away by themselves hoping titus would tell James where the money was, which captain Foy granted but soon followed them, for I, Looking out, saw captain Foy standing between them said James and titus upon which I went to him and said it was to no purpose to sound them out if he stood by them. I asked captain Foy who said he did not know but he had, but it was one's yea and the other's nay, and that they were both rogues, after which I asked our indian what titus said to him when they were together. He answered that captain Foy would not let him speak to titus, but titus escaping with such a slippery Examination would own nothing when promised to come to boston. Some considerable after I went to captain Foy's house Desiring license to search titus's chest a second time supposing titus might think the danger over, and might at Last find some of the money in his chest, but I could not obtain leave. Some time after I being at Charlestown a girl named kathrine philips told me that some short time after our money was lost, that she being in the street with money in her hand the said titus saw it, and said to her that he had more money than she had, and pulling out a pocket book showed her a bill and said it was a twenty shilling bill and said that his brother at boston had more and being desirous to have said Titus more impartially Examined my husband affirms that he procured a warrant from Edward huchinson, Esquire to Endeavor to have taken him up in this town and also made application to the several Justices at Charlestown but could not obtain any warrant from Either of them.

Lydia Draper

Suggested Reading

Bragdon, Kathleen Joan. "Crime and Punishment among the Indians of Massachusetts, 1675–1750." *Ethnohistory* 28, no. 1 (1981): 23–32.

Konig, David Thomas. *Law and Society in Puritan Massachusetts: Essex County, 1629–1692.* Chapel Hill: University of North Carolina Press, 1979.

Moore, Lindsay R. *Women before the Court: Law and Patriarchy in the Anglo-American World, 1600–1800.* Manchester, UK: Manchester University Press, 2019.

CHAPTER TWELVE

Testimony on the New York Arson Conspiracy, 1741

Introduction

The voluminous testimony of black African witnesses examined in the New York City arson trials of 1741 has largely been ignored by literary scholars. But the testimony of Sandy, Jack, Bastian, and others emphasizes both their awareness of global politics and the sense of community that sustained black Africans enduring lives in bondage.

Magistrates investigating the ten fires concluded that black African men carried out the attacks under the direction of white ringleaders. Thirteen were burned at the stake; seventeen black African men, two white men, and two white women were hanged. More than 100 black African men and women were imprisoned, interrogated, and forced to identify other conspirators. The court's proceedings were published by Daniel Horsmanden, a justice who participated in the interrogation and sentencing of alleged conspirators. Black prisoners unanimously identified a white man named John Hughson as the plot's mastermind. They described a plan to burn the city, kill its white inhabitants, and wait for the arrival of French and Spanish forces. Both the conspirators and city's officials thought of these fires as a new front in the War of Jenkins' Ear between England and Spain.

The records assembled by Horsmanden speak to a range of issues, from language and interpretation to gender. For example, Jack's testimony is a reminder that many of the accused spoke English as a second language. For this reason, court officials looked to the behavior and facial expressions of the accused to assess their guilt or penitence; thus, Horsmanden notes that Bastian seemed "touched with a remorse for his guilt." Many accounts describe alcohol as both an inducement to join the plot and a drug that impaired the judgment of conspirators. Another recurring feature of these accounts is the role of oaths; some swore on the Bible and kissed it, while others swore by God or by thunder. Although two white women were at the conspiracy's heart, the relative paucity of black African women suggests that they were intentionally excluded from the plot, and Quack's confession acknowledges that he regarded his wife as untrustworthy.

Notwithstanding the repetitive features of these testimonies—the lists of other conspirators and the commitments to kill, among others—each also preserves a unique perspective. Together, they illustrate the different ways in which enslaved black Africans negotiated the limited choices available to them. While some eagerly embraced the chance for a violent revenge, others expressed remorse for their part in the plot and spoke of their participation with regret.

Text

From Daniel Horsmanden, *The New-York Conspiracy, or a History of the Negro Plot, with the Journal of the Proceedings against the Conspirators at New-York in the Years 1741–2*. New York, 1744.

Quack's Confession at the Stake

Quack's confession at the stake. He said,

1. "That Hughson was the first contriver of the whole plot, and promoter of it; which was to burn the houses of the town; Cuffee said, to kill the people.
2. "That Hughson brought in first Caesar, Vaarck's; then Prince, Auboyneau's; Cuffee, Philipse's; and others, amongst whom were old Kip's negro; Robin, Chambers's; Cuffee, Gomez's; Jack, Codweis's and another short negro, that cooks for him.
3. "That he Quack did fire the fort, that it was by a lighted stick taken out of the servants hall, about eight o'clock at night, that he went up the back stairs with it and so through Barbara's room, and put it near the gutter, betwixt the shingles, and the roof of the house.
4. "That on a Sunday afternoon, a month before the firing of the fort, over a bowl of punch, the confederates at Hughson's (amongst whom were the confederates above named, Albany, and Tickle, alias Will, Jack and Cook, Comfort's; old Butchell, Caesar, and Guy, Horsfield's; Tom, Van Rants's; Caesar, Peck's; Worcester, and others) voted him Quack, as having a wife in the fort, to be the person who should fire the fort, Sandy, and Jack, Codweis's; Caesar and Guy, Horsfield's; were to assist him in it.
5. "That Hughson desired the Negroes to bring to his house what they could get from the fire, and Hughson was to bring down country people in his boat to further the business, and would bring in other negroes.
6. "That forty or fifty to his knowledge were concerned, but their names could not recollect [the mob pressing and interrupting.]

7. "That Cuffee, Gomez's; and Caesar, Peck's, fired Van Zant's storehouse.
8. "That Mary Burton had spoke the truth, and could name many more.
9. "Fortune, Wilkins's, and Sandy, had done the same; and Sandy could name the Spaniards, and say much more, which Cuffee particularly confirmed.
10. "Being asked what view Hughson had in acting in this manner? He answered, to make himself rich.
11. "That after the fire was over, Quack was at Hughson's house, Jack, Comfot's, a leading man, Hughson, wife and daughter present, and said, the job was done, meaning the fire; that he went frequently to Hughson's house, and met there Tickle and Albany.
12. "Quack said his wife was no ways concerned, for he never would trust her with it: and that Denby knew nothing about the matter.
13. "Jamaica, Ellis's, not concerned that he knew of, but was frequently at Hughson's with his fiddle.
14. "Said he was not sworn by Hughson, but others were."

Examination of Jack

This evening captain Jack (Comfort's negro) condemned, amongst others, to be executed to-morrow afternoon, had caused to be signified to the judges, that if his life might be spared, he would discover all that he knew of the conspiracy. From the course of the evidence, there was reason to conclude that he had been a most trusty and diligent agent for Hughson; he lived very near him, and his master was frequently absent from home for days and weeks together, which left him too much at liberty; and there was a well in his yard whereto many negroes resorted every day, morning and afternoon, to fetch tea water; and Hughson, no doubt, thought he had carried a great point when he had seduced captain Jack to his infamous schemes, for this gave him the greatest opportunities of corrupting his fellow slaves; and Jack was a crafty, subtle fellow, very well qualified for such an enterprize, and might be captivated with the fine promises and hopes given him of being not only a free, but a great man; a commander in this band of fools, of whom the greatest knaves perhaps (like fools too) projected to make a prey in the end. It was therefore thought proper, as this mystery of iniquity was yet but beginning to be unfolded, so far to accept Jack's offer as to respite his execution, till it was found how well he would deserve further favour.

Jack was examined before the judges this afternoon, and was under examination the next day, when his fellow criminals were carrying from the City-Hall to their execution. He was advised not to flatter himself with the hopes of life, without he would do the utmost in his power to deserve it, and that would be by telling freely all that he knew of the matter, and discovering all the parties concerned, to the best of his knowledge. He was told we were already let so far into this secret, as to persons and things, as to be able to give a good guess, whether he spoke the truth, and he would but deceive himself in the end if he told falsehoods. Jack looked very serious, and at length began to open, but his dialect was so perfectly negro and unintelligible, it was thought it would be impossible to make any thing of him without the help of an interpreter. There were two young men, sons-in-law to Jack's master, who were aware Jack would not be understood without their aid, and they signified their desire of being by when he was examined, from a supposition that they might be of service in interpreting his meaning, as he had been used to them, having often worked in the same shop together at the cooper's trade, whereby he was so familiarized to them, they could make a shift to understand his language, and they thought they had such an influence over him, that they were persuaded, they could also prevail upon him to make an ingenuous confession; and to do them justice, they were very serviceable in both respects, and the event well answered the expectation they had given. But notwithstanding this assistance, his examination took up as much time of three successive days, morning and afternoon, as could conveniently be spared him from other business.

Several negroes concerned in the conspiracy, having been discovered by Jack in this first sitting, were apprehended the next morning early, pursuant to orders then immediately given, but there was not time to commit his confession to writing this evening, yet it is thought proper to set the same forth as of this day. Jack desired he might be removed from the cell where his fellow criminals, condemned with him, were lodged, and his request was granted.

Examination and Confession of Jack (Comfort's) before one of the judges, No. 1.—He said,

1. "That a little after new year, on a Monday, about four in the afternoon, Ben (Capt. Marshall's) came to Comfort's house to fetch tea water, where he left his keg in the shop, and went to Hughson's house

(Hughson and his wife then gone into the country) Ben staid about two hours there, and then returned to Comfort's, and told Jack that he had met there six Spaniards, among whom were Anthony and Wan (now in Jail) and said to him, countryman, I have heard some good news: what news said Jack? Ben[1] said there were Spanish negroes at Hughson's, who told him they had designs of taking this country against the wars came; what would they do with this country? Said Jack, to which Ben answered, oh! you fool, those Spaniards know better than York negroes, and could help better to take it than they, because they were more used to war; but they must begin first to set the house [i.e. the houses] on fire.

2. "That the Sunday following Hughson and his wife came home, and brought a goose, a quarter of mutton, and a fowl home. That Ben came a little after church out, in the afternoon, to Comfort's, and told him, brother go to Hughson's, all our company is come down: he went with Ben thither, and went round the house and went in at the back door; when he came there they sat all round the table, and had a goose, a quarter of mutton, a fowl and two loaves of bread: Hughson took a flask of rum out of a case and set it on the table, and two bowls of punch were made; some drink dram; a cloth was laid:

Quash, H. Rutgers's negro; Caesar, Koertrecht's; Powlus, a Spanish negro; Toby, or Cato, Provoost's; Cato, Shurmur's; Cook, Comfort's; John, Vaarck's; York and London, Marschalk's; Ticklepitcher, Carpenter's; Francis, Bosch's; Bastian, alias Tom Peal; Scipio, Mrs. Van Borsom's; Ben, Captain Marshal's, were all present, and also six Spanish negroes, among whom were Wan and Anthony, and a negro lately belonging to John Marschalk, the three others he should know if he saw them; Hughson, and his wife, and daughter sat down on one side of the table, and the negroes on the other: two or three tables were put together to make it long; Hughson's daughter brought in the victuals, and just as he came in Sarah brought the cloth and laid it; Mary Burton did not come into the room, but Hughson said she was above making a bed; Peggy came down stairs and sat down by Hughson's wife at the table, and eat with them; when they were eating they began all to talk about setting the houses on fire, and Hughson asked Ben, who would be the head man or captain for to rise? Ben said yes, he would stand for that, and said he could find a gun, shot and powder, at his master's house, that his master did not watch him, he could go into every room: Ben asked

Quash, what will you stand for? He said he did not care what he stood for, or should be, but he could kill three, four, five white men before night.

3. "That Quash said he could get two half dozen of knives in papers, three or four swords; and that he would set his master's house on fire, and when he had done that, he would come abroad to fight.
4. "That Marschalk's York said that his mistress had scolded at him, and he would kill her before he went out to fight.
5. "London (Marschalk's other negro) said that before he went out to fight, he would set his master's house on fire.
6. "Scipio (Van Borsom's negro) said he would set his mistress's house on fire before he would got out to fight.
7. "Cato (Shurmur's negro) said he would set his mistress's house on fire, and that as the houses stand all together, the fire would go more far.
8. "Cato alias Toby (John Provoost's negro) said he would get his master's sword, and then set the house on fire, and go out to fight.
9. "The Spanish negroes he could not understand.
10. "Caesar (Kortrecht's negro) said he would set his master's bakehouse on fire.
11. "Ben said (when it was proposed to burn his master's house) no, if they conquered the place, he would keep that to live in himself.
12. "That Curacoa Dick came in just as they had done eating, but victuals enough were left for him, and he sat down and eat: when Dick had done eating, he said every one must stand to his word, and that he would get his master's gun, and after that would set his stable on fire.
13. "He (Jack) being asked to set his master's house on fire, said no, he would set his master's shingles on fire, and then go out to fight.
14. "Hughson said he would stand by what the Spanish and York negroes should do; and he would go before and be their king, and would mix them one against another when they came to fight.
15. "Hughson sat the negroes upon this discourse, and design, at the said meeting; on which the Spanish negroes agreed all to join with the York negroes.
16. "That they all swore; some said d—n, some said by G-d, and other oaths; a Spanish negro swear by thunder; Hughson swore by G-d, if they would be true to him, he would take this country; and Jack swore by G-d for his part.

17. "That Peggy went away after they had done eating, before they swore.
18. "Mary Burton took away the dishes and plates, and Sarah (Hughson's daughter) took away the cloth; Sarah (Hughson's wife) sat down by her husband, and continued there all the time.
19. "The meeting broke up just after sun down.
20. "Tickle (Carpenter's negro) said, his mistress was cross, and he worked hard, and could get no good clothes; that he would murder his mistress first, because she was not good to him, before he went out to fight.
21. "Bastian alias Tom Peal (Vaarck's) eat at Hughson's; Quash asked him if he would stand to help? he said yes, he knew that, and that was the reason he came there.
22. "Francis (Jasper Bosch's) said, he would set his master's house on fire, before he came out to fight.
23. "Comfort's Cook went with him (Jack) to Hughson's; swore, and said he would set his master's storehouse on fire; and was to go fight too, and could get a penknife or any thing.
24. "Vaarck's Jonneau stood at the door a pretty while; but when the meat ready on table, came in, and sat down at table: York asked him, what will you stand for? he said, he was not able to fight, but he would set his master's house on fire, and then his neighbours, and so on.
25. "Says, they agreed to wait a month and half for the Spaniards and French to come; and if they did not come then, they were to begin at Wenman's, next to Mr. De Lancey's, and so on down the Broadway.
26. "That they waited until this month and half was expired, and then the fort was burnt.
27. "Says, that every negro then present was to do what they engaged to do, on one and the same Sunday, when church was gone in of the morning; and if all was not done in that one day, they were to go on the Saturday following; and so, if the Spaniards and French did not come, they were to do all themselves.
28. "That at this meeting Anthony, belonging to Peter De Lancey, talked about stuff to put the houses on fire, by flinging it into the house, but heard no other negro but him talk of it; but he mentioned it every time they met, but at this meeting for the first time.
29. "That same Sunday's Monday (the next day) about sun down, all the same negroes came to Hughson's again; some brought money and gave to Hughson for drink and dram; Ben played on the fiddle; Hughson's wife and daughter danced together in one part of the

room, and the negroes in another; staid there until about seven that night: that they came there that night to frolick and merry make, and did not talk about fires, for they had agreed upon that the day before.

30. "That then one Sunday passed and no meeting any where that he knows of.
31. "The Sunday after that, there was a meeting at his master Comfort's; some negroes were in the shop, and some in the kitchen; that the kitchen and shop join to each other; the floors into each went out into the street, or into the yard; so that to go from one to the other, you must go either into the yard or on the dock; among whom were Marshall's Ben, Rutger's Quash, Provost's Cato alias Toby, Shurmur's Cato, Marschalk's York and London, Vanborsom's Scipio, Carpenter's Albany, Curacoa Dick, Kortrecht's Caesar, Burk's Sarah, Niblet's Sandy, Chamber's Robin, Gomez's Cuffee, Peck's Caesar, Comfort's Cook, Sleydall's Jack, Anthony and Wan, two Spanish negroes; Vanderspiegle's Fortune, Cowley's Cato, Jay's Brash, Bosch's Francis, Furman's Harry and Powlus: which negroes being met, they began all to talk of burning the town and killing the people; and the general conversation was to the effect of that at Hughson's and the fire to begin as aforesaid; every one being to set his master's house or stable on fire, and then go out to fight.
32. "Furman's Harry was to set his master's cowstable on fire.
33. "This conversation began, and was most talked of before Sandy came in; Sandy came into the kitchen first, being called in by him (Jack) but was loth to come; Jack asked him to drink a dram, Sandy said no; Sarah (Bark's negro wench) who was then present, said he must drink, and made him drink; and having drunk the dram, Jack asked him if he would stand to, and help them burn houses, and kill the white people? Sandy seemed afraid, they all drank a dram round, and he (Jack) brought in nine clasp knives in a paper; those that had not knives before, took knives from the paper; some went into the shop, and some came into the kitchen, and all the knives were distributed: being asked how he came by those knives, said he asked Powlus, a Spanish negro, about a week before this meeting, to give him a knife; Powlus said he would get some for him and sell him; Powlus appointed him to meet him the Wednesday before this meeting, at the meal-market, about dusk; that Powlus came, and he gave him two shillings and six pence for them.

34. "When they saw Sandy afraid, they whetted their knives in order to frighten him to say yes, to stand by them; and Jack said, if he did not stand by them he would cut his head off; to which Sarah said, he deserves it if he don't say yes; then Sandy said yes.
35. "The stone they whetted their knives on was a brown stone that lay in the yard by the door. About a week and a half after this meeting, the fort was set on fire.
36. "Soon after Sandy had consented, it growing dusk, they parted.
37. "Says he thought the bargain so sure made, that he did not make any more meetings before the fort fired.
38. "Says that some time after the fort burnt, Sleydall's Jack came to Comfort's house, and told the examinant he had put fire to Mr. Murray's haystack.
39. "That he met Provoost's negro the night that Hilton's house was burnt, and asked him what news? for he had heard that there had been fire at that end of the town; Provoost's Cato alias Toby, said he had done it.
40. "That Gomez's Cuffee set Van Zant's storehouse on fire."

Examination and Confession of Bastian

Examination and confession of Bastian, alias Tom Peal, before one of the judges, No. 1.—He said,

1. "That a little after new-year, Caesar (hanged) his fellow servant asked him to go along with him down to Hughson's house; this was of a Sunday afternoon before church was out; when he came there he found about fifteen negroes, to the best of his remembrance, in a room with Hughson, his wife and daughter (now under condemnation) Caesar (hanged) was then present, and asked him the examinant (Caesar having a pistol in his hand and clapping the same to the examinant's breast) whether he would join along with them to become their own masters? the examinant asked him, what he would have him join with him in? Caesar answered him in the plot, for that they had designed to take the country, and said they had a parcel of good hands, Spanish negroes, five or six of them (then present) who would join with the York negroes: that they expected that war would be proclaimed in a little time against the French, and that the French and Spaniards would come here, and that they (meaning the negroes present and the Hughsons) would join with them to take the place: at

first the examinant answered no, and then Caesar said if he did not join along with them, swearing, he the examinant should not go alive out of the house: then he offered the examinant something to drink, and made him drink; and then Caesar said now he had got him; and the examinant being affrighted, and very much daunted upon Caesar's offering a pistol at his breast, was forced to consent; whereupon Caesar said to Hughson, the examinant was but a weak-hearted dog; however set his name down, and I will encourage him up: Hughson answered, he would do it.

2. "Says to the same effect as Comfort's Jack [touching the meeting and entertainment at Hughson's] with this further, that there was veal, ducks, geese, a quarter of mutton and fowls to the best of his remembrance.

3. "That Hughson, his wife and daughter, sat down to eat with the negroes, with this difference, that they sat on one side of the table, the negroes on the other; that the cloth was laid on several tables put together, and some boards laid upon tubs.

4. "That Peggy went in and out of the room, but did not sit down with them, but believes she must have heard them discourse about the plot carrying on, and talked of at that meeting.

5. "That after they had done eating, the maid and the daughter helped take the things away; then John Hughson brought a bible and laid it upon the table, then opened the book, and seemed to read something out of it, which was in the nature of an oath, that the first thunder might strike them dead that discovered, or did not stand to their words to perform what they had engaged to do. Hughson swore first, then his wife, then his daughter, and all the negroes present, as well as himself, and all kissed the book; and Hughson pronounced the words they swore to, that is to say, to burn the town, and murder the people, but they were to stay till the Spaniards and French came, about a month and a half; and if they did not come in that time, they were to begin themselves, and that they were to begin with the fort first.

6. "That captain Marshall's Ben (whom Hughson and the negroes called captain Marshall) was there when the examinant came in. Jack (Comfort's) came in before the cloth was laid, and after Caesar had clapped the pistol to the examinant's breast.

7. "That Hughson took a flask of rum out of a case and put upon the table, and some punch was made of it, and some drank dry drams, and all the negroes agreed to what was proposed as before.

The negroes then present [at Hughson's] were Caesar (hanged) Prince (hanged) Philipse's Cuffee, Roosevelt's Quack, Chambers's Robin, Gomez's Cuffee, Comfort's Jack and Cook, Peck's Caesar, Marschalk's York and London, Rutgers's Quash, captain Marshall's Ben, Powlus, P. De Lancey's Anthony, Cowley's Cato, Shurmur's Cato, Kip's Harry, Carpenter's Tickle Pitcher, Bosch's Francis, captain Provoost's Cato or Toby, whom they called captain Provoost. "Every one to fire his master's house, and then to fire the fort, and to begin next Mr. De Lancey's; and those that lived at the Fly, to burn Van Zant's storehouse, and begin the fire there: those at the Long Bridge were to fire there.

8. "They broke up about nine of the clock, having made their agreement. At this meeting was the first discourse he heard about the plot.
9. "The Monday night following he went to Hughson's, where they had a frolick; no fiddle, and had the said discourse again, all to stand true to their words, &c. Most part of the same company there again; some he believes could not come out: they had agreed the night before to meet again.
10. "They met at Comfort's about a fortnight after, on Sunday. Jack asked Sandy to come in, &c. Sarah said he was an impudent boy not to do as the captain bid him; Jack fetched penknives, &c.

    Negroes present at Comfort's. He, Bastian, Curacoa Dick, Sandy, Sarah, Bosch's Francis, Albany, Roosevelt's Quack, Chambers's Robin, Comfort's Cook and Jack, Gomez's Cuffee, Kip's Harry, Peck's Caesar, Marshall's Ben, De Lancey's Albany, Sarly's Wan, Wendover's Emanuel, (Spanish negro) Shurmur's Cato, Marschalk's York and London, Sleydall's Jack.
11. "Jack (Comfort's) was to put his masters shingles on fire, &c. to the purpose as Jack said."

    Bastian seemed by his looks and behavior, upon his examination, to be touched with a remorse for his guilt, and was very ingenuous in his confession, insomuch, that he was thought an object of mercy, and would be a witness worthy of credit, therefore it was judged proper to recommend him to the lieutenant governor for a pardon.

Examination and Confession of Will

Examination and confession of Will, alias Ticklepitcher, negro, taken before one of the judges—No. 1.—He said,

1. "That he was one of the company at Hughson's with a parcel of negroes when North, the constable, came and interrupted them at a feast.
2. "That on the Sunday following, which was about Whitsontide twelve months, Tom, belonging to captain Rowe, and Quamino, belonging to the estate of Harris, in Stone-street, asked him whether he would do as they would? the examinant asked them, what was that? old Quamino answered, that they would set fire to both rows of houses in Stone-street, and he would find powder and pistol and ball: the examinant said, he would consider of it, he did not know whether he would or no: then Quamino pulled out a razor and threatened to cut his throat if he did not agree with them, upon which he was forced to consent.
3. "That about three weeks after last new year, one day about the middle of the week, he (the examinant) Albany, his fellow servant, the above named Tom, and the said Quamino, were at the house of the said John Hughson, and had a tankard of punch, which Hughson had brought to them.
4. "That they, the said negroes, together with Cowley's Cato, Vanderspiegle's Fortune, Burk's Sarah, Kelly's London, Varian's Worcester, Kip's Harry, Becker the brewer's Mars, Powlus, Debrosse's Primus, Latham's Tony, another negro (Fortune) belonging to the said Latham, captain Lawrance's tall negro (Sterling) Low's yellow fellow Wan (commonly called Indian Wan) Vaarck's Will and Bastian, Gomez's Cuffee, Groesbeck's Mink, Curacoa Dick, the fiddler, Mrs. Sims's Bill or Will, (in all he thinks between twenty and thirty) were all that he remembers to be present at this meeting at Hughson's.
5. "That the day before this meeting, the negroes above named being all present at Hughson's; he the said Hughson said to the negroes, now was a proper time to make a plot, since there were so many of them together: that is to say, they should undertake to burn the town; to burn the fort; to burn Stonestreet; almost every one agreed, and undertook to burn their master's and mistress's house; and to kill the white people as they came to extinguish the flames: he the examinant was to set his mistress's house of fire: they pitched upon him for it.
6. "Hughson brought out a great book to make them swear; Hughson swore himself and Peggy first, and then swore all the negroes; they putting their right hand every one upon the book; the purport of the

oath was, damnation to eternity to the failers, or those that brought out (i.e. discovered) what they had agreed upon.
7. "They were to bring all the goods that they could get at the fires to Hughson's house; and after all over, Hughson was to carry them (the negroes) off.
8. "Hughson, to encourage this meeting, promised to give them a barrel of cyder."

Confession of Cato

Confession of Cato, colonel Moore's negro, before one of the judges.

He said, 1. That the first that spoke to him about the conspiracy was Harmanus Rutgers's Quash and Ben, by capt. Marshall's stable, about a fortnight after Christmas, of a Sunday morning; they asked him to go down to Comfort's with them after church out in the evening, for that there was to be company there.
2. That they told him that the negroes were going to rise against the white people, and asked him to join with them? he told them at first he was not willing, he had no occasion for it, for he lived well: Quash made answer, that he himself lived as well or better than he; and Ben said so did he; but it was a hard case upon the poor negroes, that they could not so much as take a walk after church-out, but the constables took them up; therefore in order to be free, they must set the houses on fire, and kill the white people; and Ben asked him to set his master's house on fire; he told him then he was not willing to do that: they asked him to come down to Comfort's after church in the evening, which he did; there was rum there, and he drank a dram; but he did not see Jack this first time: the negroes he then saw at Comfort's were Ben, Quash, Chambers' Robin, Peck's Caesar, Cook, Marschalk's York and London, Shurmur's Cato, Crooke's Prince, Shoemaker's York, Crooke's York, Lowe's Sam, widow Fortune's Cuffee, Van Horne's Bridgwater, Bound's Scipio, Cowley's Cato, Vanderspeigle's Fortune, Provost's (hanged) Cato, Kip's Harry. The same sort of talk passed there as above mentioned; but they did not all very well agree at that time.
3. That about a fortnight afterwards, on a Sunday, he went with Pintard's Caesar, in order to meet with Albany, Tickle, Curacoa Dick and Bosch's Frank, and they went down to Hughson's one after another; when they came there, they went into a room where were

Hughson, his wife and daughter, but the latter did not stay in the room; Hughson brought them drams, which they paid for; and he talked to them about the plot for burning the houses of the town, and killing the white people; and told them there were several companies of negroes to be made up, and asked if they would be concerned; and some agreed at that time; but he and Pintard's Caesar did not, they came out of the house together after staying about half an hour.

4. That the Sunday after this, he went to Hughson's again with Albany, and Hughson carried Albany and him up stairs, and swore them upon a bible, after having told them that there were a great many concerned in this plot; that they had agreed to rise against the town, to murder the people; some to murder their masters and mistresses, and to burn their houses, and proposed to him to do the same, and destroy the whole family; which he was unwilling to agree to at first, but at last consented, and then he was sworn and kissed the book; and Albany consented to kill his mistress and the rest of the family, and to burn her house; and was sworn in the same manner: that the purport of the oath was, that they were to keep all secret, and to perform what they had severally engaged to do; and if they failed therein, they were to be damned forever.

5. That on another Sunday evening about a fortnight or three weeks after that, he went to a supper at Hughson's according to his invitation.

6. That the last time he Marschalk's Tork by Mr. De Lancey's, as he was going; when he came there there were a great number of negroes, he believes forty or fifty, among which were Fortune's Cuffee, Lowe's Sam, Bound's Scipio, Cha. Crooke's York, Van Horne's Bridgwater, Ward's Will, G. Crooke's Prince, Kortrecht's Caesar, Horsefield's Guy: that he did not sit down at the table where Hughson, his wife and daughter sat, but at a side-table with several others: after supper Hughson talked to them about the plot; they were all to be true to one another, to keep secret, and to perform what they had engaged to do: and Hughson had a book, and swore several upon it, and made them kiss it; but those that were at a distance, swore without book.

7. That the Sunday fortnight after that, he went to Comfort's, where were, he believes, about forty negroes, where they talked of the plot to the same purpose, and swore. There were Quash, Ben, Fortune's Cuffee, Wyncoop's Indian London, captain French's London, Brazier's Tony, Horsefield's Guy, Duane's Prince.

8. That Vaarck's Caesar (hanged) told him David Provost's Low was concerned in the plot, and that he was at Hughson's, at that supper on the Sunday, but don't remember he saw him there.

Confession of Prince

No. 15. Gabriel Crooke's Prince said, that Mrs. Stilwell's Pedro carried him to Hughson's, and Hughson swore them to stand by him, to kill the white people and fire the house.

2. That Marschalk's York, when the first negroes were burning, told Prince, that now it was a fit time to kill the white people; but Prince answered, no, there were too many whites to attempt it.
3. That Titus Mr. Phoenix's negro, was one day last fall on the dock with the prisoner, at one Myers's a gun-smith; that Titus asked Myers to sell him a gun to shoot partridges with; but Myers would not sell him one; that afterwards he saw Titus and asked him what he wanted to buy a gun for? That Titus told him he had been at Hughson's, and they were to rise and kill the white people.
4. That some time before the fort was burnt, he was at Mr. Masterton's; that Cataline, Mr. Masterton's negro was drunk, talking to himself in the yard, that the negroes were fools to do here as they had done in the hot country; for they all burnt and hanged for it in the hot country.[2]
5. That there were present at the same time at Hughson's, York of Gabriel Crook, Titus of Phoenix, Mr. Moore's Cato, Kip's Harry, and Furman's Harry.

Examination of Scipio

No. 1. Bound's Scipio said, that last Christmas holidays, Comfort's Jack carried him to Hughson's, where there were a great number of negroes, near thirty; that they all supped there, and after supper Hughson got a bible, and told them there was a plot going forward against the white people of the town, that the French and Spaniards were expected, and then would be a fair opportunity; that those that would swear to him to be of his side, should be his men; that they might be all free men; that he, Hughson, swore himself, his wife and daughter, and afterwards swore several of the negroes, but knows not what negroes they were; that he swore them all to secrecy, and said he would provide arms for all of them; that he, Scipio, was to kill his master and mistress. That he was afterwards at Comfort's, and saw Jack there sharpening knives, which he said were to be used to kill the white people; that several negroes were there, and afterwards Jack told him there was to be a general feast at Hughson's; that when he supped at Hughson's, the daughter of Hughson took the cloth from the table. . . .

As soon as Scipio was brought before Mr. Nicholls and Mr. Lodge to be examined, he was asked who his master was, and what was his name? he answered, master, don't you know me? I am Scipio, belonging to Mr. Robert Bound, and formerly belonged to Dr. Nichols; and it being then demanded of him, how he came to be concerned in the conspiracy? (he being a fellow that did not want sense, and had had a better education than most of his colour) he answered, it is true, sir, I ought to have known better; my first master, Dr. Nicols, brought me up from a child, sent me to school, and had me taught to read; he intended to give me to his son, who was bred a merchant, for which reason he put me to a cooper to learn that trade, but his son going to live in the country, he had no use for me in that business; my old master therefore sold me to my present master, Bound, who has likewise been very kind to me; but it was with me as it is with all my colour, who are never easy till they get a dram, and when they have one want more; this was my case on my meeting with Comfort's Jack, who carried me to Hughson's, where from drinking one dram I drank more, till I was bewitched with it, &c. as in the examination above.

Those gentlemen declared this fellow seemed to be the most sensible of any they examined, and appeared very penitent and sorry for what he had done; he had, when examined, his bible in his bosom, which he said he read in jail as often as he could.

Suggested Reading

Bond, Richard E. "Shaping a Conspiracy: Black Testimony in the 1741 New York Plot." *Early American Studies* 5, no. 1 (2007): 63–94.

Doolen, Andy. "Reading and Writing Terror: The New York Conspiracy Trials of 1741." *American Literary History* 16, no. 3 (2004): 377–406.

Lepore, Jill. *New York Burning: Liberty, Slavery, and Conspiracy in Eighteenth-Century Manhattan* (New York: Vintage Books, 2005).

Moses, William J. "Sex, Salem, and Slave Trials: Ritual Drama and Ceremony of Innocence." In *The Black Columbiad: Defining Moments in African American Literature and Culture*, edited by Werner Sollors and Maria Diedrich, 64–76. Cambridge, MA: Harvard University Press, 1994.

CHAPTER THIRTEEN

Petition of Jethro Boston for Divorce, 1741

Introduction

This series of records, documenting the marriage and divorce of two enslaved persons, is remarkable for several reasons. Marriage was widely recognized as an institution incompatible with slavery because as long as individuals were enslaved, they lacked the legal standing to enter into contracts. Accordingly, enslaved persons generally lived together in common-law marriages, rather than in unions formalized by the law. Enslaved persons rarely made formal petitions for divorce; the first and often the only recourse for enslaved men and women living in a common-law relationship was an appeal to their enslavers.

In these documents, an enslaved man named Jethro Boston requests that his marriage to an enslaved woman named Hagar, solemnized on 10 September 1731 by Samuel Sewall, be dissolved on the grounds that she had sex with a white man and gave birth to his "Molatto Bastard Child." Jethro's petition for a divorce and the two witness statements provided in support of his request describe the father of Hagar's baby as a white soldier named William Kelly, but the nature of her relationship with Kelly is unclear. This frustrating lack of clarity highlights the precarity we face when reading and examining records of black African lives in early America. Hagar may have found the prospect of a British soldier in uniform irresistible, deciding that she simply wanted to have sex with someone who was not her husband. Perhaps she had no desire to marry Jethro in the first place; enslavers sometimes gave an enslaved woman as a sexual partner and common-law wife to an enslaved man in their possession without considering the woman's agency or consulting her preferences. But her relationship with Kelly also could have been involuntary; if Kelly used the weapons given him by the state to threaten or rape Hagar, she might have had no meaningful choice in the matter of whether or not she became impregnated with his child. Whatever the reason for her relationship with Kelly, she could not escape the stigma of interracial sex.

Legal systems rarely worked to the advantage of enslaved Africans. However, both the marriage and the presumptive divorce of Jethro and Hagar are the exceptions that prove this rule. Because of the economic ramifications of their divorce, their owner tried to prevent it, but after five years of seeking a permanent separation, the two successfully ended their legal entanglement when the governor granted this petition for divorce.

Text

"Petition of Jethro Boston." *Domestic Relations*, 248–50. Massachusetts State Archives. Microfilm.

> To His Excellency William Shirley, Esquire, Captain General and Governor in Chief in and over His Majesty's Province of the Massachusetts Bay and to the Honorable His Majesty's Council for the said Province now sitting in Boston, March 1741
>
> Boston Negro Servant of Edward Broomfield of Boston, Merchant
>
> Humbly Shews That on the Tenth day of September Anno Domini 1731 he was Lawfully Married to Hagar a Negro Woman, but she not having the fear of God before her Eyes and being Instigated by a white man has been Guilty of the Detestable sin of Adultery & was during the times of Intermarriage Delivered of a Molatto Bastard Child begotten on her Body and as by Law all Controversy Concerning Marriage & Divorce are to be heard & Determined by your Excellency & Honors—
>
> Your poor petitioner humbly prays your Excellency & Honors will take the premise into Your Just Consideration & order that she the said Hagar may be Divorced from the petitioner & that the Marriage may be Declared void & of none Effect.
>
> Signed
>
> Boston Jethro

> John Gyles of Roxbury in the County of Suffolk, Esquire, espouseth & saith that he knows Jethro a Negro Servant (now belonging to Mr. Edward Broomfield) & Hagar his Wife a Negro Woman who were his Servants about five Years ago; At which Time the Said Hagar was delivered of a Female Molatto Child in the deponents House, that he Saw the Child within a few Hours after the Birth, and the said Hagar did then acknowledge that it was born of her Body & likewise said that one William Kelly (then a Soldier at St. Georges River) was the Father

of it; That this deponent has used all possible Endeavors to reconcile the said Jethro & Hagar but to no purpose.

Boston April 13 1742.

John Gyles

Boston April 13th 1742

Thomas Saunders now resident in Boston Marriner Testifieth and saith That he knew Jethro Boston Negro and Hagar his wife, that about five years ago he heard Susanna Martyn say that the said Hagar had a molatto Child born of her Body and that she was the Person that delivered her of the said Child, and that he well knows that John Gyles, Esquire whose Servants they were has used all possible Endeavors to reconcile the said Jethro & Hagar but all in vain. The Deponent further adds that said Jethro was then reputed to be a Servant to Captain Gyles & is now servant to Mr. Edward Broomfield, at Hollanderstand.

Suggested Reading

Block, Sharon. *Rape and Sexual Power in Early America*. Chapel Hill: University of North Carolina Press, 2006.

Bodle, Wayne. "Soldiers in Love: Patrolling the Gendered Frontiers of the Early Republic." In *Sex and Sexuality in Early America*, edited by Merril D. Smith, 217–39. New York: New York University Press, 1998.

Foster, Frances Smith. *'Til Death or Distance Do Us Part: Love and Marriage in African America*. New York: Oxford University Press, 2009.

Godbeer, Richard. *Sexual Revolution in Early America*. Baltimore: Johns Hopkins University Press, 2002.

Hunter, Tera W. *Bound in Wedlock: Slave and Free Black Marriage in the Nineteenth Century*. Cambridge, MA: Harvard University Press, 2017.

CHAPTER FOURTEEN

Last Will and Testament of Peter, 1743

Introduction

An enslaved man in the service of publisher Thomas Fleet, Peter worked as a pressman, artist, and delivery man. Isaiah Thomas, who also worked in the publishing industry, remembered Peter as an ingenious man who illustrated Fleet's ballads and broadsides with original woodcuts. He produced original artwork, set type for the *Boston Evening-Post* and other publications, operated the press, and delivered the newspaper each Monday evening to Fleet's subscribers. When he delivered the paper during the holiday season, some of the households he visited offered him a significant gratuity, and through thrift, Peter eventually built up a small financial reserve.

We cannot know why Peter chose to write a will in 1743, but he likely outlived the document by several years. A 1759 inventory of Fleet's estate provides a valuation of two enslaved young Black men identified by Thomas as Peter's sons. The first, named Pompey, was fourteen years of age, and the second, named Caesar, was eleven, which means that Peter was alive in 1748 and perhaps afterward. Neither was alive when the will was composed, but an older third son, Robin, was left three pounds. Peter also mentions his wife, Love, and another enslaved woman in the Fleet household, Venus.

Peter's will provides a window into the social life of the enslaved and the various avenues by which they sought relief from the trauma of bondage. Reflecting on the uses to which he might have put the money received from subscribers and as an allowance for alcohol, Peter notes that he spent little on drugs. He confesses to spending money "dealing with a wench" in the past but also asserts that he has since acquired "a little more wit than I use to have formerly amongst ye wenches." The casual misogyny of Peter's will is a reminder that unfreedom was a matter of degrees and intersectionality, rather than a Black and white binary. But it is also an indication that for Peter, intimacy and sex were forms of escapism.

That Peter is conscious of his legal and social status is clear. Even in death, he worries that he will offend his master, and his bequeaths to Fleet's children are made self-consciously, with a request that others recognize his generosity.

Text

"Will of a Boston Slave, 1743." *Publications of the Colonial Society of Massachusetts* 25:253–54. Boston, 1924.

> Here Children I leave you some thing, that's more than any Richest Master's, Servant would leave to their Master's Children considering what profit I have to my trade. Thomas Fleet jun Ten shillings and a pair of Buckles; but shall not wear them in three years from ye time he has them. John Fleet—five shillings. Anne Fleet—five shillings. Elizabeth Fleet—five shillings. Simon five shillings. Nathan Bowen jun^r five Shillings. Thomas Oliver five Shillings.
>
> What little I had thought to give it to Molley; but thought her sister Anne would make a scuable [squabble], and take it from her; that made me continue so to do, &c. —There is more than enough, yet, left for Molley, because she is very good to servants.
>
> Master and Mistres, I would not have you think that I got this money by Rogury in any thing belong'd to you or any body else, I got it honestly; by being faithful to people ever since I undertook to carry ye Newspapers, Christmas-days, & New-years days, with contribution with gentlemen sometimes 3 pounds 10/^{s} and sometimes 4 pounds 10/^{s} and in ye years 1743, 5 pounds I would Give you a true account; in my Box you may find a little cask with money, y^t I had when Mr Wollington was here, I could say when Mr Vaux was here, that I had some of his money, but I had so much dealing with a wench, y^t: I don't think that I have any of his money. One Way I and Love use to have when we had a great Work for ye Booksellers, what money we use to have for to get Drink we kept it. I am no great Drinker Nor no Smooker, and I have a little more wit than I use to have formerly amongst ye wenches. —You may find in my box a 3 pound Bill which I had for my Robin.
>
> as witness our hands
> Nathan Bowen Junr
> Thomas Oliver ye 3.
>
> All that's left is for Moley & Venis.
> Boston, June ye 2, 1743.   Peter Fleet

Sign'd Seal'd & deliver'd
in presents of us, the above
Nam'd, & deliver'd to
N. Bowen jun^r

Suggested Reading

Hardesty, Ross. "'The Negro at the Gate': Enslaved Labor in Eighteenth-Century Boston." *New England Quarterly* 87, no. 1 (2014): 72–98.

Morgan, Philip D. "The Ownership of Property by Slaves in the Mid-Nineteenth-Century Low Country." *Journal of Southern History* 49, no. 3 (1983): 399–420.

Olwell, Robert. *Masters, Slaves, and Subjects: The Culture of Power in the South Carolina Low Country, 1740–1790*, 141–80. Ithaca, NY: Cornell University Press, 1998.

Pearson, Ellen Holmes. *Remaking Custom: Law and Identity in the Early American Republic.* Charlottesville: University of Virginia Press, 2011.

CHAPTER FIFTEEN

The Trial and Execution of Mark and Phillis, 1755

Introduction

Although we often focus our attentions on the life stories of enslaved persons who attempted to escape from bondage, many persons strove toward more modest outcomes—a change of owners, for instance. When Mark and Phillis poisoned John Codman in July 1755, they did so with a hope that their lives might improve in a new household. Instead, their lives were cut short, as each was executed two months later. While Mark hung from the gallows for acquiring the poison, Phillis was burned to death for administering it—a remarkable sentence handed down on the basis of punishments established by the Treason Act of 1351 under King Edward III. By that statute, a servant who killed his master, a wife who killed her husband, or a clergyman who killed his superior was guilty of *petit treason*, a capital crime.

In the transcript of their trial, Mark and Phillis confess to killing Codman unabashedly. Phillis explains that Mark had read the Bible in its entirety and come to the conclusion that poisoning Codman would not be a sin because no blood would be shed. (See Genesis 9:6 and Ezekiel 22:4.) Mark's reasoning may have been a construct meant only to persuade his more religious co-conspirators to join him in killing the man, but it may also reflect an earnest attempt to make sense of the Bible from a non-Western, non-Christian perspective.

One of the more remarkable features of this text is its documentation of the black African community to which Mark and Phillis belonged. In addition to a third enslaved member of Codman's household, Phoebe, the pair confided in or sought supplies from a number of other enslaved individuals throughout the area. This dialogic narrative of slavery preserves a record of the social networks they and others relied upon for support in resisting and coping with their enslavement. It also speaks to the difficulty with which enslaved individuals decided whom to accept as a trusted member of this community; Phillis describes meeting an unfamiliar man who asked for Mark by name and her own mistrust of this stranger. Their social circle represented a crucial source of support but also a source of danger because the risk of exposure grew with every new confidant.

The story of Mark and Phillis was widely publicized in the newspaper, and it was also memorialized in a broadside sold at their executions, "A Few Lines on Occasion of the untimely End of *Mark* and *Phillis*."

Text

From *The Trial and Execution, for Petit Treason, of Mark and Phillis*. Cambridge, MA, 1883.

[Examination of Phillis]

> The Examination of Phillis a negro Servant of John Codman late of Charlstown deceased taken by Edmund Trowbridge and Thaddeus Mason Esq^{rs} at Cambridge in the County of Middlesex the 26th Day of July Anno Domini 1755. And ye 2^d of Augt following—
>
> Quest^n. Was Mr John *Codman* late of Charlstown decd, your Master?
> Ans^r. Yes he was.
>
> Ques^t. How long was you his servant?
> Ans^r. He my said Master bought me when I was a little girl and I continued his servant until his Death.
>
> Quest^n. Do you know of what sickness your said master died?
> Answer. I suppose he was poisoned.
>
> Ques^t. Do you know he was poisoned?
> Ans^r. I do know he was poisoned.
>
> Ques^t. What was he poisoned with?
> Ans^r. It was with that black lead.
>
> Ques^t. what black Lead is it you mean?
> Ans^r. The Potter's Lead.
>
> Ques^t. How do you know your s^d master was poisoned with that Lead?
> Ans^r. Mark got some of the said Potter's Lead from Essex Powers and my young mistress Molly found some of the same Lead in the Porringer that my Master's Sagoe [sago: a starch extracted from palm trees] was in, he complain'd it was gritty; and that made Miss Molly look into the Porringer, and finding the Lead there, she ask'd me what it was, I told her I did not know.—I cleaned the Skillet the Sagoe was boiled in and found some of the same stuff in the bottom of the skillet that was in the bottom of the Porringer.

And presently after Mark was carried to Goal, Tom brought a Paper of the Potter's Lead out of the Blacksmith's Shop, which he said he found there; and I saw it and am sure it was the same with that which Was in the bottom of the Porringer and the Skillet.

Quest. Do you know that any other Poison besides the Potter's Lead was given to your s^d master?
Answ^r. Yes.

Quest. What was it?
Answ^r. It was Water which was poured out of a Vial.

Quest. How do you know that, that Water was Poison?
Answ^r. There was a White Powder in the Vial, which Sunk to the Bottom of it.—

Quest. Do you know who put the Powder into the Vial?
Answ^r. I put the first Powder in.

Quest. Where did you get that Powder?
Answ^r. Phebe gave it to me up in the Garret, the Sabbath Day morning before the last Sacrament before my master dyed, and Phœbe at the same time told me Mark gave it to her.

Quest. What was the Powder in when Phœbe gave it to you?
Answer. It was in a White Paper, folded up Square, both ends being turn'd up, & it was tyed with some Twine.

Quest. How much Powder was there in the Paper?
Answ^r. There was a good deal of it I believe near an ounce.

Quest. Did you put all that Powder into the Vial?
Answ^r. No, I put in but a little of it, only so much as lay on the Point of a narrow Piece of flat Iron, with which I put in, which Iron Mark made & gave it to me to give to Phebe, Mark gave me the s^d Iron the Saturday before the Sabbath afores^d. I ask'd him what it was for, he would not tell me; he said Robbin gave him one, and he had lost it; and that he himself went into the shop and made this. I gave the s^d Iron to Phœbe that same afternoon, in the Kitchen; and the next morning she gave it to me in the Garret, and Quaco was there with her; she whisper'd to me and told me to take the Paper of Powder which was in the hollow over the Window, and the flat Iron which was with it and put some of it into the Vial with the Iron which I did; and she bid me put some water into it, but I did not; but she afterwards put some

in herself, as she told me, and she put it into the Closet in the Kitchen in a Corner behind a black Jug; and the same Vial was kept there untill my master dyed.

Quest. Had your Master any of that Water which was put into the said Vial given to him?
Answ^r. Yes he had.

Ques^t. How was it given to him?
Answ^r. It was poured into his barly Drink and into his Infusion, and into his Chocalate, and into his Watergruel.

Quest. Who poured the Water out of the s^d Vial into the Chocalate?
Answ^r. Phœbe did, and Master afterwards eat it.

Quest. Who pour'd it into his barly Drink?
Answ^r. I did it myself; I pour'd a drop out of the Vial into the barly Drink, & I felt ugly, and pour'd the Water out of the mug again off from the Barly, and put clean Water into the mug again & cover'd it over that it might boil quick.

Quest. Who pour'd the Water out of the Vial into the Infusion?
Answ^r. Phœbe did.

Quest. How do you know it?
Answ^r. I came into the Kitchen and saw her do it.

Quest. Did your master drink the Infusion after that water was so pour'd in?
Answ^r. He drank one Tea Cup full of it.

Quest. How do you know that Phœbe poured any of the poisoned Water out of the Vial into your Master's Chocalate?
Answ^r. She told me she had done it.

Quest. When did she tell you so?
Answ^r. That Same Day.

Quest. Was it before or after your Master eat that Chocalate that the Poison'd Water was pour'd into, that She told you so?
Answ^r. Before he eat it.

Quest. Did you see him eat that Chocalate?
Answ^r. Yes, I did, he eat it in the Kitchen on a little round Table.

Quest. Who put the Second Powder into the Vial?

Answ^r. Phœbe put it in; I left Part of the Powder she gave me in the Paper, and she afterwards put that into the Vial as she told me, as I was in the cellar drawing some Cyder, I heard Phœbe tell Mark that the Powder was all out, and all used up;

Quest. When was it that you heard Phœbe tell Mark so?
Answ^r. The Wednesday before my master dyed.

Quest. Do you know of any more Powder being got to give to your master?
Answer. Yes, but master never took any of it.

Quest. Who got this last Powder?
Answ^r. Mark got it.

Quest. What did he do with it?
Answ^r. He gave it to me; in our little House.

Quest. What Sort of Powder was it that Mark gave You?
Answ^r. I[t?] was white the same as the first.

Quest. What was it in?
Answ^r. In a Peice of Paper; he had more of that Powder than he gave me, it was in a Paper folded up in a long Square, he tore off Part of that Paper, and put Some of the Powder into it, and gave it to me and kept the rest himself and at the same time that he gave it to me he told me that Robbin said we were damn'd Fools we had not given Master that first Powder at two Doses, for it wou'd have killed him, and no Body would have known who hurt him, for it was enough to kill the strongest man living; upon which I ask'd Mark how he knew, it would not have been found out, he said that Mr. Salmon's Negros poison'd him, and were never found out, but had got good masters, & so might we.

Quest. What did you do with that Powder which Mark gave you?
Answ^r. I put it into the Vial, & set it in the Same Place it was in before, there was some of the first Powder & Water remaining in the Vial when I put this last in.

Quest. Do you know that any of the Water that was in the Vial after you put this last Powder in was given to your Master?
Answ^r. No, he never had a drop of it. The next Day after Master died Mark came into the Closet where I was eating my Dinner and ask'd me for that

Bottle, I ask'd him what he wanted it for, and he would not tell me, but insisted upon having it, upon which I told him that it was there behind the Jugg, and he took it and went directly down to the Shop in the yard, and I never saw it afterwards 'till Justice Mason shew it to me, on the Fast Day night.

Quest. Do you know where Mark got that Powder which he gave to you?
Answ^r. He had it of Robbin, Doc^{tr} Clark's Negro; that liv'd with Mr. Vassall.

Quest. How do you know that Mark had that Powder of Robbin?
Answ^r. The Thursday night before my master died Mark told me he was going over to Boston to Robbin to get some more Powder for he s^d Phœbe told him y^t the other was all out; and Mark went over to Boston, and return'd again about nine o'Clock; and I ask'd Mark if he had got it, and he told me no, he had not, but Robbin was to bring it over the next night; and between 8 & 9 o'Clock that next night, a negro Fellow came to me in our Yard & ask'd me for Mark, And I ask'd him his name but he would not tell me, and I said to him, Countryman, if you'l tell me your name I'll call for Mark, for I know where he is, but he would not, I then askt him if he was not Robbin Vassall, (for I mistrusted it was he) and upon that he laughed and said his name was not Robbin Vassall, but he came out of the Country and wanted to see Mark very much about his Child; and upon my refusing to tell him where Mark was the negro went away down to the Ferry, and I followed him at some distance & saw him go into the Ferry Boat, and the Boat put off, with him in it. That same Fryday, in the afternoon, Mark told me, if any Negro Fellow shou'd come; & say that he came out of the Country to call him, I ask'd him what negro it was that he expected wou'd come; he told me it was Robbin, and that he was to say that he came out of the Country to speak with mark about his Child, and bid me tell no Body about it.

Quest. Do you know Robbin Doct^r Clark's negro?
Answ^r. I do, and have known him for many years.

Quest. How then happen'd it that you cou'd not certainly tell whether the negro afores^d that askt for Mark was Robbin or not?
Answ^r. Because it was dark, So dark I cou'd not see his Face so as certainly to know him, but I am fully satisfied it was Robbin.

Quest. What Reason have you to be satisfied it was Robbin?
Answ^r. That same night I told Mark that a negro Fellow had been there and ask'd for him & wanted him, he ask'd me why I did not call him, I told him our Folks called me and I could not, Mark told me he was very Sorry I

did not, and asked me if he gave me any Thing, I told him he did not, he said he was very sorry he did not; then I ask'd him who it was, and he said it was Robbin, and then he told me that he thought Robbin & he had been playing blind-mans Buff, for they had been over the Ferry twice that night and mist one another; and that Elij^h Phipps & Timo Rand told him that a negro Fellow had been over the Ferry to speak with him about his Child. And then Mark told me he would the next Night go over to Robbin and get some more of the same Powder, and would bring it over on the Sabbath Day, & he went to Boston on the Saturday night, but did not return till Monday morning, when he brought it and gave it to me in the little House, as I told you before.

Quest. Did you see Robbin at Charlstown in the Time of your master's sickness or about the Time of his Death?

Answ^r. Yes, I saw him on ye Tuesday the Ship was launched, when my master catch'd Mark buying Drink at Mrs Shearman's to treat him with, & drove him away; and I saw him at Charlstown on the Saturday after my Master was buried; but I did not speak with him at either of those Times. The Tuesday he was before our Shop Door, in the Street, with Mark and had a Bag upon his shoulder; and on the Saturday in the afternoon I saw him going up the Street by our House, while Phœbe and I were washing in the back yard; I told Phœbe there was Robbin a going along this minit, and she said is he? And ask'd me what Cloaths he had on; I told her he had a bluish Coat on lined with a straw coloured or yellow lining and the Cuffs open & lined with the said Yellow lining, and that he had a black wigg on; and I told Phœbe I believed he was gone up to Mark to tell him not to own that he had given any Thing to him, and Phœbe said she believed so to; and I went into the street to the Pump with a Pail to get some Water, designing to see whether he went that Way, and I saw him go right up the main street, and I could see him as far up as Mr. Eleazar Phillips's, and I did not see him afterwards. I never see him with a Wigg on before, but as he went by us he look'd me full in the Face and I knew it was Robbin. When I told Phœbe that Robbin was going by, I thought she saw him, but she questioned whether it was he, and I told her I was sure it was he, for I had known him ever since he was a boy, and I told her I would lay a mug of Flip that it was he, but she wou'd not; and then it was that I told her I believed he was gone up to Mark &c.

Quest. Do you know what Powder that was which Mark & Phœbe gave you, and you put into the Vial?

Answ^r. Mark told me it was Ratsbane, but I told Phœbe I believed Mark lied & that it was only burnt allom, for I told her, that upon taking Ratsbane they would directly swell, and Master did not swell; and she said she believed so to.

Quest. How many Times was any of that Water, which was in the Vial afores^d, put into your master's victuals?
Answ^r. Not above Seven Times.

Quest. When was the first Time?
Answ^r. The next Monday morning after Phœbe gave me the first Powder, then it was put into his Chocalate, by Phœbe. The next was also put in to his Chocalate by Phœbe on the next Wednesday morning, and I was thinking she put in more than she should, told her her hand was heavy, and there was no more put in, that, I know of till the next Fryday, when Phœbe put some into his Chocalate, and my Master eat the Chocalate all the three times aforesaid in the Kitchen, and I was there & saw him; The next was on the Saturday following, when I put Some into his Watergruel, but I felt ugly and three it away, and made some fresh, and did not put any into that. The next was on the afternoon of the same Saturday, I made him some more Watergruel & pour'd some of the Water out of the Vial into it, and it turned yellow, and Miss Betty, ask'd me what was the matter with the Watergruel and I gave her no answer; but that was thrown away, and more fresh made, and Miss Molly was going to put the same Plumbs in again, and Phœbe told her not to do it, but she had better put in some fresh Plumbs, and she did; and no Poison was put into that; It was by Phœbe's advice that I put it into the first this afternoon. And he had no more, that I know of 'till the next Monday night, when Mark put some of the Potter's Lead into Masters Sagoe.

Quest. How do you know that Mark put any of the Potter's Lead into the Sagoe?
Answer. When I went out of the Kitchen I left the Sagoe in the little Iron Skillet on the Fire, and no body was in the Kitchen then, but when I returned, Mark was Sitting on a Form in the Corner, and I afterwards found some of that Lead in the Skillet, and neither Phœbe nor I had any such Lead.

Quest. Do you know of any other Poison prepar'd for, or given to your Master?
Answ^r. No, I do not.

Quest. Who was it that first contrived the poisoning your Master Codman?
Answ^r. It was Mark who first contrived it. He told Phœbe and I that he had read the Bible through, and that it was no Sin to kill him if they did not

lay violent Hands on him So as to shed Blood, by sticking or stabbing or cutting his Throat.

Quest. When was it that Mark first proposed the poisoning his Master?

Answ^r. Some time last Winter; he proposed it to Phœbe and I, but we would not agree to it, and told him No Such Thing should be done in the House; This before my Master brought him home from Boston.

Quest. Did he ever afterwards propose the poisoning his s^d Master?

Answ^r. Yes he did, a Week or a Fortnight after my Master brought him home from Boston, he proposed it to me first, and I would not agree to'it, and then he proposed it to Phœbe.

Quet. What Reason did Mark give for poisoning his Master?

Answ. He said he was uneasy and wanted to have another Master, and he was concerned for Phœbe and I too.

Quest. Do you know how your Master's Work house that was burnt down came on Fire?

Answ^r. Yes I do.

Quest. How came it on fire?

Answ^r. I set it on fire, but it was thro' Mark's means, he gave me no rest 'till I did it.

Quest. How did you Set your Master's Work House on fire?

Answ^r. I threw a Coal of Fire into some Shavings between the Blacksmith's Shop & the Work House, and I went away & did not see it kindle.

Quest. Who put the Shavings there?

Answ^r. Mark did.

Quest. Was any Body concern'd in the burning the Work house besides Mark and you?

Answ^r. Yes, Phœbe knew about it as well as I.

Quest. Where was Phœbe & Mark when you put the Coal of Fire into the Shavings?

Answ^r. The were up Garret in bed.

Quest. Who first proposed the Setting the Workhouse on fire? and what reason was given for doing it?

Answ^r. Mark first proposed it, to Phœbe and I; and the Reason he gave us was that he wanted to get to Boston, and if all was burnt down, he did not know what Master could do without selling us.

Quest. Why did you, when Phœbe pour'd Some of the Water out of the Vial into the Chocalate tell her, "her hand was heavy?"

Answ^r. I thought she pour'd in too much, more than she should I felt ugly and I wan't willing she shou'd put in so much and that he should be kill'd so quick. Mark's orders were to give it in two Doses, that was the Directions Robbin gave to Mark, as Mark told me, and Mark Said Robbin told him there was no more taste in it than in Cold Water.

Quest. Why did you not tell your Master or some of the Family that Phœbe had poisoned the Chocalate, and thereby prevent your Master's eating it?

Answ^r. I do not know why I did not tell.

The mark of X Phillis.

[Examination of Mark]

The Examination of Mark a Negro Servant of John Codman late of Charlstown deceased taken by Trowbridge & Thaddeus Mason Esq^rs at Charlstown in the County of Middlesex the Day of July Anno Dom: 1755.

Quest. What is your name?
Answ^r. Mark.

Quest. Are you a Servant or Freeman?
Answ^r. A Servant. Mr John Codman dec^d was my master.

Quest. How long was you his Servant?
Answ^r. For several Years before & untill his Death.

Quest. Do you know what occasion'd your s^d Master's Death?
Answ^r. He was poisoned.

q: What was he poisoned with?
a: With Poison that came from the Doctor's.

q: What Doctor?
Answ^r. Doct^r Clark that lives at the North End of Boston.

q: What sort of Poison was that?
a: It was a White Powder put up in a Paper.

q: How do you know that that Powder came from Doct[r] Clark's?
a: Robbin the Negro Fellow that belongs to Doct[r] Clark gave it to me.

q: When & where did Robbin give you that Powder?
An. A Week Day night, at his Master's Barn.

Qu. Was there any Person present with you when Robbin gave you that Powder?
An. No. The first Time, the negro man his fellow Servant called him out, it was in the Evening near 9 o'Clock.

Qu. How many Times had you such Powder of Robbin?
An. Twice only.

Qu. When was the last Time you had any such Powder of him?
An. The Sabbath Day night before my s[d] Master died, in the evening after Candle Light.

Qu. Where was it you had this last Powder of him, and what was it in?
An. He gave it to me in the same Barn, it was done up in a long square in two Papers, the outtermost Paper was brown and the inermost Paper was White, as the other was.

Qu. What did Robbin give you these Powders for?
An. To kill three Pigs belonging to Quaco as Phœbe told me.

Qu. How long ago was it Since Robbin gave you the first of these Powders?
An. I can't certainly tell.

Qu. Was it before Robbin & you were together at John Harris y[e] Potters Work house?
An. I think it was before.

Qu. How long before was it?
An. About a Week before.

Qu. Did you pay Robbin any Thing for these Powders?
An. No. I did not.

q: What did you do with them?
Ans. Phœbe had the first; and she sent Phillis for the second and I gave it to her.

Qu. When & where did you give Phœbe the first Paper of that Powder?
An. In our Garret; the same night I brought it over.

Qu. Was any Body there when you gave it to her?
An. No.

Qu. What did she do with it?
An. She took it & put it upon the Table.

Qu. Did you give her the whole of the Powder you had of Robbin the first time?
An. Yes. I gave her the Paper with all the Powder in it, as I received it of Robbin.

Qu. Did you tell her what was in the Paper?
An. No. She knew what was in it; for she told me what to get.

Qu. What did she tell you to get?
An. Something to kill three Pigs.

Qu. Did Robbin give you any Directions how to use that Powder, and tell you what Effect it would have?
Ans. He told me to put it into about 2 Quarts of Swill or Indian meal, and it would make 'em swell up.

Qu. Did you tell her how she must use the Powder? or what Effect it would have?
Answ^r. yes I told her as Robbin told me.

Qu. Do you know whether she used that Powder or any Part of it?
Answ^r. no otherwise than as Phœbe & Phillis told me Since my Master's Death.

Qu. Who did you give the Second Paper of Powder to?
An. To Phillis.

Qu. When & where did you give that Paper of Powder to Phillis?
Ans. In the little House; She came to empty a Pot over the Wharffe, and I gave it to her, The Monday before my s^d. Master died, after Breakfast in the Forenoon.

Qu. Did you then give her all the Powder you rec^d. of Robbin the Second Time?

Ans. Yes. I took off the brown Paper and gave it to her in the white Paper, that it was in, when Robbin gave it to me.

Qu. What did she do with it?
Answ^r. She carried it into the House to Phœbe as Phillis told me, She came to me & told me Phœbe sent her for that Thing that She sent me for, and thereupon I gave Phillis the Paper.

Qu. How was your Master poisoned with these Powders?
Answ^r. Phœbe & Phillis told me that they used them for that End.

Qu. When did they tell you this?
Answ^r. The next Day after my master died.

q: Were they together when they told you So?
Answ^r. No, Phillis told me of it first, and said that Phœbe used all that I brought first, that Way; and that the last was used so too by her and Phœbe; and then I went to Phœbe and ask'd her about it, and She denied it at first but when I told her that Phillis had told me all about it, then she owned it.

Ques^t. Had you no Reason before your s^d. master dyed to think that the Powders you had of Robbin were given to your master or that he was poison'd therewith?
Answ^r. No other Reason than hearing Phœbe the Saturday night before master died ask Phillis, if she had given him enough, to which she replyed, yes. I have given him enough, and will stick as close to him as his shirt to his back; but who she meant I did not then know, nor untill after master died.

Quest. Was there no Discourse had between you Phœbe & Phillis about getting more Poison, after you had the first, of Robbin?
Answ. The Fryday before my master died Phœbe told me that she had lost that stuff that I had brought to her from Robbin, and desired me to get her some more. I told her I wou'd when I went over to Boston; this was in the Forenoon, when she was washing in the back yard.

Quest. Did you get her any more of Robbin?
Ans^r. Yes, and that was it which I gave to Phillis

Quest. When did you go over to get the last Poison?
Ans. on the Saturday night before my master died; I went over after Sunset; I went directly to Robbin; & told him I wanted some of the same I had of him before for that was lost, Robbin was then at the Corner of his master's House

out in the street, he told me he could not get any then, but if I wou'd come on the Sabbath Day night he would let me have some, and I went to him on the Sabbath Day night after Candle Light, and he then gave it to me.

Quest. Was there any Body with you on the Saturday night when you ask'd for the Poison, or do you know whether any Person saw you & Robbin together that Evening?

Answ^r. No, nobody was there, and I dont know that any Body saw us together that Evening.

Quest. How long was you with Robbin at M^r. Harris's Work house?

Answ^r. I made no tarry there, but left him at the Pot house, and he and the young man that was with him followed me and overtook me a little below M^r.Waite's Slaughter house; And they went with me into the Lane leading from the market Place to the long Wharffe near M^{rs}. Shearman's, while I went into M^{rs}. Shearmans and got a mug of Toddy, in the mug I brought from M^r. Harris's Work house, and I carried it to them and they both drank with me.

Quest. Had you any Discourse with Robbin in private or between you and him alone that Day?

Ansr. No, none at all.

Quest. Where did you drink the Toddy?
Answ^r. In the Lane afores^d.

Quest. Where di you all go after you drank the Toddy?
Answ^r. We all came away together & went thro' M^r. Sprague's Yard & so thro' M^{rs}. Silence Harris's yard & Entry into the street. and they went directly down to the Ferry and I went into my master's Yard with the Pots I brought from the Potters Work house.

Quest. Did you then go with them to the Ferry or nearer to it than your master's House?
Answ^r. No, I did not.

Quest. Did Robbin give you, or did you give Robbin any Thing between the Time of your coming out of M^r. Harris's Entry and his going over the Ferry?
Answ^r. No, I did not give him any Thing neither did he give me any Thing.

Quest. After you had parted with him when you came thro' the Entry, did you call him back?
Answ^r. No, I did not.

Quest. Did your master that Day forbid Mrs Shearman's letting you have any more Drink?

Answ^r. Yes, my master told her not to sell any Drink to any of his Servants.

Quest. Did Robbin know of it?

Answ^r. Not that I know of; he see master go into M^rs. Shearman's Shop, and pass'd by Robbin in the Lane as Robbin told me.

Quest. Did you ever apply to any body else, besides Robbin for Poison?

Answ^r. No, only to Carr, Doct^r Gibbon's negro man, and then Phœbe sent me for it. She had been with Carr before on the same account, & he told her he cou'd not get her any then, as she told me;

Quest. Did you get any Poison of Carr?

Ans^r. No, he told me he wou'd not let me have any, until he had seen Quaco, and did not know whether he shou'd then or not, and I never went to him afterwards.

Quest. Did you never ask Doct^r. Rand's Cato for any Poison?

Ans^r. No, I do not know that I ever did, in the World.

Quest. Had you and Phœbe any Conversation together about your master in or near your Blacksmith's Shop or in the yard the Monday before your master died?

Answ^r. I had not, that I know of.

Quest. Did you that Day before Tom or any other of your master's Servants say that you knew that your master would dye or utter any Words to that effect?

Answ^r. No, I did not. The Day before master dyed, Phœbe came into the Shop to dress Tom's Eye & got to dancing & mocking master & shaking herself & acting as master did in the Bed; And Tom said he did not care, he hop'd he wou'd never get up again for his Eye's sake, and Scipio was there at the same time and saw her.

Quest^n. Did you ever Say that your master had been offer'd £400 for you but wou'd not take it, and now he shou'd not have a farthing or Words to that effect?

Answ^r. No I never said any such Thing.

Quest. Did you ever tell Phœbe or Phillis that the Week before your master dyed, that you went over the Ferry to see Robbin to get some more Poison, and that he came over the Ferry in another Boat and so you mist each other and that he Robbin pretended to the Ferryman that he was a Country negro and wanted to see you about your Child, or Words to that Effect?

Answ^r. I never told them or either of them so.

Quest. How came that Viall buried near your Forge in the Black-Smith's Shop, that you told M^r. Kettell of, and he found there?

Answ^r. I buried it there.

Quest. When did you bury it there?
Answ^r. In the afternoon of that Day that master dyed.

Quest. Where did you get that Vial?
Answ^r. I took it from Phillis that same Afternoon.

Quest. Did any body see you take it from her?
Answ^r. No. When I took it from Phillis she own'd that Phœbe had given the first Poison that I brought to master; and that she and Phœbe had given him all the Rest saving what was then in the Bottle. and thereupon I went to Phœbe and charged her with it, she at first deny'd it, but at last own'd it it [*sic*] and begg'd me to say nothing about it; I told her if I had known she wou'd have put it to that use I would not have got it for her; then I call'd Pompey to go down to the shop with me for I wanted to speak with him, intending to shew him the Vial, and he came into the shop but before I had an opportunity to speak with him M^r. Kettell took me.

Quest. Where was the Vial when you talked with Phœbe as afores^d?
Answ^r. I had it in my Pocket, and told her so, then I went into the shop and buried it, then I went into the House immediately to call Pompey to shew it to him.

Quest. Why did you bury the Vial before you called Pompy? or shew it to any body?
Answ^r. I buried it because I did not want any body should see it before I shewed it to him.

Quest^n. Have you lately had any Potters powder'd Lead by you or in your Possession?
Answ^r. Only that I had from Essex Powars; which was as I suppose ground to Powder.

Quest. When did you get that powder'd Lead of Essex?

Ans^r. I had it of him that Day I went there for six butter Pots, which my master's son Isaac sent me for.

Quest. What did you get that Lead for?

Answ^r. To see if it would melt in our Fire. upon a Dispute between Tom and I about it; Tom said it would melt, and I told him I did not believe it would; I carried it home and laid it upon the Wall Plate in the Blacksmith's shop, and I never moved it afterwards or thought any Thing about it, 'till it was show'd to me by the Justice.

Quet. Do you know that any Part of that Lead you had of Essex or any Lead like unto it was given to your master or put into his Victuals or Drink?

Answ^r. I do not.

Quest. Do you know of any Proposal made of poisoning your master?

Answ. No, I do not, nor ever heard any such Thing proposed by any Body.

Quest. Do you know of any Cushoe nuts being procured for that Purpose?

Answ^r. No; I have not seen a Cushoe nut since I have been in this Country.

Quest. Do you know of any Copperas or Green stuff being provided for that Purpose?

Answ^r. No I do not.

Quest. What Time on the Saturday before your master dyed was it that you heard Phœbe ask Phillis, if she had given him enough, and Phillis said she had, and would stick as close to him as his Shirt to his Back?

Answ^r. In the afternoon about Dark; and before I went to Boston.

Quest. How came you, after you had heard this Talk between Phœbe and Phillis, to get her s^d. Phœbe more Poison?

Answ^r. I did not know what she meant by their Talk, nor who they meant, by him.

Quest. Did you tell Carr that Phœbe sent you for that Poison you applied to him for?

Answ^r. She did not tell me it was Poison, but told me to ask Carr for that Thing he had promised her; he said he knew what it was and would not send it, 'till he had talked to Quaco, and did not know that he should send it afterwards; and I said no more to Carr about it.

Quest. Did you ever ask Carr at any other Time for Poison?
Ans^r. No.

Quest. Did you never ask him for something to Poison or kill a Dog?
Answ^r. No, not that I know of.

Quest. Was you ever bit by a Dog?
Anws^r. No. I never was.

Quest. Do you know any Thing more of your master's being poisoned than you have before related?
Ans^r. No, I do not.

MARK.

Suggested Reading

DeLombard, Jeannine Marie. *In the Shadow of the Gallows: Race, Crime, and American Civic Identity*. Philadelphia: University of Pennsylvania Press, 2012.

Fuentes, Marisa A. *Dispossessed Lives: Enslaved Women, Violence, and the Archive*. Philadelphia: University of Pennsylvania Press, 2016.

Rogers, Alan. *Murder and the Death Penalty in Massachusetts*. Amherst: University of Massachusetts Press, 2008.

Slotkin, Richard. "Narratives of Negro Crime in New England, 1675–1800." *American Quarterly* 25, no. 1 (1973): 3–31.

Suggs, Jon-Christian. *Whispered Consolations: Law and Narrative in African American Life*. Ann Arbor: University of Michigan Press, 2000.

Part III
Runaways

Over the last two decades, scholars have repeatedly argued that runaway slave advertisements should be regarded as slave narratives. However, because these advertisements were written by enslavers, rather than the black Africans whose escapes they recount, and because most advertisements present narratives so brief that traditional objects of literary analysis such as plot and character development are missing, relatively few readers have regarded them as worthy of study. But the advertisements we present here, many of which recount the serial escapes of a single runaway over the course of years, offer readers more lengthy and interesting narratives as well as a new perspective on the question of who is authoring those narratives.

For example, Peter, one of the men whose lives is chronicled in runaway slave advertisements, fled three times, from three different enslavers, over the course of eight and a half years. Each of the three runaway slave advertisements chronicling his life was written by a different individual, yet they clearly form a single story. If none of the enslavers who sought his capture can be considered the author of that story, then who? Peter chose the clothes he wore during his escape, the companions with whom he fled, and the destinations rumored for his flight. Peter knew that those choices would shape the formulaic language that enslavers chose to advertise for his capture and return. Thus he is, in our view, the author of the life story that emerges when we compile the various advertisements announcing his multiple escape attempts.

Since the narratives of Peter and other serial runaways included in this part develop over the course of months and years, across multiple installments, readers have an opportunity to see their stories and lives evolve. The appearance of scars and limps unmentioned in earlier advertisements and a decision to flee alone during his second recorded escape attempt, rather than with others, are tragic but tantalizing clues inviting readers to reconstruct and piece together these fragmentary accounts or to simply mull over the not-knowing. Most eighteenth-century readers would have regarded the emerging narratives as evidence of criminality, but twenty-first-century readers, perhaps, can appreciate the indomitable spirit of liberty prompting these men and women to risk life and limb in their quest for bodily autonomy and self-determination.

Because scholars have seldom written about the same advertisement or set of advertisements and because the scholarship on this body of texts is still emerging, we offer here a bibliography for this entire part, rather than appending bibliographies to each set of advertisements. The sources gathered here should enrich a reader's understanding of any of the texts that follow.

Suggested Reading

Block, Sharon. "Early American Bodies: Creating Race, Sex, and Beauty." In *Connexions: Histories of Race and Sex in North America*, edited by Jennifer Brier, Jim Downs, and Jennifer L. Morgan, 85–112. Urbana: University of Illinois Press, 2016.

Bly, Antonio T., ed. *Escaping Bondage: A Documentary History of Runaway Slaves in Eighteenth-Century New England, 1700–1789*. Lanham, MD: Lexington Books, 2012.

———. "A Prince among Pretending Free Men: Runaway Slaves in Colonial New England Revisited." *Massachusetts Historical Review* 14 (2012): 87–118.

Clavin, Matthew J. "Runaway Slave Advertisements in Antebellum Florida: A Retrospective." *Florida Historical Quarterly* 94, no. 3 (2016): 426–43.

Desrochers, Robert E., Jr. "Slave-for-Sale Advertisements and Slavery in Massachusetts, 1704–1781." *William and Mary Quarterly* 59, no. 3 (2002): 623–64.

Greene, Lorenzo J. "The New England Negro as Seen in Advertisements for Runaway Slaves." *Journal of Negro History* 29, no. 2 (1944): 125–46.

Hodges, Graham Russell, and Alan Edward Brown, eds. *"Pretends to Be Free": Runaway Slave Advertisements from Colonial and Revolutionary New York and New Jersey*. New York: Garland, 1994.

Meaders, Daniel E. "South Carolina Fugitives as Viewed through Local Colonial Newspapers with Emphasis on Runaway Notices, 1732–1801." *Journal of Negro History* 60, no. 2 (1975): 288–319.

Morgan, Gwenda, and Peter Rushton. "Visible Bodies: Power, Subordination and Identity in the Eighteenth-Century Atlantic World." *Journal of Social History* 39, no. 1 (2005): 39–64.

Newman, Simon P. *Embodied History: The Lives of the Poor in Early Philadelphia*, 82–103. Philadelphia: University of Pennsylvania Press, 2003.

———. "Hidden in Plain Sight: Escaped Slaves in Late Eighteenth- and Early Nineteenth-Century Jamaica," *William and Mary Quarterly*, 3rd ser., digital edition (June 2018), https://oieahc.wm.edu/digital-projects/oi-reader/simon-p-newman-hidden-in-plain-sight/.

Prude, Jonathan. "To Look upon the 'Lower Sort': Runaway Ads and the Appearance of Unfree Laborers in America, 1750–1800." *Journal of American History* 78, no. 1 (1991): 124–59.

Schneider, Rebecca. "'He Says He Is Free': Narrative Fragments and Self-Emancipation in West Indian Runaway Advertisements." *European Romantic Review* 29, no. 4 (2018): 435–47.

Smith, Billy G., and Richard Wojtowicz, eds. *Blacks Who Stole Themselves: Advertisements for Runaways in the Pennsylvania Gazette, 1728–1790*. Philadelphia: University of Pennsylvania Press, 1989.

Waldstreicher, David. "Reading the Runaways: Self-Fashioning, Print Culture, and Confidence in Slavery in the Eighteenth-Century Mid-Atlantic." *William and Mary Quarterly* 56, no. 2 (1999): 243–72.

———. *Runaway America: Benjamin Franklin, Slavery, and the American Revolution*. New York: Hill and Wang, 2004.

Winans, Robert B. "Black Musicians in Eighteenth-Century America: Evidence from Runaway Slave Advertisements." In *Banjo Roots and Branches*, edited by Winans, 194–213. Urbana: University of Illinois Press, 2018.

Windley, Lathan, ed. *Runaway Slave Advertisements: A Documentary History from the 1730s to 1790*. 4 vols. Westport, CT: Greenwood, 1983.

CHAPTER SIXTEEN

Penelope, 1704

Introduction

When Joseph Campbell distributed the first issue of the first newspaper published in North America on 24 April 1704, he announced that the paper would finance itself at least in part by printing advertisements. Campbell wrote that "all Persons who have any Houses, Lands, Tenements, Farmes, Ships Vessels, Goods, Wares or Merchandizes, &c. to be Sold or Lett; or Servants Run away; or Goods Stoll or Lost, may have the same Inserted at a Reasonable Rate; from Twelve Pence to Five Shillings and not to exceed." This price for describing an escaped slave or an enslaved person to be sold was low. In the early eighteenth century, five shillings represented approximately one day of skilled agricultural labor; in exchange, these advertisements circulated throughout the Atlantic world, as the captains of outbound vessels frequently carried copies of Campbell's *Boston News-Letter* and other papers with them to ports along the coast of North America and in the Caribbean, Europe, and Africa.

The first runaway advertisement, published just two months later, was unusual in that it described a woman—one of just a handful of advertisements seeking escaped black African women that were published in the first decades of the eighteenth century. That the stories of black African women were rarely preserved in this genre is a sign of the way in which their stories typically differed from those of enslaved men. Many male runaways had contacts in maritime industries; the work they did enabled their escape, while the domestic and agricultural labor of black African women rarely provided similar opportunities. Women who did run often fled with their children in tow, but men seldom attempted to escape with dependents, suggesting that familial ties also disproportionately kept women from running. Finally, women who escaped on their own risked violence and sexual assault without whatever protections the proximity of other women or potential witnesses of an attack might have afforded.

This advertisement, seeking a woman named Penelope, names her homeland, Madagascar, as a cue for recognizing her. Although eighteenth-century colonists believed that all Africans shared a racial identity as "negroes," the grooming, language, and physiognomy of different African nations were thought to be distinctive enough to serve as a reliable marker of racial subcategories. She may have been easy to identify and was likely retaken quickly, but Penelope's forced journey from Madagascar to Massachusetts was only prelude to a new, second trip—this one of her own planning.

Text

The Boston News-Letter 26 June 1704.

> Ran-away from Capt. *Nathanael Cary*, of *Charlstown*, on *Saturday* the 17th Currant, a well set middle sized *Maddagascar* Negro Woman, called *Penelope*, about 35 years of Age: With several sorts of Apparel; one whereof is a flowered damask Gown; She speaks English well. Whosoever shall take up said Negro Servant, and her Convey to her abovesaid Master, shall have sufficient Reward.

CHAPTER SEVENTEEN

George, 1704

Introduction

Most advertisements seeking the help of a white public in identifying and detaining runaway slaves were written by enslavers. These advertisements provided information that enslavers believed might be used to identify the runaway; readers could guess at further details of enslaved individuals' lives and imaginatively reconstruct their experiences of slavery, but a sense of subjectivity—of the names they claimed for themselves as well as their thoughts and feelings—was often absent from newspaper copy authored by enslavers.

However, occasionally a public official or postmaster would advertise the capture of an enslaved person who had escaped—or, perhaps, a freeman without papers attesting to the truthfulness of his claims and wrongfully imprisoned because of the color of his skin—in the hope that an enslaver would self-identify as his or her owner. In such cases, an advertisement might document the runaway's own account of life as a freeman or, alternatively, of enslavement and escape. For example, the second runaway slave advertisement published in the *Boston News-Letter* offers an account of a man named George and the story he used to explain why he was traveling without a pass. The story of George's escape and transformation, captured in this advertisement, preserves George's sense of self as well as his imaginative ventures into the broader Atlantic world, as an independent Englishman.

Text

The Boston News-Letter 17 July 1704.

> There is a Negro man taken up supposed to be Run-away from his Master; he said he was a free Negro, and lived at *Bristol*, but upon being sent to Prison, he owned he was a Servant and made his escape from his Master *Matthew Howard* at *Seaconet*, about 5 Weeks ago: he is a Lusty Fellow, says his name is *George*: upon paying the Post-master for this Advertisement the owner may be informed where he is, and also upon paying the charge and reward for taking him up, may have said Negro again.

CHAPTER EIGHTEEN

Mother of Four, 1706

Introduction

The unique challenges facing female runaways are evident in this advertisement for an unnamed mother of four children. For more than a decade, she either had been pregnant or was the mother of an infant. Childcare would have been an additional responsibility, beyond the labor required of her by enslavers, who expected her to work regardless of her maternal sensibilities and needs. "Lately weaned" suggests that she left as soon as she was neither pregnant nor nursing, and thus better able to travel quickly and to endure the hardships of flight.

The flight of this unnamed woman separated her children from their fathers and illustrates the divisive impact of slavery on nuclear families, and the language of this advertisement highlights the callous disregard of enslavers for familial ties while also revealing the way in which enslavers exploited those ties to dissuade the enslaved from fleeing. Repeatedly, Nathaniel Niles writes that he seeks the recovery of "any of them," whether or not they remain together as a family unit. Further, he suggests that those who succeed in capturing one or more of the children might "send notice thereof to her"—the unnamed woman—in order to lure her back to bondage by exploiting her maternal affection. Small wonder that enslaved females, who were often raped and impregnated as teenagers, ran far less often than their male counterparts.

Text

The Boston News-Letter 14 October 1706.

> Ran away from their Master Nathaniel Niles Junior of Point-Judith in Narraganset, a Negro Woman with 4 small Childreen, three of them are Molatto's, and the youngest a Negro that sucks or is lately weaned: The Woman is of a middle Stature and thick set. The Eldest of the Children is not above 10 or 11 year old, the two eldest are Girls, the other two Boyes. Whosoever shall apprehend the said Negro Woman & her Children, or any of them, and do bring and Convey her or them or any of them to their said Master, or secure her or them, or any of them, and send notice thereof to her or their said Master, shall be sufficiently rewarded and satisfyed for their pains.

CHAPTER NINETEEN

Peter, 1705–1714

Introduction

Often those enslaved made common cause with those suffering different forms of unfreedom, escaping with indentured servants, impressed seamen, and others seeking liberty or opportunity. Peter, a serial runaway whose life is chronicled in four newspaper advertisements over the course of ten years, made his first escape in 1705 with a Native American sailor and, probably, a Welsh soldier. Because each was advertised separately, the story of Peter's escape evolved, for readers, from the resistance of a single enslaved person into an interracial collaborative project. All three were outsiders in the English colonies, but they made common cause to escape oppression.

The announcement of Peter's capture several months later, in 1706, suggests the efficacy of eighteenth-century newspapers in circulating the likenesses and life stories of runaways. Peter traveled to South Carolina and, if he had fled just two years earlier, he might have relocated permanently and anonymously. But the *News-Letter* made him into a minor celebrity, so he was recognized a thousand miles from home, detained, and sent back to Maine.

Over the next six and a half years, Peter was sold three times, likely because he continued to run away. By 1712, he was living in Middletown, Connecticut, where he convinced three other men to join him in an escape attempt. We know that he was caught because two years later a fifth enslaver placed an advertisement in the *News-Letter*, announcing that Peter had once again run away. This final advertisement presents Peter as a man with whom many readers will be familiar, recalling his former masters and escape attempts. But the Peter introduced in 1714 is a man markedly different from the one introduced to readers in 1705. The writer does not mention the "pretty brown Complexion" which distinguished him ten years earlier; instead, Peter is identified in 1712 and 1714 as a "thin fac'd" man "with a Slit on one of his Ears" who "goes a little Lame" and has "lost his Fore-upper Teeth." These injuries and defacements possibly were inflicted by vindictive enslavers or others associated with Peter's several captures (reference the mutilation of ears in the runaway advertisement of John in chapter 22 of this volume.) His story, revealed in multiple installments over the course of a decade, illustrates the physical price of an unwavering resistance to the institution of slavery, even when that resistance is a collaborative effort made with the support of others seeking freedom.

Text

The Boston News-Letter 10 December 1705.

> Ran-away from his Master William Pepperil Esqr. At Kittery, in the Province of Maine, a Negro Man-Slave named Peter, aged about 20, speaks good English, of a pretty brown Complexion, middle Stature, has on a mixt gray home-spun Coat, white home spun Jacket and Breeches, French fall Shoes, sad coloured Stockings, or a mixt worsted pair, and a black Hat. Whosoever shall take up said Negro, and bring or convey him safe to his said Master, or secure him and send notice of him either to his Master, or to Andrew Belcher Esqr. at Boston, shall be well rewarded for his pains, and all reasonable charges paid besides.
>
> Lately Deserted Her Majesties Service in the Province of Main, an Indian Man (under the command of Cap. Joseph Brown) named Isaac Pummatick, was seen at Newbury, in Company with the above Runaway Negro; he is a short Fellow not very thick, speaks very good English, he liv'd formerly with Mr. Samuel Thackster of Hingham; he has on English Cloaths, a sad coloured old coat, or else a new light coloured drugget Coat with buttons, holes and lining of Black, black breeches, gray yarn Stockings, a black hat almost new. Whosoever shall apprehend said Indian, & him convey to his said Captain, or to Andrew Belcher Esqr. at Boston, shall have a sufficient reward besides his Charges.
>
> Lately Deserted Her Majesties Service at Kittery Garison in the Province of Maine, David Thomas Souldier, a Welsh-man, aged about 30 years, pretty short and thick stature, dark brown coloured hair; hath on a new white Cape cloth Watch Coat, under that an old sad coloured strait bodied Coat and Jacket, gray yarn stockings, and an old black Hat. Whosoever shall apprehend said Deserter, and him safely convey to his said Post, or to Andrew Belcher Esqr. at Boston, shall have satisfaction to Content, besides his Charges.

The Boston News-Letter 22 April 1706.

In *December* last, There was Advertisements of a Negro man Slave, and an Indian's Running away from Mr. *William Pepperil* of Kittery in the Province of Main, desiring they might be apprehended where ever they came, and by virtue of said Advertisements coming (in the News Letter) to *South-Caralonia*, whither the said Negro and Indian had travelled, The Governour of said place has secured the said Runaways for the Owner.

The Boston News-Letter 18 August 1712.

Ran-away from their Masters in Connecticut Colony the following Negro's and a Spanish Indian, *viz.* from Mr. *George Phillips* in Middletown Two Negro Men one Named *Irankilo* aged about Thirty years, of a middle stature, speaks good English, well Apparelled, one finger of one hand Stump'd. The other Negro Named *Harry* aged about 20 years, streight Lim'd, has on a blew Shirt, Red Jacket, Castor Hat, Speaks broken English, and well Apparelled.

Ran-away also from Mr. *Jehiel Hauley* of Durham, A Spanish Indian Man, Named *Peter* aged about Twenty years, of a Middle Stature, a Cheridary Wastcoast, A Soldiers blew Coat fac'd with red, the Cape taken off, he speaks very good English.

And on the 18th of July, Ran-away from Mr. *Ebenezar Hubbard* of said Middletown, a Negro Man nam'd *Peter*, aged about 28 years, a Slim Fellow, thin fac'd, having a Skare on the back of one of his hands near the Nuckles, with a Slit on one of his Ears, speaks good English.

Whoever shall apprehend said Run-aways or any of them, and him or them safely convey to his or their said Masters, or give any true Intelligence, of them or either of them, so as their Masters may have them again shall have Fourty Shillings reward, for each Servant, besides all necessary Charges paid.

The Boston News-Letter 14 June 1714.

Ran-away on Wednesday the 26th Day of May last at Beverly, from his Master *Joseph Tuck*, A Negro Man Servant, Named *Peter*, a slim Fellow not very Tall, goes a little Lame, lost his Fore-upper Teeth, has on a close-bodied Coat, and Pale Copper-coloured Jacket, Coat and Jacket tarr'd in some Places, white Worsted Stockings, Leather Breeches, and French fall Shoes, the heels goes much back: He was formerly Servant to Mr. *Pepperel* of Kittery, Mr. *Boreman* Tanner in Cambridge, Mr. *Morecock* in Boston, and Mr. *Hubbard* of Middleton.

Whoever shall apprehend the said Run-away, and him safely Convey to his said Master, or to Mr. *Nathan Howell* Merchant in Boston, or give any true Intelligence of him so as his Master may have him again, shall be Sufficiently Rewarded, besides all necessary Charges paid.

CHAPTER TWENTY

Daniel, 1712–1714

Introduction

As a "Molatto Man," Daniel was fathered by a white man upon the body of an enslaved black African woman. It is possible that Daniel's mother spoke English well enough and was familiar enough with the Bible to name him Daniel, after the boy prophet who rose to power and prominence in captivity, far from his ancestral homeland.

Enslaved men and women who made serial escape attempts were often sold or otherwise transferred to new masters, and the story conveyed in the three advertisements announcing that Daniel had left his enslavers provides clues as to how running away offered the enslaved advantages beyond the possibility of freedom. After Daniel's first recorded escape attempt, Edward Wanton—the Quaker owner of a Massachusetts shipyard where Daniel worked—transferred custody of Daniel's person to John Scott, his son-in-law and the captain of a Rhode Island trading sloop. This transfer of ownership likely also entailed a shift in Daniel's obligations and the material circumstances of his life. During his first escape, Daniel possessed fairly modest clothing—a "home made dy'd Coat" and a "strip'd home-spun Jacket." But by the time of his second escape attempt, two years later, Daniel had acquired several changes of apparel, including "Sea Cloths and Bedding, and other good Cloaths." Daniel probably traveled with Scott on one or more of his voyages to the Caribbean and apparently enjoyed an improved standard of living. His first escape attempt may have been conceived with the ultimate goal of obtaining his freedom, but it also became a bargaining chip whereby he secured a preferable situation.

Of course, Daniel's second and third escape attempts make it clear that freedom was always the object he sought. Although Wanton and Scott were both Quakers, they were slow to embrace the antislavery position of George Fox, the sect's founder, so Daniel assumed responsibility for his own emancipation. If he succeeded in escaping, he likely relied upon knowledge and contacts gained during his time at sea; bargaining for a transfer to Scott's custody was the first step to freedom.

Text

The Boston News-Letter 29 September 1712.

> Ran away from his Master *Edward Wanton* of Scituate Ship Carpenter, the Second of this Instant September A Molatto Man Servant, Named *Daniel*, about 19 years of Age, pretty Tall, speaks good English, thick curl'd Hair with a bush behind, if not lately cut off, black Hat, [cotton] and linen Shirt: he had with him two Coats, one a home made dy'd Coat, the other a great Coat dy'd a muddy color, strip'd home-spun Jacket, Kersey Breeches, gray Stockings, french fall Shoes.
> Whosoever shall take up said Runaway Servant and [him] safely Convey to his above-said Master at Scituate, or [give] any true Intelligence of him, so as his Master may have [him] again, shall have Satisfaction to Content, besides all necessary Charges paid.

The Boston News-Letter 24 May 1714.

> Ran-away from his Master *John Scott* of Newport Rhode-Island, a Molatto Man named *Daniel* born in New-England, and by Trade a Ship Carpenter, formerly belonging to *Edward Wanton* of Situate, he is about 20 years of Age, indifferent tall, and slender bushy hair, carried with him white and speckled Shirts, Sea Cloaths and Bedding, and other good Cloaths as a Cinnamon coloured Broad-Cloth Coat trim'd with Froggs, Ticking Breeches, Worsted Stockings &c. Whoever shall apprehend the said Runaway and bring him to his said Master, or secure him and give notice to his Master aforesaid that he may have him again shall have reasonable Satisfaction and Charges paid.

The Boston News-Letter 23 August 1714.

> Ran away from his Master *John Scott*, the 17th of this Instant August, A Molatto Man named *Daniel*, formerly belonging to *Edward Wanton* of Situate; he is indifferent Tall and Slender, by Trade a Shipwright, but 'tis thought Designs for Sea. Whosoever shall stop, take up, or secure the said Run-away, and bring him or give Notice of him to his said Master at Newport, Rhode-Island, shall be well rewarded, and reasonable Charges paid.

CHAPTER TWENTY-ONE

Jethro, 1719–1720

Introduction

Enslaved men and women often made common cause, fleeing in groups. But the case of Jethro hints at some of the downfalls of a joint escape. During his first escape in 1719, Jethro ran away from his enslaver on a Wednesday; his companion, Pero, did not run until Friday. That delay of two days meant Jethro had to remain undetected for forty-eight hours in the vicinity of his enslaver and any search parties that had been organized. Escaping jointly would also require the runaways to carry or scavenge for twice as much food and water while avoiding detection. Further, if they were stopped and asked to identify themselves, they would require a cover story explaining why two black African men might be traveling together through the New England countryside, without a pass or free papers. The challenges of traveling unobserved or of evading capture increased significantly as the number of escapees increased, and Jethro may have believed that running away with Pero contributed to his ultimate failure.

An increased risk of capture may explain why Jethro chose to flee by himself a year later, but his second attempt was similar to the first in at least one key respect. Both escapes took place in September, and while the timing may be coincidental, it also suggests that Jethro left in the early fall for a reason. He may have left in the early autumn because his enslaver, George Webb, regularly hired out his time for the winter months on board a ship or because he found the work at harvest time more disagreeable than that which he performed in other months of the year. The early autumn may also have provided more opportunities for escape than during the winter months, when snow preserved a runaway's tracks and ice blocked harbors.

Text

The Boston News-Letter 28 September 1719.

> Ran-away from George Webb of Kingstown in Naraganset the 13th of this Instant September, A Negro Man Named Jethro; Aged about 24 Years, a well set tall Fellow; a scar upon his upper Lip; having on a dark coloured Jacket and grey Kersey Breeches and a Felt Hat.

Ran away from Samuel Brown of Kingston aforesaid the 15th Instant, a Negro Man Named Pero; Aged about 24 Years, of a middling Stature and Pox broken very much; white Jacket & Breeches, and whitish coloured Coat, & Hat; the said Negro Men both Speaks good English; and are supposed to be both together; and both to have Stocking & Shoes on. Whosoever shall take up & secure said Negro Men & bring or send them, or give Notice to their said Masters; so as they may have them again, shall receive sufficient Satisfaction & reasonable Charges allowed them by George Webb & Samuel Brown.

Boston News-Letter 5 September 1720.

Ran-away from his Master George Webb of Kingston in the Colony of Rhode-Island, the Seventh day of August past, A Negro Man called Jethro, a tall, well set Fellow, a scar upon his upper Lip, speaks very plain English, has a dark coloured broad cloth Coat, and striped Jacket and Breeches, a Castor Hat, aged about 25 Years; whoever shall apprehend the said Negro, and him safely convey to his said Master, or secure him in Irons and send his Master Notice, so as that his Master may have him again, shall be well paid for so doing, besides all reasonable Charges.

CHAPTER TWENTY-TWO

John, 1719–1720

Introduction

John, or Johnny, ran away from Phillip Ludwell at least two times. The advertisements memorializing these escape attempts offer the usual descriptions of a runaway's clothes and hair, but those descriptions provide an unusually suggestive narrative of coercion and resistance. In both of the advertisements, Ludwell alerts readers that John's body is distinctive in two ways. First, John has a lump—perhaps a lipoma—on the "small of his left Leg." Second, his ears have been mutilated, and each is distinguished by a small hole. While the lump may have been a natural occurrence, Ludwell concedes, in the second advertisement, that he physically altered John's ears, both to inflict pain as a punishment and to make identifying the enslaved man easier if he should run away a second time. This form of mutilation may have been inspired by the Bible, in which Israelites were instructed that when an enslaved person has been freed, if he or she desires to remain in bondage, "then thou shalt take an awl, and thrust it through his ear" (Deuteronomy 15:17). By boring through John's ears, Ludwell might have intended to signal, cruelly, that his opportunity for freedom had already passed. Although many runaway slave and slave-for-sale advertisements mention scars or injuries, this candor on the part of enslavers is rare.

Also preserved in these advertisements is a sense of how John may have resisted Ludwell's control. The first advertisement stipulates that John wears "short Dark hair," but the second makes no mention of his hair—perhaps because in the nine intervening months John had grown it long enough to cover his upper ears and hide the holes left there by Ludwell. In the absence of those distinguishing marks, it is unclear how anyone would identify John as a slave; by Ludwell's own admission, he "is as white as any Englishman." The story told in these advertisements emphasizes the fragility of slavery as an institution because of its reliance on signs whose absence or concealment renders the master powerless to identify or claim another human being as property. At least one of Ludwell's white readers must have realized that the only thing differentiating him or her from John was two small holes in his ears.

Text

The American Weekly Mercury 29 December 1719.

> Run a way from his Master, *Phillip Ludwell* of *Green-Spring*, in *Virginia*, on Saturday the fourth of *July* 1719. A Mallato Man named *Johney*, but of a very White Complexion, aged a bout Twenty Two Years he is tall and well Limb'd, he has a little lump on the small of his left Leg, and small holes Punched in the upper part of each Ear, short Dark hair and broad Teeth, (he is my Coach-Man) Whosoever shall take up said Mallato Slave, and bring him to his said Master at *Virginia* or to *Henry Evans* at *Philadelphia*, or Give Notice thereof so that he may be had again shall have Five Pounds as a Reward, with all Reasonable Charges paid by *Phillip Ludwell* or *Henry Evans*.

The American Weekly Mercury 29 September 1720.

> I do hereby certify that I will pay ten pounds Current money and reasonable charges to any Person that shall take up and bring home, my slave named *John* who was my Coachman, and ran away from *Green Spring July* the 4th 1719, he is a Lusty young man aged about 23 years, is as white as any Englishman, has very broad teeth, a Small bump on the Small of his left Legg and a Small hole made in the upper part of each Ear, made with a short punch when he ran away before. Or if any person shall give me certain, intelligence where he is, so as I may take him I will give such person five pounds Current mony reward, given under my hand in *Virginia* the 16th day of *June* 1720.   *Phil. Ludwell*

CHAPTER TWENTY-THREE

Richard Molson, 1720

Introduction

This advertisement introduces six people to the reader, but the story it tells is clearly Molson's; he is its protagonist. The fluidity of affiliations in Molson's story illuminates the difficulties of treating accounts of slavery from the early eighteenth century with expectations shaped by nineteenth-century slave narratives, in which black Africans and their descendants are generally the only individuals who suffer unfreedom. Molson, Mary, and Garrett and Jane Choise apparently regarded their shared experience of bondage—varied though it may have been—as a more important marker of identity than the differing hues of their skin.

Given his status as a "Mullata," Molson was likely the son or grandson of Thomas Molson, who emigrated from England to Maryland in 1663 and owned land in Sussex County, Delaware, just a few miles from Richard Tilghman's land in Queen Anne's County, Maryland. Like other early colonists, Thomas Molson acquired wealth by transporting others—often indentured servants, like Mary, Jane, and Garrett Choise—to North America and selling or exploiting their labor. Indeed, the neighbor to whom these three were indentured may have been Thomas Molson. The term of their servitude was fixed; at the end of a defined period, they would be free to earn wages and purchase land. Although their legal status was different, indentured servants and enslaved individuals often made common cause, escaping together.

Richard Molson's biracial background may have made him a more plausible "husband" for "a White Woman" like Mary, but his choice of traveling companions speaks more broadly to the fact that unfreedom was not yet understood as a condition endured only by black Africans. While scholars are careful to draw distinctions between the term-limited contractual obligations of white laborers and the indefinite, multigenerational bondage of enslaved black Africans, close-knit multiracial groups such as this one suggest that some enslaved black Africans and white indentured servants cared more about their shared circumstances than racial divides.

That Molson and his companions were thought to have escaped south also challenges expectations shaped by popular understanding of slavery in the nineteenth century. At a time when slavery was legal throughout North

America, this group's best chance to escape notice was, paradoxically, to travel to places where a greater percentage of the population had descended from enslaved Africans—where Richard Molson might go unnoticed. For many runaways in the eighteenth century, freedom meant turning your back to the North Star and fleeing south.

Text

The American Weekly Mercury 11 August 1720.

> Run away in *Aprill* last, from *Richard Tilghman* of *Queen Anns* County in *Maryland* a Mullata slave, Named *Richard Molson*, of Middle stature, about forty Years old, and has had the small Pox, he is in Company with a White Woman named *Mary*, who 'tis suppos'd now goes for his wife, and a white Man Named *Garrett Choise*, and *Jane* his Wife, which said White People are servants to some Neighbors of the said *Richard Tilghmans*, The said fugatives are Supposed to be gone to *Carolina* or some other of his Majestys Plantations in *America*. Whoever shall apprehend the said Fugatives and cause them to be committed into safe costedy, and give Notice thereof to their Owners shall be well rewarded. The white man has one of his fore fingers disabled,
>
> Whoever shall convey them to the Sheriff of *Philadelphia* shall have Twenty Pounds current mony paid him or them or whoever shall convey the Mollata to the said Sheriff shall have Tenn Pounds, or whoever shall convey the Mollata to the said *Richard Tilghman* shall have Fifteen Pounds, reward.

CHAPTER TWENTY-FOUR

Fransh Manuel, 1722

Introduction

The narrative of Fransh Manuel is told secondhand in this advertisement penned by William Yard, but Yard suggests that he had possession of an original, written by the runaway. Manuel, Yard writes, "has told me [his story] since he has run away." Unless the two held a long-distance conversation, Manuel must have left that story for Yard to find after his escape. This advertisement, then, preserves Manuel's perspective on and experience of enslavement; although mediated, it can only be described as a slave narrative.

Manuel explains to Yard that he discovered a mine and was emancipated by his previous owner in gratitude. This type of interaction was relatively common, at least in the public imagination. For example, newspapers on both sides of the Atlantic reported that "A Negro named Papaw, belonging to Mrs. Little page in Virginia, having discovered a certain Remedy for the Venereal Disease, by which he has wrought very speedy and surprising Cures, the Governour and Council have purchased him his Freedom, and settled on him an Annuity of Twenty Pounds per Annum" (*New-England Weekly Journal*, 22 December 1729). Manuel's claim was thus plausible but, predictably, rejected by Yard. However, Manuel's previous enslaver was likely a land surveyor named John Raymond (1665–1737) of Norwalk, a small town in Fairfield County, Connecticut. In his work as a surveyor, Raymond would have searched the countryside for exploitable natural resources; while working for him, Manuel would have had ample opportunity to look for mineral lodes.

Whether or not Manuel discovered a mine and extracted from Raymond a promise of freedom in exchange for its location, his story of betrayal and, then, self-determination suggests the fragility of freedom. When personal liberty is contingent upon the textual authority of a pass identifying its bearer as a freeman, freedom is only as secure as the literacy and storytelling skills establishing its authenticity. Although we cannot read the narrative left by Manuel with Yard, this advertisement is a testament to its existence and to the ways in which narrative authority was foundational to life and liberty in colonial North America.

Text

The American Weekly Mercury 15 November 1722.

> *Run away from William Yard of Trenton in West-Jersey the Fifth Day of this Instant November, a Negro Man named* Fransh Manuel, *but commonly called* Manuel, *of a pretty tall Stature, and speaks indifferent English. He wears a dark coloured home-spun Coat; an Ozenbrig Jacket, old Leather Breeches, Sheeps-russet Stockings, new Shoos and an old Beveret Hat. He pretended formerly to be a Freeman, and had Passes; but he did belong to one John Raymond of Fairfield in New England, and I bought him of the said Raymond. And the said Negro has told me since he has run away, That he had found a Body of Ore for his Master, and that his Master had given him free. Whoever takes up the said Negro, secures him and brings him to Mr William Bradford of New-York, or to Mr. William Burge of Philadelphia, or to his said Master at Trenton, shall have Forty Shillings Reward, besides all reasonable Charges, paid by me,*
>
> William Yard.

CHAPTER TWENTY-FIVE

Quam, 1722–1723

Introduction

These two advertisements, which recount the escape attempts of an enslaved man named Quam, are remarkable in part because neither actually identifies Quam as a runaway. In both cases, Samuel Beaks—the enslaver who seeks assistance in locating Quam—accuses the white servants with whom Quam has escaped of stealing or taking his property. Although Quam runs during the same month two years in a row, the second time with an entirely new group of white servants, Beaks cannot conceive of his "property" as an agent with the capacity to plan, organize, and execute an escape attempt. In the context of a multiracial group, Beaks cannot recognize a black African man as a leader; Quam and other enslaved individuals used this prejudice to act unnoticed, knowing that some white observers would be unable to acknowledge their exercise of subjectivity.

Alternatively, these advertisements that deny Quam's participation in the escape planning might be read as attempts to deflect blame away from Beaks for Quam's suffering and dissatisfaction. Beaks acknowledges, in the first advertisement, that Quam has been disfigured at some point in the past, but he also provides an explanation for that disfigurement. This narrative interlude is unusual and, apparently, irrelevant to the advertisement's rhetorical function: helping readers identify a missing body. However, this brief explanation of a scar's origins plays another role, stripping narrative authority from Quam; he cannot claim that the scar was acquired recently or through Beaks's cruelty without contradicting or dramatically altering an extant account of its acquisition. Both his insistence that Quam was kidnapped and his explanation for the scar on Quam's hand deflect the reader's attention from Beaks and his status as an enslaver, preemptively denying that he might have given Quam reason to run.

Text

The American Weekly Mercury 21 June 1722.

> Run away from William Hunt of Bucks County, a Servant Man named Benjamin Hillyard, *a Blacksmith, aged about* 25 *Years. Pretty lusty and*

tall, with a grey Broadcloth Coat, and a brown Home-spun Drugget Coat, an Ozenbrig Jacket, Leather Breeches, with Glass Buttons, black Stockings with round-toed Shoos, wearing a Wig or Cap, having no Hair on. And the said Hillyard *hath stolen or taken with him a lusty well-set Negro Man, belonging to* Samuel Beaks, *called* Quam, *aged about 22 Years, having on a brown short Kersey Coat with Horn Buttons, a fine red-striped Vest and Breeches, grey Stockings; Castor Hat and Garlicks Shirt, having his Right Hand burnt, between his Fore Finger and Thum when a Child. Whoever can take up the said Servant Man and Negro, and secure them so that their said Masters may have them, and gives notice to their said Masters, shall have Three Pounds current Money paid them, By*

Delaware Falls,   William Hunt, *and*
June 17, 1722   Samuel Beaks.

The American Weekly Mercury 13 June 1723.

Run away the 2d of this Instant June, from Robert Harris and William Hunt, at the Falls in Bucks County in Pennsylvania, Two Servant Men, the one named John Bealey, he is a tall Man, swarthy Complexion, dark short hair, wears a black and white Kersey Coat, homespun Shirt and Drawers, yearn Stockings and Pumps. The other named David Reeves a short well set fellow fresh Complexion light hair, wears a Blue Gray Druget Coat, strip'd Jacket home spun shirt and Drawers, yearn stockings & round to'd shooes, he is a Husbandman. Run away at the same time from Samuell Bonham of Trent Town in west Jersey, a servant man named Charles Brown a middle siz'd man fresh Complexion, light Brown hair, wears an old Stuff coloured Jacket, Leather Breeches with Brass buttons bluish stockings, new round to'd shooes, by trade a Baker, they have taken with them a Negro man named Quam belonging to Samuell Beaks of the Falls in Bucks County, he is a Lusty well sett fellow wears a black and white Kirsey Coat, Osinbrigs Jacket and Drawers, home spun shirt and round to'd shooes, they are all about the age of Nineteen or Twenty (they are supposed to have taken Guns with them) Whosoever secures the said Servants or either of them so that their said *Masters* may have them again shall have a Pistole reward for each and Reasonable Charges paid by their said *Masters.*

CHAPTER TWENTY-SIX

Tom, 1723

Introduction

Slave-for-sale and runaway slave advertisements regularly comment on the linguistic abilities of the individual in question; in this case, Joseph Coleman attests that Tom "speaks very good English." However, these advertisements rarely comment on the uses to which such linguistic proficiency might be put. Language acquisition was conceived of, by enslavers, in strictly economic terms, but it also unlocked the imaginative or narrative capacities of the enslaved.

Without a "very good" command of English, Tom's escape would have been foiled long before Coleman managed to publish an advertisement. His success depends on an ability to speak persuasively, bringing to life an alternative reality for his listeners. Tom weaves a fictive, counterfactual account, one that he may have imagined even before he had been sold to Coleman by Captain Palmer, and he quite literally speaks it into existence. If the Coleman advertisement is a slave narrative, the story told by Tom might be characterized as a freeman's narrative—a genre defined not by its documentation of facts and history but by its preservation of an unfettered imagination. An advertisement like this one, which includes the counternarrative of the enslaved, demonstrates the linguistic power wielded by Tom and is evidence of its potency.

Text

The American Weekly Mercury 11 July 1723.

> Run away from Joseph Coleman in the Great Valley, in Chester-County, a Negro Man, named Tom, aged about 30 Years, of a middle Stature, he speaks very good English, having on a white Shirt, Stockings and Shoes a great riding Coat tyed round him with a blew Girdle. He was seen by several Persons in *New-York*, about the latter end of *June* last, who was well acquainted with him and suspected his being Run away, but he told them his former Master Capt. *Palmer* had sold him to a Person in the Great Valley, who had given him his Freedom,

then he pull'd out a forged Pass, which, to the best of their remembrance was Signed by one William Hughs. Whosoever takes up the said Negro and puts him into any Goal, and gives nitice thereof to his said Master, or to *William Bradford* in *New-York*, or to Messrs. *Steel* or *Bethune* Merchants in Boston, shall have *Three Pounds* Reward and all Reasonable Charges.

Those that take him are desired to Secure the Pass.

CHAPTER TWENTY-SEVEN

Timothy, 1726–1727

Introduction

The stories of enslavement reported in newspaper advertisements are necessarily fragmentary, narrative scraps in search of an ending. But such endings or continuations of a story rarely appear, and sometimes it is unclear whether a subsequent text is the next installment in a serial history or a separate story of slavery with overlapping details. The two advertisements below require readers to decide whether the Timothy who escaped from Daniel Johannot of Boston, in December 1726, is the same man who escaped from Job Green of Warwick, Rhode Island, eight months later. While the ages and names of these two men match, their builds may differ; the enslaved man who ran from Johannot was "a pretty Tall fellow," while the man who ran from Green was "a well set Fellow, of middle Stature." Their racial status may also differ; Johannot identifies his runaway as a "Negro Man," while Green asks readers to find "a Molatto Man." The word *negro* was used to describe any individual of African ancestry and could refer either to an individual with two African parents or to an individual with a mixed European and African parentage. However, such differences are perspectival; the same man might appear tall or of middle stature to different masters. Similarly, racial designations generally depend on the prejudices and experience of an observer. The difficulty in determining whether these advertisements refer to the same man highlights the challenge these narrative fragments posed to readers. What identified a human being as a slave? If runaways secured different clothes or changed their names, would they still be recognizable from a brief textual description?

The matter of naming is a shared concern for the men in these advertisements. Both report a name given or recognized by the white community as well as a name preferred by the enslaved and in common use. This struggle for control over the most basic component of an individual's identity reflects the way in which resistance was not solely—or even primarily—concerned with bodily autonomy. The enslaved sought self-determination in every aspect of their lives, including in the matter of what names enslavers, acquaintances, and friends would use to address them. So if these two advertisements do recount escape attempts by the same man, they show that Timothy gained at least a measure of self-determination: whether or not he secured his freedom, Timothy gained control over the use of his name.

Text

The Boston News-Letter 29 December 1726.

> *Ran away the 24th of this Instant December from his Master Mr.* Daniel Johannot *of Boston, Distiller, A Negro Man Named* Jupeter, *but calls himself by the Name of* Timothy, *is a Cooper by Trade; formerly belonged to Mr.* Chadock *of Bradford, a pretty Tall fellow, speaks very good English, aged about* 35 *Years; had on a Leather Jacket & Breeches, two pair of yarn Stockings, a pair of square To'd Shoes, a very dark, almost black double breasted frize Jacket, with a white flannel Lining, a very good Felt Hat. Whosoever apprehends the said Run away & him Convey to his abovesaid Master, shall have* Forty Shillings *reward and all necessary Charges paid.*

The Boston News-Letter 24 August 1727.

> *Ran away from his Master Maj.* Job Green *of* Warwick, *in the Colony of* Rhode-Island, *the* 31st *of* July *past, A Molatto Man (born of a Negro Woman) Named* Timothy, *commonly called* Tim, *about* 35 *Years of Age, a well set Fellow, of middle Stature, speaks good English: He had on when he went away, a Cinnamon coloured Camblet Coat; a check'd Cherry derry Jacket, Leather Breeches, a Garlick Holland Shirt, grey worsted Stockings, wooden heel Shoes, and a felt Hat. Whoever shall take up the said Run away, and him Convey to his abovesaid Master, or keep him in Custody so that his Master may have him again, shall have* Five Pounds *Reward, and all necessary Charges paid.*

CHAPTER TWENTY-EIGHT

Chocolate Grinder, 1727–1728

Introduction

It seems appropriate that we do not know the name of the young man who ran away from the Boston chocolatier James Lubbuck in 1727 because the predominant theme of his story, as it unfolded in two advertisements, is the different treatment experienced by white and Black, propertied and destitute, able and disabled runaways. The young man who flees from Lubbuck was described as "battle-ham'd," a phrase that describes both genetic and acquired defects in the hips, knees, and ankles. He is a "Negro" whose few possessions are "old" and in poor condition. Lubbuck's advertisement accordingly promises a smaller reward. He offers three pounds rather than the five given in exchange for the capture of other runaways. Because the young man can be identified visually, Lubbuck does not identify his runaway by name; he is a piece of missing property, not an individual with agency.

Although we cannot know with any certainty the outcome of this escape attempt, Lubbuck likely recovered the young man. Still, we can be reasonably sure that the youth fled Boston a second time, just nine months later. However, this second experience as a fugitive was far different from his first. When the young man left Boston in 1728, he did so *with* Lubbuck, as the white chocolate maker fled Boston with four enslaved persons and considerable property to escape from his creditors. The irony of Lubbuck relying on and replicating his enslaved young man's experience as a runaway is delicious. But the difference between Lubbuck's own advertisement for a disabled young Black man and the advertisement published by Lubbuck's creditors delineates the limits of any power inversion that might have taken place during this episode. Unlike the enslaved young man, Lubbuck is offered an inducement to return. He need not worry about debtor's prison or being sold as an indentured servant to recoup lost capital; while a reward is offered for his capture, an even larger reward is offered to Lubbuck himself, if he will only return. The young man and his three enslaved associates, who accompanied Lubbuck from Boston, must have expected some form of compensation for assisting Lubbuck in his escape. Perhaps he promised them their freedom. And since Lubbuck's name disappears from the public record after his flight from Boston, he may have lived to enjoy his freedom after all.

Text

The New-England Journal 4 September 1727.

> Ran-away from his Master Mr. *James Lubbuck* of Boston, Chocolate-Grinder, on the 28th of last Month, A Young Negro Man-Servant, about 20 Years of Age, a short Fellow, speaks pretty good English, has thick Lips, battle-ham'd, and goes something waddling: he had on an old Hat, no Coat, a blue baze [baize] Jacket, a white Ozenbriggs Shirt, open knee'd long Canvas Breeches, pretty large Shoes, with a slit in the side of one of them. Whoever shall take up the abovesaid Runaway, & him safely convey to his abovesaid Master, living near Mr. *Colman's* Meeting-House, shall have *Three Pounds* Reward, and all necessary Charges paid.
> Boston, Sept, 4th. 1727.

The Boston News-Letter 2 May 1728.

> *Whereas* James Lubbuck *of* Boston, *Chocolate-maker, has lately Absconded & Carried away with him* Four *Negro's, and sundry other Effects to a Considerable Value, and his Creditors having met on said Occasion, do Promise to Reward any Person who shall Secure said* Lubbuck, *Negro's, &c. with Twenty Pounds, Money, besides necessary Charges; and in case said* Lubbuck *will Return & Surrender himself & Effects to his Creditors, they Promise to Allow said* Lubbuck *the Sum of* One hundred Pounds *out of the Effects to set him up again, and Suspend any further Prosecution.*

CHAPTER TWENTY-NINE

Stephen, 1728–1729

Introduction

As Frederick Douglass and others attest, some white plantation owners gave the enslaved license to celebrate Christmas with a feast, supplying victuals and alcohol. In escaping from the Maryland plantation of Charles Carroll during this period, Stephen might have thought to disappear undetected for a week or more, placing distance between himself and anyone who might be looking for him. But Carroll seems to have noticed his absence immediately, publishing an advertisement for Stephen's capture on Christmas Eve.

Although he was suspected of stealing a horse, Stephen likely was not responsible—or if he was responsible, he didn't use the horse to travel any significant distance. Instead, he hid on the estate of Charles Calvert, a former colonial governor whose brother, Benedict Calvert, succeeded him as the colony's chief executive. While the black African overseer of Charles Calvert's plantation was punished for aiding and abetting Stephen in his escape, the Calverts advocated for leniency in the punishment of Stephen. He—with another local runaway named Cora (see chapter 32)—was sentenced to death in April 1729 for one or more of the "Villanies" he confessed to committing during his month of freedom. Stephen may have started one or more of the fires that burned down local homes and barns in the weeks after his disappearance, but whatever Stephen's supposed crimes, Benedict Calvert issued a reprieve two months later, in June. More than mercy, this stay of execution was likely a means of preserving Carroll's capital investment in Stephen; if Stephen had been executed, Carroll would receive no compensation from the state for funds he had spent in purchasing, feeding, and clothing the man he claimed as human capital.

Text

The Maryland Gazette 24 December 1728.

> Run away from Mr. *Charles Carroll*, at *Annapolis*, a Negroe Man Named *Stephen*, a Cooper by Trade; suspected to be at present, about the Fork of *Patuxent*. Whoever secures the said Negroe, so that he may

be brought to his Master, at *Annapolis*, or to *Daniel H*a*n* at Mr. *Carroll*'s Plantations beyond *Elk Ridge*, shall (over and above the Allowance by Act of Assembly,) receive 20 Shillings Reward.

The Maryland Gazette 31 December 1728.

> Stolen out of the Stable of Mr. *Geo Neilson*, in *Annapolis*, this Day Fortnight at Night, a Bay Horse, about 13 Hands and a half high, branded on the near Shoulder and Buttock, with the Letters AP joyn'd close together, with a Sprigg Tail, and his Fore Feet newly shod. Whoever secures the said Horse to Mr. *Neilson* aforesaid, shall have Half a Pistole Reward; paid by Geo. Neilson.
>
> N.B. *'Tis suspected he was taken away by a* Negro, *belonging to* Cha. Carroll, *Esq; who ran away about the same Time, and was advertis'd in the last Week's* Gazette.

The Maryland Gazette 21 January 1729.

> The Negroe *Stephen*, belonging to *Charles Carroll*, Esq; who was lately advertis'd in this Paper, for a Run-away, was brought to Town last Night, and carried before the Hon. B Tasker, Esq; who committed him to Prison. He has confess'd several Villanies which he has been guilty of. It seems he has been for some Time harbour'd at the Plantation of the Hon. *Charles Calvert*, Esq; in *Prince George*'s County, by the Negroes there, and the Overseer (who is a Negroe) was also brought to Town, and has been punished with a severe Whipping.

CHAPTER THIRTY

John Mallott, 1729

Introduction

Because the Atlantic world frequently brought the inhabitants of different countries and of British colonies from the Caribbean to Canada into contact with one another for the first time, personal identity in an eighteenth-century seaport was a fluid construct, potentially subject to revision at a moment's notice. Unless a new arrival was already personally known to the city's inhabitants, he or she might plausibly claim to have arrived from any one of a dozen cities. This latitude created both opportunities and dangers for individuals of African descent.

On the one hand, newly arrived enslaved individuals might plausibly claim to be free. All that would have been necessary is a plausible explanation for how they came to be present in a port far from their place of residence and, potentially, papers attesting to their legal status. On the other hand, enslavers could—and did—take advantage of these circumstances to kidnap and enslave free men and women of color. The difficulty of determining whether individuals had been legally enslaved, as prisoners of a just war, or kidnapped unlawfully was a key consideration in Samuel Sewall's 1700 essay questioning the morality of slavery, *The Selling of Joseph*, and this same difficulty animates the following advertisement.

Some Bostonians clearly believed that John Mallott, a free man, had been wrongfully detained as a slave. They harbored him from Samuel Bass in an effort to preserve his liberty. But Samuel Bass, the author of the advertisement, and Habijah Savage, a local magistrate, believed that Mallott was a fictional identity assumed by an enslaved man named Caesar in an attempt to bluff his way to freedom. Modern readers cannot know which story was true any more than eighteenth-century readers could; this account captures the narrative complexity of slavery, in which legal status was often shaped by the storytelling abilities of both the enslaved and the enslavers.

Text

The New-England Weekly Journal 24 March 1729.

> *Whereas my Negro Man* Caesar, *has assumed the Name of* John Mallott, *Pretending he was Freeborn, and the Son of* John Mallott *a Free Negro in* Jamaica, *and ship'd by the way of* Barbados *here for his Education: This may Certifie the several Persons to whom my said Negro has spread this Report that the same is false & groundless, and that upon Examination before* Habijah Savage *Esq; One of His Majesties Justices; said Negro after being catch'd in Numberless Lies, Confess'd himself Born in* Guinea, *and brought into* Barbados *for Sale as a Slave, and was Sold accordingly, Also acknowledg'd the Authors of two forged Letters found with him. Now I desire the several Persons to whom he has Resorted, no longer to Entertain him, and hope no Master of Vessel will Ship him, as he must expect to Answer the same at his Peril.*
>   Boston, March 22, 1729.   Samuel Bass.

CHAPTER THIRTY-ONE

Boy, 1729

Introduction

Not all of those sought by their masters and advertised for in newspapers escaped intentionally. In this advertisement, an unnamed boy without any identifying marks has been missed, but he is so small that the advertiser rejects the possibility that he meant to leave. Instead, the advertiser assumes the boy has "Stray'd" or been kidnapped. This language speaks to the lost boy's status on the plantation; he is a piece of livestock allowed to age and fatten until he is of value to his owner, a point driven home by the advertisement that immediately follows, which uses the same language to describe a missing horse: "Stray'd or stol'n about the 25th of *September* last, from Mr. *Alexander Contee's* in Prince George's County, a Grey Mare, branded on the rear Buttock." The proximity and similarity of these two advertisements communicates the boy's status as a farm animal with devastating efficacy. But unlike a horse or dog, which can generally be trusted to avoid dangers and to return to its home in the evening, most human toddlers cannot care for themselves. Left unsupervised, the boy likely wandered off and, given the plantation's proximity to a creek, may have drowned or suffered some other tragedy. But such a death may have been preferable to the alternative; because the boy was still years from developing into an economic contributor, any kidnapper likely would have taken the boy for other, unsavory reasons. If his mother or a free black African father had stolen him away, the advertiser would have been able to recover him fairly quickly, so the boy probably suffered an untimely death.

Text

The Maryland Gazette 20 May 1729.

> Stray'd or stolen, the 2d Inst. from the Plantation of Mr. *Richard Hall*, near *Hall's Creek*, in *Calvert* County, a Negroe Boy between 3 and 4 Years old, of a very Black Complexion. Whoever secures the said Negroe to me, at the Plantation aforesaid, shall have Two Pistoles Reward.
>
> *Richard Hall*

Stray'd or stol'n about the 25th of *September* last, from Mr. *Alexander Contee's* in *Prince George's* County, a Grey Mare, branded on the rear Buttock thus H. with a sprig Tail, about 24 Hands high. Also a White Horse, branded on the near Buttock thus R. with a sprig Tail, about 13 Hands high: They us'd the Plantation of the said Mr. *Contee*, near *Zeckia Swamp*. Whosoever secures the said Mare and Horse, so that the Subscriber may have them again, shall have half a Pistole Reward, or in Proportion for either; paid by me,

William Parks

CHAPTER THIRTY-TWO

Cora and Joe, 1728–1751

Introduction

Although the story of runaways is broadly presumed to be a quest for liberty, some escapees sought freedom of movement for the purpose of revenge, not resettlement. And for others, escape was an option pursued almost incidentally, after violence against their enslavers left them with no other option. For Cora, the death of his master, Aquila Hall, was a more important outcome than his own freedom. He made multiple attempts, first with an ax and then with a gun. Local newspapers omitted the names of Cora and another enslaved person, who similarly killed his enslaver and her children, perhaps with the hope of discouraging imitators. However, Cora's name was clearly known to many and is familiar today because of a Massachusetts paper's report on events in Maryland.

Cora's escape and his attack on Aquila Hall was one of several incidents leading to the passage of legislation in August 1729 legalizing the torture and disfiguration of enslaved people convicted of murder, arson, and other crimes. Before death, those convicted could have a hand amputated, and after death, they could be drawn and quartered, with their bodies displayed publicly as a reminder of the violence promised against enslaved persons who rebel. That legislation offers commentary on the character of Cora and those who committed similar acts of violence, alleging that they acted "because they have no Sense of Shame, or Apprehension of future Rewards or Punishments," regarding only "the Rigour and Severity of Punishment." This complaint hints at a failure of religious instruction as the root cause of Cora's desire for revenge; although the enslaved often framed such acts of violence as retributive justice, the law is a reminder that religious instruction and literacy were sometimes denied to individuals like Cora.

This piece of legislation is one of two epilogues to the story of Cora's escape. The second came more than twenty years later, when his brother Joe ran from and then killed an enslaver, named Edward Taylor. Local commentators understandably drew attention to the similarities in their stories, but they also seem to have expected that a broader readership would remember Cora, even two decades later. Their belief that readers would remember Cora suggests that runaways occasionally became local celebrities whose fame was much broader than the brief textual notices that are, today, the only record of their notoriety.

Text

The Maryland Gazette 31 December 1728.

> *Annapolis, Dec.* 31. There is a Report in Town, that Mr. *Aquila Hall*, of *Baltimore* County, was unfortunately shot to Death on Christmas-Day in the Morning, as he was walking in his Orchard, by one of his Negroes, who had been run away some Time before; and lay in Ambush to [execute] this barbarous Murder; since which he has made his Escape. It seems this was not the first Time this Villain had attempted his Master's Life, having before struck at him with an Ax, which cut him over the Eye brow, and had certainly split his Skull, if he had not suddenly mov'd his Head.

The Maryland Gazette 8 April 1729.

> *Annapolis, April* 7. A few Days ago, a Negroe Man, belonging to one *Aldridge*, in Prince *George's* County, without any provocation, barbarously murder'd his Mistress, and two of her Children, whilst his Master was absent; After which, he took Two Guns out of the House, with all the Powder and shot he could find, and made his Escape. He was speedily persued by his Master and his Neighbours, for several Days, and at last was taken, after an obstinate Resistance of the Negroe, who in the Fray shot his Master thro' the Hand.
>
> We have an Account, from *Baltimore* Assizes, that the Negroe who shot his Master, Mr. *Aquila Hall*, pleaded Guilty upon his Tryal, and received Sentence of Death.

The Maryland Gazette 22 April 1729.

> *Annapolis, April* 21. It being represented, that the Negroe belonging to John Aldridge, who murder'd his Mistress and 2 Children, was so ill in Prison, that 'twas though he could not live till the Assizes, and consequently not receive lawful Punishment for his horrid Crimes; his Excellency was pleased to Order a special Commission for trying him, which was accordingly done; he confessed the murdering his Mistress

and one Child, but said, the youngest was killed by a Fall of its Mother upon it; he received Sentence of Death, was executed at Marlborough last Friday, and on Saturday was hung in Chains in the old Fields near Capt. Murdock's. The Negroe who kill'd his Master, Mr. Aquilla Hall, is also to hang in Chains. Which Examples 'tis hoped will be a Means to terrify such wicked Wretches from the like Practices for the future.

The New-England Weekly Journal 23 June 1729.

> *Annapolis, (in Maryland) May* 13. We hear the Ludlow Castle Man of War is arrived in Virginia, from the West-Indies. An Embargo is laid on the Ships there not to sail till the last of June, when she is to convoy the Ships home.
>
> Dead Warrants are issued out for the Execution of the Negro Cora, (who kill'd Mr. Aquila Hall,) on the 26th. Inst. and he is to be hang'd in Chains. Also for Rich. Dowman, for Felony. And for Charles Smith, & Tho. Garnet, who shot Capt. Dickenson of Talbot County.
>
> The Negro who kill'd his Mistress and 2 Children was executed at Marlborough on Friday the 18th of April last; and on Saturday was hung in Chains. His Trial & Execution was sooner than was intended, by reason of his Illness, that 'twas tho't he could not live till the Assizes, & was try'd by a special Commission from the Governour.

"An ACT for the more effectual punishing of Negroes and other Slaves; and for taking away the Benefit of Clergy from certain Offenders." 8 August 1729. Bacon, Thomas. *Laws of Maryland at Large.* Annapolis: Jonas Green, 1765.

> Whereas several Petit-Treasons, and cruel and horrid Murders, have been lately committed by Negroes, which Cruelties they were instigated to commit, and hereafter may be instigated to commit with the like Inhumanity, because they have no Sense of Shame, or Apprehension of future Rewards or Punishments: And that the Manner of Executing Offenders, prescribed by the Laws of *England,* is not sufficient to deter a People from committing the greatest Cruelties, who only consider the Rigour and Severity of Punishment: **Be it therefore Enacted,** *by the Right Honourable the Lord Proprietary, by and with the Advice and Consent of his Lordship's Governor, and the Upper and Lower Houses of Assembly, and the Authority of the same,*

That when any Negro, or other Slave, shall be convict, by Confession, or Verdict of a Jury, of any Petit-Treason, or Murder, or willfully Burning of Dwelling Houses, it shall and may be lawful for the Justices before whom such Conviction shall be, to give Judgment against such Negro, or other Slave, to have the Right Hand cut off, to be Hanged in the usual Manner, the Head severed from the Body, the Body divided into Four Quarters, and Head and Quarters set up, in the most public Places of the County where such Fact was committed.

The Pennsylvania Gazette 29 January 1751.

Dec. 19. *The Beginning of this Month a Murder was committed in Cæcil County, by a Molattoe Man. He had run away from his Master, Mr. Edward Taylor, and was pursu'd by him and another Man, who overtook and were just going to take him, but he having a loaded Gun, shot his Master dead on the Spot. He was afterwards taken and put into Prison, but is since broke out. This Molattoe is Brother to him who was hang'd some Years ago for shooting Mr. Aquila Hall, in Baltimore County.*

The New-York Gazette Revived in the Weekly Post-Boy 18 February 1751.

Jan. 2. *We hear from Cæcil County, that the Mulatto Man Joe, who murder'd his Master Mr. Edward Taylor, is again apprehended, and in that County Goal: A special Commission is gone up, to hold a Court of Oyer and Terminer, for his Trial.*

The Pennsylvania Gazette 26 February 1751.

Feb. 13. *On the first Instant, the Mulatto Man Joe, for the Murder of his Master, was executed in Cecil County, pursuant to his Sentence.*

Part IV
Life and Travel Writing

The impulse of black Africans to tell their life stories marked the early American literary archive, reflected in a variety of forms, most notably the antebellum slave narrative but also in poetry, conversion narratives, criminal (or gallows) narratives, fiction, nonfiction essays, letters, travel narratives, and so forth. Many of the texts we have included throughout this reader fall into the tradition of Black life writing. Consider, for example, the seventeenth-century court cases of Elizabeth Key and John Casor and the conversion narrative of the Blackmore maid from "New England's First Fruits." From the moment black Africans arrived in the British North American mainland, they endeavored to tell their life stories.

In this final part, we note the emergence of a Black life writing tradition by presenting a series of texts that narrativize black African lives. We settled on the particular grouping of texts in this part based on the fact that they, even more so than the others placed elsewhere in this reader, present biographical accounts of black African lives. That is to say, the texts included here narrate singular experiences of early Black Africans with a focus on individual agency and deeds that contain an element of the heroic. These narratives do not offer birth-to-death accounts of black African subjects, which is usually the scope of biographies. Also, the narratives are not shaped by a Black consciousness. In other words, the figures do not craft their life stories with a sense of a collective, shared Black experience. Their texts do not (at least not overtly) challenge slavery or the racism that creates the obstacles and traumas they must overcome. These are not abolitionists' texts, not in the vein of the antebellum slave narrative, which remains the centerpiece of critical studies of early African American life writing. For the figures in this part, their lives seem to make it into print as singular expressions that we nonetheless can read within the larger context of a Black life writing tradition because they illustrate the efforts early on of black Africans to make meaning out of their experiences in early American spaces.

By collaborating with amanuenses, they self-fashion as Black subjects. It should be noted that their subjectivities are dependent on factors beyond their racial difference. Those factors include regionalism, class, gender, and ethnicity—their proximity to systems of power. The complexities of their subject positions remind us of the dangers of essentializing Blackness, especially in these earlier literary periods. The narratives point to a long history of life writing in African American literature.

CHAPTER THIRTY-THREE

Jethro and King Philip's War, 1676

Introduction

On 1 July 1676, during King Philip's War, Wampanoag-allied forces raided the home of a white colonist living in Swansea, a town south of Boston. They killed the home's owner and took as prisoner the man's black African servant, Jethro. Five days later, Jethro escaped. During his brief time as the captive of the Wampanoag chief Metacomet, Jethro, who could understand their language, learned a great deal about Wampanoag war strategy and resources. Upon his return, he told the English that Metacomet, known to the English as King Philip, was in good health but that a thousand or so of his followers were sickly and dying. He also brought back news of Metacomet's plan to attack the town of Taunton, not far from Swansea. The English staged a successful counterattack, which turned the tide of war. Later that year, a court decree manumitted Jethro.

Jethro's deeds are recorded in at least three contemporary accounts: Samuel Sewall's diary, Increase Mather's *A Brief History of the Warr with the Indians in New-England*, and William Hubbard's *A Narrative of the Indian Wars in New England*. In each instance, the text renders Jethro's actions in a single paragraph; two of the three do not mention his name. The accounts appear as snippets that provide little biographical specificity. His representation appears wholly mediated through the Puritanical lens of these writers, who deem his actions a particular divine providence.

Despite the gaps, the biographical sketch provides glimpses of Jethro's life and motivations; one can ascertain, for example, that he spoke multiple languages. Also, although the accounts do not provide details about how he escaped, one must assume that he was resourceful. If one were inclined to infer about his motives, one could surmise that Jethro possessed a certain political savvy and brokered information to improve his lot in the colony. A less cynical guess might be that he acted out of a sense of loyalty and care for those in Swansea and the surrounding community. Perhaps, most likely, a combination of factors motivated him. The point is this: Jethro's deeds created a literary presence and afterlife. His actions and motivations insinuated him into the literary imagination of colonial New England. In terms of a Black life writing tradition, Jethro's textual representation strains conventional notions of the tradition that center on authorship.

Text

From Increase Mather, *A Brief History of the Warr with the Indians in New-England* (1676). An Online Electronic Text Edition. Royster, Paul, ed. *Faculty Publications*, University of Nebraska Lincoln Libraries, accessed Apr 14, 2020, digitalcommons.unl.edu/libraryscience/31.

> July 11. A Party of Indians (tis conjectured that there were about two hundred of them) assaulted *Taunton*. And in probability, that Town had at this time been brought under the same desolation other places have experienced, had not the Lord in his gracious providence so ordered, that a Captive *Negro*, the week before escaped from *Philip* and informed of his purpose speedily to destroy *Taunton*; whereupon Souldiers were forthwith sent thither, so that the enemy was in a little time repulsed, and fled, after they had fired two Houses: but not one English Life was lost in this Ingagement. What loss the enemy sustained is as yet unknown to us. There was a special providence in that *Negroes* escape, for he having lived many years near to the *Indians*, understood their Language, and having heard them tell one another what their designs were, he acquainted the English therewith, and how *Philip* had ordered his men to lie in *Ambuscadoes* in such and such places, to cut off the English, who by meanes of this intelligence escaped that danger, which otherwise had attended them. (64)

From William Hubbard, *A Narrative of the Indian Wars in New-England, from the First Planting Thereof in the Year of 1607, to the Year 1677: Containing a Relation of the Occasion, Rise and Progress of the War with the Indians in the Southern Western, Eastern and Northern Parts of Said Country, 1677.* Boston, 1775. Early English Books Online Text Creation Partnership, 2011, accessed Apr 14, 2020, http://name.umdl.umich.edu/N11149.0001.001.

> For on the 1st of July, 1676, a party of [Metacoment's] Indians committed a horrid and barbarous murder upon Mr. Hezekiab Willet, of Swanzey, an hopeful young gentleman as any in those parts. They used frequently to keep a sentinel on the top of their house from a watch-house built thereon, whence they could discover any Indians before they came near the house, but not hearing of the enemy in those parts for a considerable time, that necessary piece of circumspection was omitted

that day, whereby that deserving person was betrayed into their cruel hands; for within a quarter of an hour after he went out of his own door, within sight of his house, he was shot at by three of them at once, from every one of whom he received a mortal wound; they after their barbarous manner took off his head, and carried it away with them (which however was soon after recovered) leaving the trunk of his body behind, as a sad monument of their inhuman cruelty. The same Indians, not being above 30 in number, took away a negro belonging to the same family, who being faithful to his master's and the country's interest, ventured his life to make his escape, which was the preservation of many others; for the said negro being a little acquainted with their language, discovered to the English after his escape, Philips purpose to seize such and such places: In the first place to assault Taunton, which in all probability had been in great danger, if their treacherous plots and purposes had not so wonderfully been made known beforehand. The said negro affirmed, that there was near a thousand of them; for he observed that altho' they had killed 20 head of neat cattle over night, yet there was not any part of them left the next day at eight o'clock in the morning. By this special providence the enemy was defeated of their purpose, and never after had an opportunity of doing any considerable damage to the English in that part of the country. So, after this day, we may truely date the time of our deliverance, and beginning of revenges upon the enemy; now is their own turn come, when it shall be done unto them as they have done unto us. (164)

From Samuel Sewall, *The Diary of Samuel Sewall, 1674–1729*, ed. M. Halsey Thomas, vol. 1 (New York: Farrar, Straus and Giroux, 1973), 18.

Saturday, July 1, 1676. Mr. Hezekiah Willet slain by Naragansets, a little more than Gun-shot off from his house, his head taken off, body stript. Jethro, his Niger, was then taken: retaken by Capt. Bradford the Thorsday following. He saw the English and ran to them. He related Philip to be sound and well, about a 1000 Indians (all sorts) with him, but sickly: three died while he was there. Related that the Mount Hope Indians that knew Mr. Willet, were sorry for his death, mourned, kombed his head, and hung peag [wampum, or beads] in his hair. (14)

From Nathaniel Bradstreet and David Pulsifer, eds., *Records of the Colony of New Plymouth, in New England*. Vol. 5. Boston, 1855. *Internet Archive*, August 2008, accessed April 14, 2020, https://archive.org/details/records ofcolony005newp/page/230/mode/2up.

> In reference unto a negro named Jethro, taken prisoner by the Indians, and retaken againe by our army, which said negro appertained to the estate of the successors of Capt Willett, deceased, our Generall Court haue agreed with Mr. John Saffin, adminnestrator of the said estate, mutually, that the said negro doe forthwith betake himself to his former service, and to remaine a servant vnto the successors of the said Captaine Willett, vntill two yeers be expired from the date hereof, and then to be freed and sett att libertie from his said service, provided, alsoe, that during the said tearme of two yeers, they do find him meat, drinke, and apparel fitting for one in his degree of calling, and att the end of his said service, that hee goe forth competently prouided for in reference to apparel. (216)

Suggested Reading

Brooks, Lisa. *Our Beloved Kin: A New History of King Philip's War*. New Haven, CT: Yale University Press, 2018.
Cantor, Milton. "The Image of the Negro in Colonial Literature." In *Images of the Negro in American Literature*, edited by S. L. Gross and J. E. Hardy, 29–53. Chicago: University of Chicago Press, 1966.
Flores De Apodaca, Roberto. "'Jethro, Who Saved Taunton': An African Man's Captivity Narrative during King Philip's War." *Journal of American Studies* (2020): 1–24.
Green, Lorenzo Johnston. *The Negro in Colonial New England, 1620–1776*. 2nd ed. New York: Atheneum, 1968.
Rezek, Joseph. "Author." *Early American Studies: An Interdisciplinary Journal* 16, no. 4 (Fall 2018): 599–606.
Warren, Wendy. *New England Bound: Slavery and Colonization in Early America*. New York: W. W. Norton, 2016.

CHAPTER THIRTY-FOUR

Onesimus and the Small Pox, 1711–1716

Introduction

A black African man named Onesimus finds his way into the early American textual archives largely by way of the prominent Puritan minister Cotton Mather, to whom Onesimus was enslaved for nearly a decade. Onesimus entered the Mather household in 1706, a gift presented by members of Mather's North Church in Boston. In his diaries and in letters, Mather makes several passing references to Onesimus that offer clues about how the enslaved man navigated life as part of Mather's household. Mather, for instance, mentions that Onesimus had a wife and a child (possibly two) who died young. Onesimus also learned to read and write in English, part of Mather's efforts to convert him to Christianity. Also, as part of the conversion process, Onesimus learned a catechism. He, however, seemed a reluctant study. In 1711, Mather accused Onesimus of stealing five pounds from him, and in a diary entry dated 1 July 1716, Mather describes him as "wicked" and "useless." That same year, Onesimus secured his freedom from Mather by purchasing another black African man (or boy) to serve Mather in his place and receiving, in return, his liberty.

Despite Mather's negative assessment of Onesimus, he did find valuable Onesimus's knowledge about preventive treatments for smallpox. Onesimus described a process of inoculation, common in regions of Africa, in which the skin of a healthy person is exposed to a small amount of secretion from the pustule of an infected person. Onesimus told Mather that he, himself, had undergone such a procedure in his homeland. Mather writes that Onesimus was from Guramantese, which might or might not be a reference to the Gold Coast region of West Africa. Onesimus's testimony, which Mather conveyed in a letter to the Royal Society of London in 1716 and then referenced in a medical treatise after a smallpox outbreak swept through Boston in 1721, took center stage in medical debates that raged in the colony. Mather staked his own credibility on the testimony of this black African man. The image of Onesimus that emerges from Mather's recording of his actions and knowledge emphasizes the hybrid nature of Black life in early America. Onesimus arrived in Boston with a store of experiences that informed his encounters in the colony.

Text

From Cotton Mather, *Diary of Cotton Mather 1681–1708*. Vol. 7. Boston: Massachusetts Historical Society, 1911. *Google Books.* accessed April 15, 2020, https://www.google.com/books/.

> Dec. 13, 1706: This day, a surprising Thing befel me. Some Gentlemen of our Church, understanding (without any Application of mine to them for such a Thing,) that I wanted a *good Servant* at the expence of between forty and fifty Pounds, purchased for me, a very likely *Slave*; a young Man, who is a *Negro* of a promising Aspect and Temper, and this Day they presented him unto me. It seems to be a mighty Smile of Heaven upon my Family; and it arrives at an observable Time unto me. I putt upon him the Name of *Onesimus*; and I resolved with the Help of the Lord, that I would use the best Endeavours to make him a Servant of Christ, and also be more serviceable than ever to a Flock, which laies me under such Obligations. (579)

From Cotton Mather, *Diary of Cotton Mather 1709–1724*. Vol. 8. Boston: Massachusetts Historical Society, 1912. *Google Books.* accessed April 15, 2020, https://www.google.com/books/edition/Collections_of_the_Massachusetts_Histori/rwMQAQAAMAAJ?hl=en&gbpv=0.

> Dec. 9, 1711: . . . I must keep a strict Eye on my Servant Onesimus; especially with regard unto his Company. But I must particularly endeavour to bring him unto Repentance, for some Actions of a thievish Aspect. Herein I must endeavour that there be no old Theft of his unrepented of, and left without Restitution. But then, upon every observable Miscarriage of any Person in my Family, I must make my Flight unto the Blood of my Saviour, as a Family-Sacrifice; that so the Wrath of God may be turned away from my Family. (139)

> Dec. 20, 1713: There are several Points, relating to the Instruction and Management of my Servant Onesimus, which I would now more than ever prosecute. He shall be sure to read every Day. From thence I will have him go on to Writing. He shall be frequently Catechised. I would also invent some advantageous Way, wherein he may spend his Liesure-hours. (271–72)

July 1, 1716: My Servant Onesimus, proves wicked, and grows useless, Froward, Immorigerous. My Disposing of him, and my Supplying of my Family with a better Servant in his Room, requires much Caution, much Prayer, much Humiliation before the Lord. Repenting of what may have offended Him, in, the Case of my Servants, I would wait on Him, for his Mercy. (363)

Memorandum of Onesimus's Manumission

My servant Onesimus, having advanced a Summ, towards the purchase of a Negro-Lad, who may serve many occasions of my Family in his Room, I do by this Instrument, Release him so far from my Service and from the claims that any under or after me might make unto him, that he may Enjoy and Employ his whole Time for his own purposes, and as he pleases. But upon these conditions. First, that he do every Evening visit my Family, and prepare and bring in, the Fuel for the day following, so Long as the Incapacity of my present Servant, shall oblige us to Judge it necessary: As also, in great snows, appear seasonably with the help of the Shovel, as there shall be occasion. "Secondly, that when the Family shall have any Domestic Business more than the Daily affairs, he shall be ready, upon being told of it so far to Lend an helping Hand, as will give no Large nor Long Interruption to the Business, of his own, to which I have dismissed him; As particularly, to carry corn unto the mill, and help in the fetching of water for the washing, if we happen to be destitute. And in the piling of our wood, at the season of its coming in. "Whereas also, the said Onesimus has gott the money which he has advanced as above mention'd, from the Liberties he took, while in my Service, and for some other Considerations, I do expect, that he do within six months pay me the sum of Five Pounds, wherein he acknowledged himself Endebted unto me. (363)

From George Lyman Kittredge, ed., *Some Lost Works of Cotton Mather*. Cambridge: Cambridge University Press, 1912. *Internet Archive*, accessed April 11 2020, archive.org/details/39002086341758.med.yale.edu/page/422/mode/2up/search/negro.

(A letter written to John Woodward of the Royal Society of London, July 12, 1716)

All that I shall now add, will be my Thanks to you, for communicating to the Public in Dr *Halley's* Transactions, the Account which you had from Dr. *Timonius*, at *Constantinople*, the Method of obtaining and procuring the *Small-Pox*, by *Insition*; which I perceive also by some in my Neighbourhood lately come from thence, has been for some time successfully practiced there. I am willing to confirm you, in a favourable Opinion, of Dr. Timonius's Comunication; And therefore, I do assure you, that many months before I mett with any Intimations of treating the *Small-Pox*, with the Method of Inoculation, any where in *Europe*; I had from a Servant of my own, an Account of its being practiced in *Africa*. Enquiring of my Negro-man *Onesimus*, who is a pretty Intelligent Fellow, Whether he ever had the *Small-Pox*; he answered, both, *Yes*, and, *No*; and then told me, that he had undergone an Operation, which had given him something of the *Small-Pox*, & would forever preserve him from it; adding, That it was often used among the Guramantese, & whoever had the Courage to use it, was forever from the fear of the Contagion. He described the Operation to me, and shew'd me in his Arm the Scar, which it had left upon him; and his Description of it, made it the same, that afterwards I found related unto you by your *Timonius*. (422)

Suggested Reading

Herbert, Eugenia W. "Smallpox Inoculation in Africa." *Journal of African History* 16, no. 4 (1975): 539–59.

Koo, Kathryn S. "Strangers in the House of God: Cotton Mather, Onesimus, and an Experiment in Christian Slaveholding." *Proceedings of the American Antiquarian Society* 117 (April 2007): 143–76.

Niven, Steven J. "Onesimus." In *African American Lives*, edited by Henry Louis Gates and Evelyn Brooks Higginbotham, 640–41. Oxford: Oxford University Press, 2004.

Wisecup, Kelly. *Medical Encounters: Knowledge and Identity in Early American Literatures.* Amherst: University of Massachusetts Press, 2013.

CHAPTER THIRTY-FIVE

Titus in the Caribbean, 1714–1716

Introduction

The story of Titus, as preserved in a series of letters and depositions seeking to recover the cost of his illegal sale by Zachariah Fowle, documents this enslaved man's efforts to determine the course of his own life, even as his legal status and racial identity rendered him vulnerable to the whims of the various white men who assumed control of his movements. Like many enslavers in seaport cities, Edward Lyde rented the right to Titus's person and labor to a sea captain, Fowle. But when Fowle and Titus shipwrecked and washed up on the beaches of Hispaniola, Fowle pretended that he owned Titus and sold him to purchase his passage back to Boston. In the absence of papers attesting to his ownership, Fowle was only able to sell Titus to a man named Fay because Titus's racial identity made Fowle's claim of ownership plausible. Blackness marked Titus as an enslaved person—property in search of an owner.

Of course, Titus could have protested and might even have been able to foil Fowle's plans. Instead, Titus may have agreed to pose as an enslaved person belonging to Fowle because Titus preferred life in the Caribbean to living with Lyde, in Boston. But when Fay sent him to St. Martinique and tried to sell him to the French planters of that island, Titus circumvented the transaction by pretending to be ill; presumably, returning to Lyde would have been preferable to working in French sugarcane fields and refineries. He exercised a degree of control over his living conditions.

After he was identified by a sailor who knew he belonged to Lyde, Titus was sold by Fay to a merchant named William Fenton, who assumed responsibility for returning Titus to Boston. Conscious that Fenton considered him to be Lyde's property, Titus stole wine and "played several rogue tricks," confident that Fenton would not punish him severely and thereby damage another man's property. Titus could not liberate himself, but he exploited the circumstances of his enslavement to secure more favorable living conditions and to steal from enslavers without suffering in full the consequences that typically attended such infractions.

Text

"Case of Titus." *Domestic Relations*, 170–73. Massachusetts State Archives. Microfilm.

St. Thomas, July 26, 1714,

This is to Certify that one Captain Fowles belonging to Boston being cast away upon St. Domingo has saved one negro man Titus belonging to the ship and brought here with him to this Island and wanting money has sold him to one Mr. Antony Fay merchant of St. Christophers given under our hands the day and date above mentioned

Charles Egan
J. Magens

To Mr. William Harris, Merchant.

In Boston
Mr. William Harris, St. Christophers, Sept. the 5[th,] 1714

Sir,
I received yours of the 22nd of May and observed What you Write Concerning your Friend's Negro Man Titus, Mr. Fay (who had Bought him of the Master as you Mentioned) sent him to Martinique for sale among the French, but the fellow feigned himself sick which Prevented his being sold there. At his Return I went to Fay & Demanded him for such a Person. He told me the Negro Cost him forty-one Pounds, and he would not Part with him Except I would Pay him the Whole; I find he designed the Fellow for a Second Venture so that I have Promised to pay him the aforesaid Sum, and shall send him you at the Next good opportunity. But I Expect you will Send me your Note or order for said Sum, in Consideration that we are all Mortal. I have not to add at Present but that I am

Sir, Your Most Humble Servant,
William Fenton

Mr. William Harris, St. Christophers, June 3rd, 1715

Sir,

I have by Mr. William Smith sent your friend's Negro Man Titus. I formerly Charged your Account for the forty-one pounds I paid Mr. Fay for him with Commission, the Whole being forty-three pounds one Shilling and now have received the said sum from the Estate of Major Crip, with a Small Matter over which I have placed to your Account Credit & will make it up with my kinsman William Fenton of Nevis. I have reason to Wish I had sent the Negro sooner to you for he has played several rogue tricks with me to my Loss. He broke my Storehouse & Stole a considerable Quantity of Wine & other things. I made bold to give him a Small Matter of Correction & Satisfied myself with that, having a Value for your friendship; the fellow is to work onboard Mr. Smith's Ship but he leaves it to Mr. Lyde what to Allow him for his passage. I wish him Safe to your hands being
    Sir, your most Humble Servant,
        William Fenton

Jonathan Mason of the Island of St. Christophers, now resident in Boston in New England, Mariner, being of full age; Testifieth and saith That sometime in the year 1714 at St. Christophers aforesaid, he saw Titus a Negro Man formerly slave to Mrs. Ann Pollard, and afterwards belonging to Edward Lyde of Boston, aforesaid Esquire, And the Deponent asking the said Titus how he came there; he Replied That his Master Lyde had sent him to sea with Captain Zachariah Fowles in the Ship *Adventure* which was Cast away off of Hispaniola And that they got to St. Thomas's in a Boat and that the said Fowles sold him there to Mr. Anthony Fay of St. Christophers, Merchant, And soon after the said Fay told this Deponent that he bought the said Negro at St. Thomas of the said Captain Fowles & Affirmed the said Negro to be his slave and pretended he wanted money and therefore he sold him. And further the Deponent saith not.
      Jonathan Mason

April 3d 1716, Sworn in Inferior Court at Boston. Attention. John Ballantine, Clerk.

Suggested Reading

Aljoe, Nicole N. "Testimonies of the Enslaved in the Caribbean Literary History." In *Literary Histories of the Early Anglophone Caribbean: Islands in the Stream*, edited by Aljoe, Brycchan Carey, and Thomas W. Krise, 107–24. New York: Palgrave Macmillan, 2018.

Bennet, Andrew. *The Author*. Abingdon: Routledge, 2005.

Lindsay, Lisa A., and John Wood Sweet. *Biography and the Black Atlantic*. Philadelphia: University of Pennsylvania Press, 2014.

CHAPTER THIRTY-SIX

John Williams and the Atlantic World, 1724

Introduction

The man who called himself John Williams and was known as Pompey to the white men who held him in bondage was a fugitive whose story begins with a runaway slave advertisement. But his escape and subsequent travels are so well documented that it makes more sense to think of his documented experiences as a narrative of travel.

Working for Captain Richard Trevett aboard the shallop *Ann*, Williams was well acquainted with the rhythms of maritime life and used that specialized knowledge of sloops and sailors to stow away on a transatlantic voyage and make his escape aboard Captain John Moffatt's ship *Morehampton*. Massachusetts law threatened ship captains with hefty fines if they helped enslaved or indentured servants to escape, so when Moffatt and his crew found Williams aboard the ship, they made plans to send him back to his master once they arrived in England. Imprisoned, briefly, in the seaport of Lynn, Williams was then sent aboard another ship to Bristol for transport back to Massachusetts. He escaped when the vessel made port in Dover and signed on as a sailor aboard the *Clapham* under Captain Francis Thorne. Unfortunately for Williams, when the *Clapham* made port in Cádiz, Spain, he was recognized as a runaway by another sea captain and remanded to Massachusetts.

Williams's story was preserved because, after his return, Trevett sued Moffatt for the price of Williams's labor during the period Williams was gone. For modern readers, his story is notable less for its legal implications than because it documents the actual methodology of Williams's escape and because it demonstrates the relative smallness of the eighteenth-century Atlantic world. Like Titus, who was recognized as an enslaved man from Massachusetts, and Briton Hammon, a black African whose 1760 *Narrative* documents his recognition by a Massachusetts enslaver in England, Williams was identified an ocean away from the enslaver and legal status he was seeking to escape. For Williams and many others, running away was only the beginning of their quest for freedom. No matter where in the Atlantic world they sought refuge, there was always a significant chance that they would be recognized as another person's property and returned to bondage. Williams's memorable lament, "must [I] stay with [my] Master all Days of [my] life?" is a haunting reminder that reenslavement was a constant threat for those who escaped, no matter where they ran.

Text

Boston News-Letter 6 August 1724.

> *Ran-away from his Master Capt.* Richard Trevett *of* Marblehead, *A Negro Man Named* Pompey, *about Twenty-two Years of Age, a Lusty, Tall Fellow: He had on when he went away, a striped homespun Jacket, Cotton & Linen Shirt, dark coloured Kersey Breeches, grey yarn Stockings, round To'd Leather-heel Shoes, and Felt Hat.* Note, *He deserted his Masters Service in the Shallop Ann, at Plymouth. Whoever shall apprehend the said Run away, and him safely convey to his said Master at Marblehead, or to Mr.* Francis Miller *in Boston, near the Green Dragon, shall have* Fifty Shillings *Reward and all necessary Charges paid.*

"Case of Pompey." *Domestic Relations*, 182–95. Massachusetts State Archives. Microfilm.

Captain Richard Trivett, Cádiz Bay, July 31

Sir, arrived here five Days ago from Bristol & Cork & am bound up the Straits as far as Naples and hope to be with you the next Spring. The first Time of my going a Shore I met with your Negro, and Spake to him and asked him, what was the Reason he run away? He told me, must he stay with his Master all Days of his Life? I told him he must or during his Master's Pleasure. I likewise asked him what ship he belonged to He told me to a Brigantine but that did not Satisfy me, so inquired further and found he belonged to a London Gally, Captain Francis Thorne Commander, called the *Clapham* Gally so went to my Merchant, Mr. William Jacks, & consulted Methods how to recover him, which Mr. Jacks was very Diligent in getting of him Clear. We went to the Consul & took Nathaniel Stacy to give Oath that he was your Slave; likewise went to the Merchant that the said Thorne was Consigned to and made all the Interest we Could and to several Masters of his acquaintance, and got Them to make Intercession for Us. He made very much Scruple to Clear him, but Mr. Jacks has given him Security for all Damage that will accrue attending to this Slave, which will be none I believe. He went by the name of John Williams and told Captain Thorne that he was Christened and a Freeman, but that we Proved to the Contrary. I beg the Favor that You would be favorable to Him, which I know your Temper leads you to Nothing Else, for as he will Inform you he was Deluded away.

I. M. and likewise one belonged to you.

He likewise tells me He was kept four Days in the Country hid, when Judas Curry went on board to Search, for he tells me he was hidden under the Master's Cabin. It is a Thing that I should not Care to been guilty of for a large Sum, and Cannot see which way They can be off from paying for his absent Time from You. I am very glad twas my good Fortune to meet with him and make Such friends to get him Clear, which I did Scruple once. This I would do to serve any of my Friends in Marblehead and will as much more was I capable of It. And likewise I think I have served my friend C.I.M. I mention no name, & likewise desire that my name would not be much mentioned in the Matter. I have not agreed with Captain Gall, for his Passage; I presume you and he will not fall out for I believe he will be very favorable to you or C.I.M. As soon as I got Pompey clear I would not trust him on board Captain Gally but took him on board my own Ship 3 or 4 Nights and Set a good watch over him. Notwithstanding believe he will not run away, for he Seems very willing to go home. My Service to your Spouse, Sons, and Daughters, and to all Friends in Marblehead. This is all that offers from your very humble Servant,

John Hastie

P.S. Captain Francis Thorne of the *Clapham* Gally of London that Pompey belonged to, he has Stopped the half of his Wages, which You may write for to your friend in London. Any reason of my not coming to New England this Year is partly in the Death of my wife and a great Deal of Sickness that I had my Self as before. J. H.

Cádiz, 11th August 1724
To Richard Trivett, Esquire

Sir,
This is the first time I have had the honor to write You and is occasioned by Captain John Hastie, Commander of the *New Phoenix* meeting by accident your Slave Pompey in this Port, and the Captain

informing me of your Worth and the unjust action of the Person who carried off your Slave, I left no Stone unturned to get him Cleared but with no Small Difficulty, all which I went through with the utmost alacrity and have given my obligation to Captain Francis Thorne, Commander of the *Clapham*, Gally, who Shipped him in old England, to indemnify him of all Claims and Demands whatsoever in said Place, with my Promise that I would request of You not to use him ill upon this Score. Nor do I think he is so much to blame as the Captain that carried him out of that Country contrary to the Laws of the Same whose name you will learn in time and ought to be made to pay heartily for the Same for Example to others. Honest Captain Gally, by whom this goes, was very Zealous and Cordial in your Interest and merits your Thanks as well as Captain Hastie. The Wages due your Slave as a Foremost Man may be about 4 or 5£ Sterling, and I have consented that the Captain may keep the half in his hands to Satisfy his Landlady at home if he is Indebted (which is very frequent; if not he is to hold the Same at your Disposition when You may think fit to Demand the Same). Captain Hastie will likewise write you by this Ship more of this History.

My hearty Service to honest Captain Abram Howard, and when You and any one friend with your Recommendation honor me with your Commands they shall be both faithfully and punctually Executed.

Your Most Humble Servant, William Jacks

At his Majesty's Inferior court of Common pleas begun and held at Salem for and within the said county of Essex on the last Tuesday being the 28th day of December anno Domini 1725—

Richard Trivett of marblehead within the county of Essex Cord Winder Quitam, the Plaintiff, Against John Moffatt of Kittery within the County of york mariner, Defendant, In a plea of Debt for that whereas in and by One Certain Act of the Province of Massachusetts Bay made and passed by the Great & General Court of the said province begun and held at Boston upon Wednesday the 28 of May 1718 and Continued by Several Prorogations unto Wednesday the 29th day of October following and then Met, Entitled An Act for the preventing of persons under age, apprentices or Servants being transported out of the province without the consent of their masters Parents or Guardians, it is among other things then and there Enacted that every master of any Outward bound Ship or Vessel that shall thereafter Carry or Transport out of this province any persons underage or bought or hired Servants or Apprentice to any parts beyond the Seas without the Consent of Such master parent or guardian Signified in writing Shall forfeit the Sum of fifty pounds, the one half to and for the use of him that shall Inform or Sue for the same, as in and by the said act Preference thereto being had more fully and at large it doth and may appear, Yet never the less the said John moffat on or about the last day of July 1724 the aforesaid act of the said general court not Regarding, or the penalty in the Same Contained not minding at plymouth in the County of Plymouth being then master of the said Ship *Morehampton* then bound for Oporto in Portugal One Negro man Servant named pompey of the Plaintiff Richard Trivett and to him belonging did then and from thence carry away and transport in the said Ship *Morehampton* out of the Said province of the Massachusett Bay to Oporto aforesaid without the Plaintiff's Richard Trivett's consent Signified in writing, as by the Said Act is Required, and against the true Intent and meaning of the Aforesaid Recited Act whereby the Defendant hath by Law Incurred the penalty and forfeiture of fifty pounds to be Distributed as the Said Law in Such Cases directs the nonpayment whereof as aforesaid, though often by the plaintiff requested, is to the damage of the Said Richard Trivett Inferior as well for the King as for himself in this behalf as he saith the Sum of One hundred pounds—

This Action was first brought forward at an Inferior Court of Common pleas begun and held at Newbury for and in this County of Essex the last Tuesday of September last past and from thence continued by consent of both parties to this court, both parties now appeared and the Defendant saving his pleas in abatement which were overruled for he pleaded not guilty whereupon after a full hearing the cause was Committed to the Jury who were Sworn according to Law to try the Same who returned with their Verdict as follows that is to Say, the Jury find for the Plaintiff the fifty pounds as Sued for and costs of Court.

The Declaration of John Moffatt of Kittery in the County of York Mariner

This Declarant saith that in the month of July 1724 he was Commander of a Ship loading Fish at Plymouth in New England and bound for Oporto, That after he had been there some time, there came in a Shallop from Marblehead, and while they lay there, the people belonging to the shallop came to this Declarant & Complaining they had lost a Negro man, whereupon the Declarant gave an order to his Mate to let them search the Ship & to assist them therein, strictly charging them not to harbor any such Fellow as they described, which they promised to observe. The day before the Ship sailed this Declarant desired some of the Shallop's Crew to give him a Cast on board his Ship, and when they were on board, he told them if they had any Jealousy that the said Negro Fellow was on board he desired they would search the ship again and Commanded the people to assist them, which they did, but found nothing of him, & all the Ship's Crew then Declared they knew nothing of the said Negro, nor did they ever see him, neither did this Declarant ever see the said Negro before he sailed out of Plymouth. But it so happened that the Second day after the Ship Sailed, when at sea with a fair Wind, some of the people found the said Negro on board stowed away in the Fore Castle behind some Wood and Covered up with some things to conceal him (as they told the Declarant), to this, the Declarant's, very Great Surprise. But he having then a Loaden Ship and a fair Wind, dare not Venture to return back to set the said Negro on shore. When the Ship Arrived at Oporto he, the Declarant, agreed with Captain Davie to give him three Moidores [Portuguese gold coins] for the passage of the said Negro home to New England, but Captain Davie refusing to take charge of him till he was just ready to Sail, and Sailing before the Declarant knew anything of it, he missed that Opportunity of Sending the said Negro home, which he fully Intended, so that the Declarant was obliged to carry him in his Voyage. When the ship arrived at Lyme Regis she was sold & the Declarant put the said Negro in Prison whilst an Opportunity offered to send him to Bristol (whither he was then bound in order to his return to New England), but so it happened the ship the said Negro went in from Lyme Regis, in her passage to Bristol, put in to Dover, where after some time the said Negro Departed the said Ship and the Declarant as well as the Master of the said Ship, that they used

Considerable pains and were at Great Cost to obtain the said Negro, yet they never could. But the said Negro some time afterwards was secured in Cádiz (as the Declarant was informed) by one Captain Hastie of Bristol who knew him to belong to Captain Richard Trevitt of Marblehead, he having seen him there, & accordingly sent him home to his said Master in one Captain Legally, and the said Trevitt has since sold and disposed of him. And further the Declarant saith not.

John Moffatt

Boston June 20th 1727

Suggested Reading

Beckles, Hilary. "Running in Jamaica: A Slavery Ecosystem." *William and Mary Quarterly* 76, no. 1 (January 2019): 9–14.

Linebaugh, Peter, and Marcus Rediker. *The Many-headed Hydra: Sailors, Slaves, Commoners, and the Hidden History of the Revolutionary Atlantic.* Boston: Beacon, 2000.

Rupprecht, Anita. "'He Says That if He is Not Taught a Trade, He Will Run Away': Recaptured Africans, Desertion, and Mobility in the British Caribbean, 1808–1828." In *A Global History of Runaways: Workers, Mobility, and Capitalism, 1600–1850*, edited by Marcus Rediker, Titas Chakraborty, and Matthias van Rossum, 178–98. Oakland: University of California Press, 2019.

Wong, Edlie L. *Neither Fugitive nor Free: Atlantic Slavery, Freedom Suits, and the Legal Culture of Travel.* New York: New York University Press, 2009.

CHAPTER THIRTY-SEVEN

A Short Account of the Life of Elizabeth Colson, 1727

Introduction

Elizabeth Colson, described in records as a "molatto woman," was born in Weymouth, Massachusetts. She was apparently the free daughter of a school teacher who sold her into an indenture or apprenticeship at an early age, with the idea that Colson's master would educate her. Colson never received that education, an oversight she blames for her self-described acts of sin and murder. On 22 May 1727, she was convicted of killing her illegitimate baby and was executed in Plymouth. Colson was surrounded by ministers, one of whom preached an execution sermon hours before her hanging, and in front of the gallows, she offered her own penitent prayer. In the days before her execution, she dictated her autobiography to a jail mate F. The as-told-to account was published a month later in the *New-England Weekly Journal*, a Boston newspaper founded in 1727 that printed mostly literary and religious content. In printing the narrative, the newspaper's editor notes that it was printed "without the addition of one word," authenticating Colson's voice. The brief autobiography, appearing below in its entirety, follows several generic traditions. It is an infanticide narrative, with mostly oblique references to her baby's death. It also is a criminal execution narrative. A kind of gallows literature, these typically brief, tabloid-esque narratives offered biographical accounts of the lives of convicted criminals, with a special emphasis on their criminal pasts and, if applicable, their spiritual conversion and repentance. Of particular note is Colson's determination to tell her own story, which appears in a printed form because she marshals the resources around her, employing the narrative form to signify her life experiences. Her story does not have the weight of a Puritan minister who shapes her words on the page, as was the case with Joseph Hanno, whose account appears in chapter 3 in this reader. Also unlike Hanno, Colson seems to affirm the importance of proselytizing black Africans. Repeatedly, she references her own lack of education and her ignorance about spiritual matters, which made her particularly susceptible to the powers of Satan. She seeks the reader's sympathy even as she catalogues her sins—stealing, lying, fornicating, and ultimately committing murder.

Text

Elizabeth Colson, "A Short Account of the Life of Elizabeth Colson, a Molatto Woman, Who Now Must Dye for the Monstrous Sin of Murdering Her Child." *New-England Weekly Journal*, no. XIII, 19 June 1727, p.[2]. Readex: America's Historical Newspapers, accessed June 11, 2021, infoweb.newsbank.com/apps/readex/.

A Short Account of the Life of Elizabeth Colson, a Molatto Woman, Who Now Must Dye for the Monstrous Sin of Murdering Her Child

> I was born at Weymouth and my Mother put me out to Ebenezer Prat, who was to learn me to read, but I fear they never took that pains they should have done to instruct me, my Mother being School-Mistress was loth I should come to School with other children, and so I had not that Instruction I wish I had in my Youth. I was carry'd very hardly too by my Mistress, and Suffer'd hunger and blows, and at last was tempted to Steal, for which I have reason to lament, for although I stole at first for Necessity as I tho't, yet the Devil took that Advantage against me, and led me further into Sin, for one Lord's Day the People being gone to Meeting, I broke into a Neighbour's House, and stole some Victuals, and looking for more I saw a piece of Money, which I took, and afterwards telling a Lye, & saying I found it; so was led by one Sin to another.
>
> After-wards I was Sold to Lieut. Reed, where I had some good Examples set me, but having got a habit of Sin, I still grew worse & worse & worse; and was left to fall into the Sin of Fornication, and after my Time was out with Master Reed, I was in great distress what to do with my Child, but carried it about from place to place, till I left it at Dighton and ran away from it, and soon fell again to that shameful & Soul destroying Sin of Fornication the Second time; and not having the Fear of God before my Eyes, I was justly left of God to this horrid Sin the Third time, that led me, together with the Instigation of the Devil, and the wretchedness of my own Heart, to that monstrous Sin for which I must now Dye: And so I have not only brought my Body to dye a Shameful Death, but my Soul in danger of Death & Damnation.
>
> O that all people would be Warned to flee from the Sins I have been Guilty of, least they run themselves into more terrible Distresses than they can easily imagine, amongst their ungodly Companions, who will

not be able to help them out of their Distresses, when they have left God and God hath left them. I would therefore earnestly intreat all Young People to watch against the beginnings of Sin and themselves, for you know not where you will stop this side Hell if once you allow your selves to Sin, tho' you may think you can: For I remember that when I was Young I heard of a Woman that murdered her Child, and I said, I never would do so. I may say to you as my Mistress did to me, you do not know what you may be left to. Therefore I would intreat all Young People to beware of Stealing, Lying, and especially that Shameful sin of Uncleanness, which hath been the leading Sin to that horrid Sin for which I must Dye. O then take this Advice from a poor Dying Malefactor, who must suffer a Shameful Death as the just demerits of a Sinful Life.

O that all People would take Warning by me, of grieving the Holy Spirit of God by sinning against the light of their own Consciences, and of Prophaning the Sabbath Day and not regarding the Warnings of Christ's faithful Embassadours, but be now advised to take fast hold of Instruction, and let it not go, keep it for it is thy Life: And let them then that think they stand, take heed lest they fall.

Suggested Reading

Braxton, Joanne. *Black Women Writing Autobiography: A Tradition within a Tradition*. Philadelphia: Temple University Press, 1989.

DeLombard, Jeannine Marie. *In the Shadow of the Gallows: Race, Crime, and American Civic Identity*. Philadelphia: University of Pennsylvania Press, 2012.

Foster, Frances Smith. *Written by Herself: Literary Production of African American Women, 1746–1892*. Bloomington: Indiana University Press, 1993.

Foster, Frances Smith, and Larose Davis. "Early African American Women's Literature." In *The Cambridge Companion to African American Women's Literature*, edited by Angelyn Mitchell and Danille K. Taylor, 15–31. Cambridge: Cambridge University Press, 2009.

Hine, Darlene Clark. "Rape and the Inner Lives of Black Women in the Middle West." *Signs* 14, no. 4 (Summer 1989): 912–20.

Schorb, Jodi. "Uncleanliness Is Next to Godliness: Sexuality, Salvation, and the Early American Woman's Execution Narrative." In *The Puritan Origins of American Sex: Religion, Sexuality, and National Identity in American Literature*, edited by Magdalena J. Zaborowska and Nicholas F. Radel, 72–92. United Kingdom: Taylor & Francis, 2014.

CHAPTER THIRTY-EIGHT

Ayuba Suleiman Diallo, 1734

Introduction

Ayuba Suleiman Diallo (or Job ben Solomon) was one of the estimated 10 to 15 percent of black Africans captured and enslaved in early America who were also Muslim. Diallo was the son of a wealthy and prominent priest in the town of Bundu, part of the kingdom of Futa-Toro in present-day Senegal. In 1730, he was kidnapped by Mandinka slave traders along the Gambia River while he, himself, was conducting a trade in humans. The Mandinka sold him to agents of the Royal African Company. Despite his declarations about his prominent status and his father's wealth, Diallo was shipped off to Maryland in 1731. While enslaved on a Maryland plantation, he remained faithful to Islam. His devotion so impressed the enslaver that Diallo was granted space on the plantation to pray. Upon discovering his literacy skills, that Diallo could write and read in Arabic, the enslaver also granted him permission to pen a letter to his father in Bundu. The letter made it to London, into the hands of James Oglethorpe, a director of the Royal African Company. Diallo's literacy skills so impressed Oglethorpe that he became one of Diallo's chief benefactors. He offered to purchase Diallo and in 1733 sent him to London in the company of an Anglican minister named Thomas Bluett. A year later, Diallo secured his freedom and returned to his home in Senegal. Bluett transcribed Diallo's story and published it in London in 1734. Three years later, Francis Moore, an agent with the Royal African Company, published a coda of sorts that details Diallo's experiences upon his return to Bundu. He returned to find his father had died and that other members of his family had moved on, assuming that he was forever lost to them.

    Diallo's *Memoirs* emphasize his noble status and suffering. They tell a story of captivity and redemption. The narratives do not, however, critique the system of slavery itself. Rather, they condemn the enslavement of one particular man. In this way, his story does not serve as a precursor to the slave narrative genre with the overarching goal of condemning and dismantling slavery. Yet, Diallo is not completely an outlier in an early African American literary tradition. He anticipates the life writing endeavors of figures such as Briton Hammon, John Marrant, and Olaudah Equiano. Diallo, who told his story to Bluett, Oglethorpe, and others, clearly appreciated the power of narrative to shape a self.

Text

From Thomas Bluett, *Some Memoirs of the Life of Job, the Son of Solomon the High Priest of Boonda in Africa*. London, 1734. *Documenting the American South*. 1999. The University of North Carolina at Chapel Hill, accessed Apr 10, 2020, docsouth.unc.edu/neh/bluett/bluett.html.

Bluett's Introduction

> HAVING had occasion to inform my self of many considerable and curious Circumstances of the Life of JOB, the African Priest, in a more exact and particular Manner than the Generality of his Acquaintance in England could do; I was desired by himself, a little before his Departure, to draw up an Account of him agreeable to the Information he had given me at different Times, and to the Truth of the Facts, which I had either been a Witness to, or personally concerned in upon his Account. I have been solicited also by several Gentlemen, who were Benefactors to JOB, to publish what I knew of him: And I am of opinion such an Account is pretty generally wanted; at least it cannot but be agreeable to those Persons, who were pleased to do kind Offices to this Stranger, merely from a Principle of Humanity, before any particular Account of him could be had. Therefore I have at length resolved to communicate to the World such Particulars of the Life and Character of this African Gentleman, as I think will be most useful and entertaining; intending to advance nothing as Fact, but what I either knew to be such, or have had from JOB's own Mouth, whose Veracity I have no reason to doubt of.
>
> Pursuant to this Resolution, I shall not trouble my Reader with any very long and particular Detail of the Geography, History, or Rarities of that Country of Africa which JOB belongs to; nor shall I meddle any farther with these Matters, in the present Account, than to relate such Observations concerning them, as JOB himself made to me in Conversation; being either not generally known, or so curious as to bear a Repetition here, consistently with the Design of these Memoirs. However, I shall endeavour to make the whole as agreeable as the Nature of the Subject, and the Limits of this Pamphlet will allow; and therefore, without any farther Preface, shall proceed to the Thing propos'd.

Sect. I: An Account of the Family of JOB; his Education; and the more remarkable Circumstances of his Life, before he was taken Captive

... JOB, who is now about 31 or 32 Years of age, was born at a Town called Boonda in the County of Galumbo (in our Maps Catumbo) in the Kingdom of Futa in Africa; which lies on both Sides the River Senegal, and on the south Side reaches as far as, the River Gambia. These two Rivers, JOB assured me, run pretty near parallel to one another, and never meet, contrary to the Position they have in most of our Maps. The Eastern Boundary of the Kingdom of Futa or Senega is the great Lake, called in our Maps Lacus Guarde. The Extent of it, towards the North, is not so certain. The chief City or Town of it is Tombut; over against which, on the other side of the River, is Boonda, the Place of JOB's Nativity.

About fifty Years ago Hibrahim, the Grandfather of JOB, founded the Town of Boonda, in the Reign of Bubaker, then King of Futa, and was, by his Permission, sole Lord Proprietor and Governor of it, and at the same Time High Priest, or Alpha; so that he had a Power to make what Laws and Regulations he thought proper for the Increase and good Government of his new City. Among other Institutions, one was, that no Person who flies thither for Protection shall be made a Slave. This Privilege is in force there to this Day, and is extended to all in general, that can read and know God, as they express it; and it has contributed much to the Peopling of the Place, which is now very large and flourishing. Some time after the Settlement of this Town Hibrahim died; and, as the Priesthood is hereditary there, Salumen his Son, the Father of JOB, became High Priest. About the same Time Bubaker the King dying, his Brother Gelazi, who was next Heir, succeeded him. Gelazi had a Son, named Sambo, whom he put under the Care of Salumen, JOB's Father, to learn the Koran and Arabick Language. JOB was at this Time also with his Father, was Companion to Sambo, and studied along with him. Sambo, upon the Death of Gelazi, was made King of Futa, and reigns there at present. When JOB was fifteen Years old, he assisted his Father as Emaum, or Sub-priest. About this Age he married the Daughter of the Alpha of Tombut, who was then only eleven Years old. By her he had a Son (when she was thirteen Years old) called Abdolah; and after that two more Sons, called Hibrahim and Sambo. About two Years before his Captivity he married a second Wife, Daughter of the Alpha of Tomga; by whom he has a Daughter named Fatima, after the Daughter of their Prophet Mahommed. Both these Wives, with their Children, were alive when he came from Home.

Sect. II: Of the Manner of his being taken Captive; and what followed upon it, till his Return

IN February, 1730, JOB's Father hearing of an English Ship at Gambia River, sent him, with two Servants to attend him, to sell two Negroes and to buy Paper, and some other Necessaries; but desired him not to venture over the River, because the Country of the Mandingoes, who are Enemies to the People of Futa, lies on the other side. JOB not agreeing with Captain Pike (who commanded the Ship, lying then at Gambia, in the Service of Captain Henry Hunt, Brother to Mr. William Hunt, Merchant, in Little Tower-Street, London) sent back the two Servants to acquaint his Father with it, and to let him know that he intended to go farther. Accordingly, having agreed with another Man, named Loumein Yoas, who understood the Mandingoe Language, to go with him as his Interpreter, he crossed the River Gambia, and disposed of his Negroes for some Cows. As he was returning Home, he stopp'd for some Refreshment at the House of an old Acquaintance; and the Weather being hot, he hung up his Arms in the House, while he refresh'd himself. Those Arms were very valuable; consisting of a Gold-hilted Sword, a Gold Knife, which they wear by their Side, and a rich Quiver of Arrows, which King Sambo had made him a Present of. It happened that a Company of the Mandingoes, who live upon Plunder, passing by at that Time, and observing him unarmed, rush'd in, to the Number of seven or eight at once, at a back Door, and pinioned JOB, before he could get to his Arms, together with his Interpreter, who is a Slave in Maryland still.

. . .

JOB was brought with the rest of the Slaves to Annapolis in Maryland, and delivered to Mr. Vachell Denton, Factor to Mr. Hunt, before mentioned. . . . Mr. Vachell Denton sold JOB to one Mr. Tolsey in Kent Island in Maryland, who put him to work in making Tobacco; but he was soon convinced that JOB had never been used to such Labour. He every Day shewed more and more Uneasiness under this

Exercise, and at last grew sick, being no way able to bear it; so that his Master was obliged to find easier Work for him, and therefore put him to tend the Cattle. JOB would often leave the Cattle, and withdraw into the Woods to pray; but a white Boy frequently watched him, and whilst he was at his Devotion would mock him, and throw Dirt in his Face. This very much disturbed JOB, and added to his other Misfortunes; all which were increased by his Ignorance of the English Language, which prevented his complaining, or telling his Case to any Person about him. Grown in some measure desperate, by reason of his present Hardships, he resolved to travel at a Venture; thinking he might possibly be taken up by some Master, who would use him better, or otherwise meet with some lucky Accident, to divert or abate his Grief. Accordingly, he travelled thro' the Woods, till he came to the County of Kent, upon Delaware Bay, now esteemed Part of Pensilvania; altho' it is properly a Part of Maryland, and belongs to my Lord Baltimore. There is a Law in force, throughout the Colonies of Virginia, Maryland, Pensilvania, &c. as far as Boston in New England, viz. That any Negroe, or white Servant who is not known in the County, or has no Pass, may be secured by any Person, and kept in the common Goal, till the Master of such Servant shall fetch him. Therefore JOB being able to give no Account of himself, was put in Prison there.

...

When JOB had been some time confined, an old Negroe Man, who lived in that Neighbourhood, and could speak the Jalloff Language, which JOB also understood, went to him, and conversed with him. By this Negroe the Keeper was informed to whom JOB belonged, and what was the Cause of his leaving his Master. The Keeper thereupon wrote to his Master, who soon after fetch'd him home, and was much kinder to him than before; allowing him a Place to pray in, and some other Conveniencies, in order to make his Slavery as easy as possible. Yet Slavery and Confinement was by no means agreeable to JOB, who had never been used to it; he therefore wrote a Letter in Arabick to his Father, acquainting him with his Misfortunes, hoping he might yet find Means to redeem him. This Letter he sent to Mr. Vachell Denton, desiring it might be sent to Africa by Captain Pike; but he being gone to England, Mr. Denton sent the Letter inclosed to Mr. Hunt, in order to be sent to Africa by Captain Pike from England; but Captain Pike had sailed for Africa before the Letter came to Mr. Hunt, who therefore kept it in his own Hands, till he should have a proper Opportunity of sending it. It happened that this Letter was seen by James Oglethorpe, Esq; who, according to his usual Goodness and Generosity, took Compassion on JOB, and gave his Bond to Mr. Hunt for the Payment of a certain Sum, upon the Delivery of JOB here in England. Mr. Hunt upon this sent to Mr. Denton, who purchas'd him again of his Master for the same Money which Mr. Denton had formerly received for him; his Master being very willing to part with him, as finding him no ways fit for his Business.

. . .

On our arrival in England, we heard that Mr. Oglethorpe was gone to Georgia, and that Mr. Hunt had provided a Lodging for JOB at Limehouse. After I had visited my Friends in the Country, I went up on purpose to see JOB. He was, very sorrowful, and told me, that Mr. Hunt had been applied to by some Persons to sell him, who pretended they would send him home; but he feared they would either sell him again as a Slave, or if they sent him home would expect an unreasonable Ransom for him. I took him to London with me, and waited on Mr. Hunt, to desire leave to carry him to Cheshunt in Hartfordshire; which Mr. Hunt comply'd with. He told me he had been apply'd to, as JOB had suggested, but did not intend to part with him without his own Consent; but as Mr. Oglethorpe was out of England, if any of JOB's Friends would pay the Money, he would accept of it, provided they would undertake to send him home safely to his own Country. I also obtained his Promise that he would not dispose of him till he heard farther from me.

. . .

About the latter end of July last he embark'd on Board one of the African Company's Ships, bound for Gambia; where we hope he is safely arrived, to the great Joy of his Friends, and the Honour of the English Nation.

Sect. III: Some Observations, as related by JOB, concerning the Manners and Opinions of his Countrymen

I Don't pretend here, as I hinted before, to trouble the Reader or my self with a full and regular History of JOB's Country. Those who have the Curiosity to inform themselves more particularly in the History of those Parts of the World, may consult the Voyages that are already published on that Subject. I shall only take Notice of some occasional Remarks upon the Customs of the Country, as I had them in Conversation from JOB himself.

It is pretty commonly known that the Africans in general, especially those in the inland Countries, are inured from their Infancy to a hard and low Life, being great Strangers to the Luxury and Delicacy of most of the Countries of Europe. They have the Necessaries of Life, 'tis true, and might have many of the Conveniences of it too; but such is the Simplicity of their Manners, occasioned chiefly by their Ignorance, and want of Correspondence with the politer Part of the World, that they seem contented enough with their plain Necessaries, and don't much hanker after greater Matters, tho' their Country in many Places is capable of great Improvements.

In JOB's Country the Slaves, and poorer sort of People, are employed in preparing the Bread, Corn, &c. And here they labour under a great many Difficulties, having no proper Instruments either for Tilling the Ground, or reaping the Corn when it is ripe; insomuch that they us'd, in Harvest-time, to pull it up, Roots and all. To reduce their Corn to Flower, they rub it between two Stones with their Hands, which must be very tedious. Nor is their Fatigue in Building and Carriage less, for they perform the whole by mere Dint of Strength, and downright Labour. The better Sort of People, who apply themselves to Study and Reading, are obliged to read whole Nights together by the Light of the Fire, (having no Candles or Lamps, as we have) which must be very troublesome in that hot, sultry Country. These, and several other Difficulties which these People labour under, we hope will be removed by JOB's Return; his Friends here having suited their Presents very judiciously to the Necessities of his Country-men; and there is scarce any Tool or Machine, that can be of real Use to them, which JOB has not had from some Friend or other, and their several Uses have been shewn to him with a great deal of Care.

Some of those People spend a great Part of their Time in Hunting; particularly after the Elephants, with whose Teeth they drive a great Trade. One of those Hunters affirmed to JOB, that he had seen an Elephant surprize a Lion (to which Beast, it seems, the Elephant bears a very great Hatred) and carry him to a Tree, which he split down, and putting the Lion's Head thro', let the Tree close again on the Lion's Neck, and there left him to perish. JOB did not say that he knew this Fact to be true; but it seems to be the more probable, upon account of what he assured me he had been a Witness to himself, viz. that an Elephant having catch'd a Lion, carried him directly to a great Slough, and thrusting the Lion's Head under the Mud, held him there till he was smothered.

Of JOB's Person and Character

JOB was about five Feet ten Inches high, strait limb'd, and naturally of a good Constitution; altho' the religious Abstinence which he observed, and the Fatigues he lately underwent, made him appear something lean and weakly. His Countenance was exceeding pleasant, yet grave and composed; his Hair long, black, and curled, being very different from that of the Negroes commonly brought from Africa.

His natural Parts were remarkably good; and I believe most of the Gentlemen that conversed with him frequently, will remember many Instances of his Ingenuity. On all Occasions he discovered a solid judgment, a ready Memory, and a clear Head. And, notwithstanding the Prejudices which it was natural for him to have in favour of his own religious Principles, it was very observable with how much Temper and Impartiality he would reason in Conversation upon any Question of that kind, while at the same Time he would frame such Replies, as were calculated at once to support his own Opinion, and to oblige or please his Opponent. In his Reasonings there appeared nothing trifling, nothing hypocritical or overstrained; but, on the contrary, strong Sense, joined with an innocent Simplicity, a strict Regard to Truth, and a hearty Desire to find it. Tho' it was a considerable Disadvantage to him in Company, that he was not sufficient Master of our Language; yet those who were used to his Way, by making proper Allowances, always found themselves agreeably entertained by him.

. . .

His memory was extraordinary; for when he was fifteen Years old he could say the whole Alcoran [Qur'an] by heart, and while he was here in England he wrote three Copies of it without the Assistance of any other Copy, and without so much as looking to one of those three when he wrote the others. He would often laugh at me when he heard me say I had forgot any Thing, and told me he hardly ever forgot any Thing in his Life, and wondered that any other body should.

From Francis Moore, *Travels into the Inland Parts of Africa*. London, 1738.

James Fort, Aug. 22. 1734.

Sir,
The good Opinion we have of your Integrity and Zeal to serve the Company, induces us to appoint you their Chief Factor at the Company's Settlement at Joar, now under the Direction of Mr Brooke Gill. And as the Commissions, Salary, and Allowance of Diet, is much augmented of late by the Company at the Factory, purposely to promote and encourage an honest and reputable Conduct, in regard to the high Trust reposed in you by them; so we promise ourselves that you will so far be a Friend to yourself and your own Reputation, as to do the Company the Strictest Justice agreeable to your most Solemn Engagement you have voluntarily obliged yourself to perform. At your Arrival at Joar you are to deliver to Mr Brooke Gill our Orders for him to resign up the Company's Factory and all their Effects in your Custody, which you are immediately to inventory, and give him two proper Discharges for the Particulars and Amount thereof: One of which Mr Gill and you are to send to us per first Opportunity.

As you have been for some Years past conversant in Business at Our-Factories, so we shall now only repeat, that you stick to such Orders as have been formerly given you.

By this Conveyance comes one Black Free Man, by Name Job Ben Solomon; whom you are to use with the greatest Respect, and all the Civility you possibly can. We are
Your Loving Friends

RICH. HULL,

H. HAMILTON

. . . *JOB Ben Solomon* having a Mind to go up to *Cower* to talk with some of his Countrymen, went along with me. In the Evening we weighted Anchor, saluting the Fort with five Guns, which return'ed the same Number.

On the 26th we arrived at the Creek of *Damasensa*, and having some old Acquaintances at the Town of *Damasensa*, *Job* and I went up in the Yawl; in the Way, going up a very narrow Place for about half of Mile, we saw several

Monkeys of a beautiful Blue and Red, which the Natives tell me never set their Feet on the Ground, but live entirely amongst the Trees, leaping from one to another at so great Distances, as any one, were they not to see it, would think improbable.

In the Evening, as my Friend *Job* and I were sitting under a great Tree at *Damasensa*, there came by us six or seven of the very People who robb'd and made a Slave of *Job*, about thirty Miles from hence, about three Years ago; *Job*, tho' a very even-temper'd Man at other times, could not contain himself when he saw them, but fell into a most terrible Passion, and was for killing them with his broad Sword and Pistols, which he always took care to have about him. I had much ado to dissuade him from falling upon the six Men; but at last, by representing to him the ill Consequences that would infallibly attend such a rash Action, and the Impossibility of mine or his own escaping alive, if he should attempt it, I made him lay aside the Thoughts of it and persuaded him to sit down and pretend not to know them, but ask them Questions about himself; which he accordingly did, and they answer'd nothing but the Truth. At last he ask' them how the King their Master did; they to him he was dead, and by further Enquiry we found, that amongst the Goods for which he sold *Job* to Captain *Pyke* there was a Pistol, which the King used commonly to wear flung about his Neck with a String; and as they never carry Arms without being loaded, one Day this accidentally went off, and the Balls lodging in his Throat, he died presently. At the Closing of this Story *Job* was so very much transported, that he immediately fell on his Knees, and returned Thanks to *Mahoment* for making this Man die by the very Goods for which he sold him into slavery; and then turning to me, he said, 'Mr *Moore*, you see now God Almighty was displeas'd at this Man's making me a Slave, and therefore made him die by the very Pistol for which he sold me; yet I ought to forgive him, *says he*, because had I not been sold, I should neither have known any thing of the *English* Tongue, nor have had any of the fine, useful and valuable Things I now carry over, nor have known that in the World there is such a Place as *England* nor such noble, good and generous People as Queen *Caroline*, Prince *William*, the Duke of *Montague*, the Earl of *Pembroke*, Mr *Holden*, Mr *Oglethorpe*, and the Royal *African* Company.'

On the 1st of September we arrived at *Joar*, the Freshes being very strong against us. I immediately took an Inventory of the Company's Effects, and gave Receipts to Mr *Gill* for the same. After which we unloaded the Sloop, and then I sent her up to *Yanimarew* [a port town along the Gambia River] for a Load of Corn for *James* Fort, where she stayed till the 25th, and then came back to Joar, during which time I made some Trade with the Merchants, though at a pretty high Price.

On *Job's* first Arrival here, he desired I would send a Messenger up to his own Country to acquaint his Friends of his Arrival. I spoke to one of the *Blacks* which we usually employ upon those Occasions, to procure me a Messenger, who brought to me a *Pholey*, who knew the High Priest his Father, and *Job* himself, and express'd great Joy at seeing him in safety returned from Slavery, he being the only Man (except one) that was ever known to come back to this Country, after having been once carried a Slave out of it by White Men. *Job* gave him the Message himself, and desired his Father should not come down to him, for it was too far for him to travel; and that it was fit for the Young to go to the Old, and not for the Old to come to the Young. He also sent some Presents by him to his Wives and desired him to bring his little one, which was his best beloved, down to him. After the Messenger was gone *Job* went frequently along with me to *Cower*, and several other Places about the Country; he spoke always very handsome of the English, and what he said, took away a great deal of the Horror of the *Pholeys* for the State of Slavery amongst the *English*; for they before generally imagined, that all who were sold for Slaves, were generally either eaten or murdered, since none ever returned. His Description of the English gave them also a great notion of the Power of *England*, and a Veneration for those who traded amongst them. He sold some of the Presents he brought with him from England for Trading-Goods, with which he bought a Woman-Slave and two Horses, which were very useful to him there, and which he designed to carry with him to *Bundo*, whenever he should set out thither. He used to give his Country People a good deal of Writing-Paper, which is a very useful Commodity amongst them, and of which the Company had presented him with several Reams. He used to pray frequently, and behaved himself with great Mildness and Affability to all, so that he was very popular and well-beloved. The Messenger not being thought to return soon, *Job* desired to go down to *James* Fort to take care of his Goods, I promising to send him word when the Messenger came back, and also to send some other Messengers, for fear the first should miscarry.

On the 26th I sent down the *Fame* Sloop to *James* Fort, and *Job* going along with her, I gave the Master Orders to shew him all the Respect he could.

...

On the 29th came up from *Damasensa* in a Canoa *Job Ben Solomon*, who, I forgot to say, came up in the *Fame* Sloop along with me from *James* Fort on the

26th of December last, and going on Shore with me at *Elephants* Island, and hearing that the People of *Joar* were run away, it made him unwilling to proceed up hither, and therefore he desired *Conner* to put him and his things ashore at a Place call'd *India*, about six Miles above *Damansensa*, where he was continued ever since; but now hearing that there is no farther Danger, he thought he might venture his Body and Goods along with mine and the Company's and so came up.

On the 14th a Messenger, whom I had sent to *Job's* Country, return'd hither with Letters, and Advice that *Job's* father had died before he got up thither, but that he had liv'd to receive the Letters sent by *Job* from *England*, which brought him the welcome News of his Son's being redeemed out of Slavery, and the Figure he made in *England*. That one of *Job's* Wives was married to another Man, but that as soon as the Husband heard of *Job's* Arrival here, he thought it advisable to abscond: That since *Job's* Absence from his Country, there has been such a dreadful War, that there is not so much as one Cow left in it, tho' when *Job* was there, it was a very noted Country for numerous Herds of large Cattle. With this Messenger came a good many of *Job's* old Acquaintance, whom he was exceeding glad to see; but notwithstanding the Joy he had to see his Friends, he wept grievously for his Father's Death, and the Misfortunes of his Country. He forgave his Wife, and the Man that had taken her; *For*, says he, *Mr Moore, she could not help thinking I was dead, for I was gone to a Land from whence no Pholey ever yet returned; therefore she is not to be blamed, nor the Man neither*. For three or four Days he held a Conversation with his Friends without any Interruption, unless to sleep or eat.

Suggested Reading

Bennett, Herman. *African Kings and Black Slaves: Sovereignty and Dispossession in the Early Modern Atlantic*. Philadelphia: University of Pennsylvania Press, 2018.

Gomez, Michael A. "Muslims in Early America." *Journal of Southern History* 60, no. 4 (1994): 671–710.

Harris, Will. "Phillis Wheatley: A Muslim Connection." *African American Review* 48, no. 1/2 (Spring/Summer 2015): 1–15.

Moody, Joycelyn. "Early Black Men's Spiritual Autobiography: Marriage and Violence." In *Reading African American Autobiography: Twenty-First-Century Contexts and Criticism*, edited by Eric D. Lamore, 41–65. Madison: University of Wisconsin Press, 2017.

Sweet, James H. *Recreating Africa: Culture, Kinship, and Religion in the African-Portuguese World, 1441–1770*. Chapel Hill: University of North Carolina Press, 2003.

Thornton, John K. *Africa and Africans in the Making of the Atlantic World, 1400–1800*. Cambridge: Cambridge University Press, 1998.

Notes

Introduction

1. See, for example, William L. Andrews, *To Tell a Free Story: The First Century of Afro-American Autobiography, 1760–1865* (Urbana: University of Illinois Press, 1986); Henry Louis Gates Jr., *Signifying Monkey: A Theory of Afro-American Literary Criticism* (New York: Oxford University Press, 1988); Frances Smith Foster, *Written by Herself: Literary Production of African American Women, 1746–1892* (Bloomington: Indiana University Press, 1993); Rafia Zafar, *We Wear the Mask: African-Americans Write American Literature, 1760–1870* (New York: Columbia University Press, 1997); and Vincent Carretta and Philip Gould, eds., *Genius in Bondage: Literature of the Early Black Atlantic* (Lexington: University Press of Kentucky, 2001). See also April Langley, *The Black Aesthetic Unbound: Theorizing the Dilemma of Eighteenth-Century African American Literature* (Columbus: Ohio State University Press, 2008); Cedrick May, *Evangelism and Resistance in the Black Atlantic, 1760–1835* (Athens: University of Georgia Press, 2008); Michael J. Drexler and Ed White, eds., *Beyond Douglass: New Perspectives on Early African-American Literature* (Lewisburg, PA: Bucknell University Press, 2008); and Laura Langer Cohen and Jordan Alexander Stein, eds., *Early African American Print Culture* (Philadelphia: University of Pennsylvania Press, 2012).

2. Jeannine Marie DeLombard, "Apprehending Early African American Literary History," in Cohen and Stein, *Early African American Print Culture*, 93. In an effort to de-center the slave narrative in discussions about the origins of African American literature, Delombard asks, "What would happen, though, if we were to think of the genre distinguished by the opening line 'I was born' not as heralding the birth of a fully formed African American literature after a century-long gestation but as the second-generation scion of an important (if sometimes forgotten) and influential (if not always illustrious) literary family?" (94). Dickson Bruce similarly challenges the centrality of slave narratives in *The Origins of African American Literature, 1680–1865* (Charlottesville: University of Virginia Press, 2001).

3. During the period represented in this text, individuals born in Africa and transported to the Americas as human chattels still thought of themselves primarily in terms of the different national, religious, and linguistic affiliations from which they had been torn by slavery. A collective, diasporic racial identity of Blackness only became the predominant heuristic in the late eighteenth century, as a second or third generation of enslaved people born in the Americas gradually outnumbered those still arriving via the Middle Passage. The lowercase element in the phrase "black Africans," which we use throughout the reader, is meant as a reminder that many of the individuals whose stories we tell were born in Africa and had not yet relinquished their particular national, religious, and cultural identities to claim the label "Negro" or "Black" as a racial marker for themselves. However, when we refer to a diasporic or African American consciousness, we capitalize Black in recognition of a self-determined racial identity and shared culture.

4. In describing "literary black Africans," we borrow from and modify the term "literary Indians" that Angela Calcaterra employs to describe "connections in literary productions" and the "multilateral aesthetic choices that guided moments of encounter" between Natives and Euro-American settlers. Similarly, this reader highlights the consequences of encounter between black Africans and settlers in early America. See Angela Calcaterra, *Literary Indians: Aesthetics and Encounter in American Literature to 1920* (Chapel Hill: University of North Carolina Press 2018), 8.

5. Toni Morrison, *Playing in the Dark: Whiteness and the Literary Imagination* (Cambridge, MA: Harvard University Press, 1992).

6. Stephen Greenblatt, "Invisible Bullets: Renaissance Authority and Its Subversion, *Henry IV* and *Henry V*," in *Political Shakespeare: Essays in Cultural Materialism*, ed. Jonathan Dollimore and Alan Sinfield, 2nd ed. (Manchester: Manchester University Press, 1994), 35.

7. Gene Andrew Jarrett, *Representing the Race: A New Political History of African American Literature* (New York: New York University Press, 2011), 4.

8. For more on this critical impasse, see Saidiya Hartman, "Venus in Two Acts," *Small Axe* 12, no. 2 (June 2008): 1–14 and Ed White, "Invisible Tagkanysough," *PMLA* 120, no. 3 (May 2005): 751–67, which responds to Greenblatt's "Invisible Bullets" essay. For more on the potential to craft more meaningful literary histories by reading beyond the impasse, see Kelly Wisecup, *Medical Encounters: Knowledge and Identity in Early American Literatures* (Amherst: University of Massachusetts Press, 2013). Nicole Aljoe offers strategies for reading mediated texts in the Caribbean; she proposes that the words of black Africans that have been edited or transcribed by others belong to a syncretic form she calls *testimonio*, which relates communal experience rather than the individual triumph over conditions of bondage. See Nicole N. Aljoe, *Creole Testimonies: Slave Narratives from the British West Indies, 1709–1838* (New York: Palgrave Macmillan, 2012).

9. For more on the material world and textuality in terms of early black African representations, see Cassander L. Smith, *Black Africans in the British Imagination: English Narratives of the Early Atlantic World* (Baton Rouge: Louisiana State University Press, 2016).

10. See again Calcaterra, *Literary Indians*; Wisecup, *Medical Encounters*; and Smith, *Black Africans in the British Imagination*. Those studies harken back to the work of Myra Jehlen and Neil Whitehead, who in the 1990s and early 2000s acknowledged that cultural encounters registered on multiple levels beyond the linguistic or discursive, leaving a mark on the literary record. See Myra Jehlen, *Readings at the Edge of Literature* (Chicago: University of Chicago Press, 2000) and Neil L. Whitehead, "Anthropology and Colonial Text," in *Sir Walter Ralegh, The Discoverie of the Large, Rich, and Bewtiful Empyre of Guiana* (Manchester: Manchester University Press, 1997), 33–38.

11. Foundational studies include Ira Berlin, *Generations of Captivity: A History of African American Slaves* (Cambridge, MA: Belknap Press of Harvard University Press, 2003); Ira Berlin, *The Making of African America: The Four Great Migrations* (New York: Viking, 2010); Paul Gilroy, *The Black Atlantic: Modernity and Double Consciousness* (Cambridge, MA: Harvard University Press, 1993); and Jane Landers, *Black Society in Spanish Florida* (Champaign: University of Illinois Press, 1999).

12. Andrew Bennett, *The Author: The New Critical Idiom* (Abingdon: Routledge, 2005).

13. Olaudah Equiano, *The Interesting Narrative of the Life of Olaudah Equiano, or Gustavus Vassa, the African*, rev. ed. (New York: Penguin, 2003), 1.

14. Phillis Wheatley, *Complete Writings* (New York: Penguin, 2001), 8.

15. This approach to authorship in African American literary studies is similar to the "authors are actors" model that Joseph Rezek argues has dominated the study of book history. Authors, Rezek argues, "are embedded in and susceptible to historically specific circumstances and influences" and are "strategic in their navigations of the world of media and communication." See Rezek, "Author," *Early American Studies: An Interdisciplinary Journal* 16, no. 4 (Fall 2018): 600.

16. John Sekora, "Black Message/White Envelope: Genre, Authenticity, and Authority in the Antebellum Slave Narrative," *Callaloo* 32 (Summer 1987): 482–515.

17. Kenneth W. Warren, *What Was African American Literature?* (Cambridge, MA: Harvard University Press, 2011), 42.

18. Jarrett argues specifically that "from the late eighteenth century to the present, African American literature has come to define, demonstrate, and even succeed in political action." See Jarrett, *Representing the Race*, 4.

19. See Roland Barthes, "The Death of the Author," in *Image, Music, Text*, trans. Stephen Heath (New York: Hill and Wang, 1977), 142–48 and Michel Foucault, "What Is an Author," in *The Foucault Reader* (New York: Pantheon Books, 1984), 101–20.

20. Heather Hirschfeld, "Early Modern Collaboration and Theories of Authorship," *PMLA* 116, no. 3 (May 2001): 614.

21. David D. Hall, "The Chesapeake in the Seventeenth Century," in *A History of the Book in America*, vol. 1: *The Colonial Book in the Atlantic World*, ed. H. Amory and David D. Hall (Chapel Hill: University of North Carolina Press, 2009), 76.

22. Julie Sievers, "Drowned Pens and Shaking Hands: Sea Providence Narratives in Seventeenth-Century New England," *William and Mary Quarterly* 63, no. 4 (2006): 748.

23. For readings restoring the experience of enslaved Africans in the Caribbean to our sense of the slave narrative tradition, see Aljoe, *Creole Testimonies*.

24. The kind of archival oversight this reader endeavors to redress is complemented by recent work in early African American cultural history and digital humanities. See, for example, the scholarly forum that appeared in *William and Mary Quarterly* 76, no. 1 (January 2019). The forum featured Simon Newman's article "Hidden in Plain Sight: Escaped Slaves in Late Eighteenth- and Early Nineteenth-Century Jamaica," which was published through the journal's OI Reader app a year earlier (https://oireader.wm.edu/). Newman and those scholars contributing to the forum discussion, including Hilary Beckles, Jessica Marie Johnson, Sharon M. Leon, and Celia E. Naylor, contemplate the potential for historical discovery and study of early black African lives based on digitally based analytical tools and platforms that make legible the presences of Black bodies often "hidden in plain sight" in historical archives. *The Earliest African American Literatures* echoes the forum's call for new methodological frames.

25. This omission is surprising, as studies of nineteenth-century African American literature have devoted significant resources to the recovery and examination of newspaper accounts. See, for example, Eric Gardner, *Black Print Unbound: The Christian Recorder, African American Literature, and Periodical Culture* (New York: Oxford University Press, 2015); Hannah Wakefield, "'Let the Light Enter!': Illuminating the Newspaper Poetry of Frances Ellen Watkins Harper," *Legacy* 36, no. 1 (2019): 18–42; and Brian Baaki, "White Crime and the Early African American Press: Elements of Reprinting and Reporting in New York's *Freedom's Journal*," *American Periodicals* 29, no. 2 (2019), 121–34.

26. Charles E. Clark, "Periodicals and Politics," in Amory and Hall, *History of the Book in America*, 355.

27. *New-England Weekly Journal*, 20 March 1727.

28. Toni Morrison, "Rememory," in *The Source of Self-Regard: Selected Essays, Speeches, and Meditations* (New York: Alfred A. Knopf, 2019), 322–25.

29. Barthes, "Death of the Author."

30. Joseph Addison, *The Tatler*, 14 September 1710, in *The Works of Joseph Addison* (New York: 1868), 3: 67.

31. See David Waldstreicher, "Reading the Runaways: Self-Fashioning, Print Culture, and Confidence in Slavery in the Eighteenth-Century Mid-Atlantic," *William and Mary Quarterly* 56, no. 2 (1999): 243–72.

32. *Boston News-Letter*, 24 December 1724.

33. Elaine K. Ginsberg, "Introduction: The Politics of Passing," in Ginsberg, ed., *Passing and the Fictions of Identity* (Durham, NC: Duke University Press, 1996), 5. On the performance of class among the enslaved, see William L. Andrews, *Slavery and Class in the American South: A Generation of Slave Narrative Testimony, 1840–1865* (New York: Oxford University Press, 2019).

34. *Boston News-Letter*, 3 March 1718.

35. *Boston Evening-Post*, 18 May 1741.

36. In addition to the voluminous English-language archive we survey here, there are records in French, Spanish, Dutch, and other languages that feature literary black Africans in North America. Our emphasis here on the British American mainland and texts originally written in English is designed as an opening statement, one we hope will generate further dialogue across languages.

37. These, and many other relations we have omitted from *The Earliest African American Literatures*, are even more abbreviated than the passages preserved in this anthology: "*April, 1. 1699.* Mr. Jnº Wait was here and express'd his earnest desire that Bastian might have Jane, Mr. Thair's Negro. I spake to Jane on Monday." And "*Friday, Janʸ 10. 1700/01.* Mr. John Wait came to me, and earnestly desired me to hasten consummating the Marriage between his Bastian and Jane, Mrs. Thair's Negro." See Samuel Sewall, *The Diary of Samuel Sewall, 1674–1729* (New York: Farrar, Straus and Giroux, 1973), 1:408, 443.

38. Although scholarly readers have disagreed as to the meaning of Hammon's status as a servant, most now accept that he was a slave. His apparent liberty to enter into a labor contract taking him to the Caribbean might suggest that Hammon was a free man who received wages from General John Winslow, but Robert Desrochers Jr. explains that enslaved black Africans living in New England frequently received permission to enter into such arrangements during the winter months. Vincent Carretta republished Briton Hammon's *Narrative* in *Unchained Voices: An Anthology of Black Authors in the English-speaking World of the Eighteenth Century* (University Press of Kentucky, 1996), and his introduction suggests that Hammon was a free man. On the question of Hammon's legal status, see Robert Desrochers Jr., "'Surprizing Deliverance'?: Slavery and Freedom, Language and Identity in the *Narrative* of Briton Hammon, 'A Negro Man,'" in *Genius in Bondage: Literature of the Early Black Atlantic*, ed. Vincent Caretta and Philip Gould (Lexington, KY: University Press of Kentucky, 2001), 153–74.

39. Curiously, Hammon's narrative has garnered more critical attention as a "literary" first than has the as-told-to memoir of Ayuba Suleiman Diallo, *Some Memoirs of the Life of Job, the Son of Solomon the High Priest of Boonda in Africa* (1734). Published in London more

than two decades before Hammon's *Narrative*, it recounts Diallo's capture and enslavement in Maryland. The scholarly preference for Hammon's narrative may be a function of its link to the Indian captivity narrative, as described in John Sekora, "Briton Hammon, the Indian Captivity Narrative, and the African American Slave Narrative," in *Where Brer Rabbit Meets Coyote: African–Native American Literature*, ed. Jonathan Brennan (Urbana: University of Illinois Press, 2003), 141–57.

40. Briton Hammon, *Narrative of the Uncommon Sufferings, and Surprizing Deliverance of Briton Hammon, a Negro Man*, in *Unchained Voices: An Anthology of Black Authors in the English-Speaking World of the 18th Century*, ed. Vincent Carretta, 2nd ed. (Lexington: University Press of Kentucky, 2004), 21, 24.

41. Laurel Thatcher Ulrich, "Vertuous Women Found: New England Ministerial Literature, 1668–1735," *American Quarterly* 28, no. 1 (1976): 20.

42. *Boston News-Letter*, 16 April 1711.

43. See Jacob D. Wheeler, *A Practical Treatise on the Law of Slavery* (New York: 1837), 7.

44. In this runaway ad, the simple insertion of a possessive pronoun illustrates the collaborative nature of writing. Without the specific details, we can nonetheless ascertain that something about Jack's actions compels the master's textual deviation. The material circumstances to which the advertisement alludes—the clothing, the fiddle, Jack's musical abilities, his very choice to run—circumscribe the writer's imagination.

45. On the English acquisition of the *asiento* and its role in provoking hostilities between England and Spain in the late 1730s, see James A. Rawley and Stephen D. Behrendt, *The Transatlantic Slave Trade: A History*, rev. ed. (Lincoln: University of Nebraska Press, 2005), 59–62.

46. Please note that very few of the texts in this reader have received sustained critical attention. Consequently, when constructing a list of suggested reading relevant to each text, we selected secondary readings that speak to larger historical and cultural contexts appropriate to the text in question.

47. Lisa A. Lindsay and John Wood Sweet, "Introduction: Biography and the Black Atlantic," in *Biography and the Black Atlantic*, ed. Lindsay and Sweet (Philadelphia: University of Pennsylvania Press, 2014), 14.

48. The retheorization of these terms is all the more crucial as scholars of early African American cultural studies and history turn increasingly to the digital humanities to make more accessible data, images, and texts relevant to early black African lives. See, for example, the recent launch of the *Colored Conventions Project*, cofounded by P. Gabrielle Foreman and Jim Casey (https://coloredconventions.org/). This digital resource tracks nineteenth-century black American political gatherings and activism. See also the massive database project *Slave Voyages*, the result of some sixty years of data collection and scholarly collaboration across the Atlantic world (https://www.slavevoyages.org/). See also *The Early Caribbean Digital Archive*, a repository of early Caribbean texts and images that are especially relevant to this anthology's concern with literary mediation (https://ecda.northeastern.edu/).

49. One can make a similar argument about Briton Hammon's narrative.

Part I

1. Equiano, *The Interesting Narrative of the Life of Olaudah Equiano, or Gustavus Vassa, The African Written by Himself*. Sollors, Werner, ed. New York: Norton & Company, 2001: 69.

Chapter Four

1. Transcription reprinted by permission of *William and Mary Quarterly*.

Chapter Five

1. Transcription reprinted by permission of *William and Mary Quarterly*.

Chapter Six

1. Transcription reprinted by permission of *William and Mary Quarterly*.

Chapter Seven

1. Transcription reprinted by permission of University of North Carolina Press.

Chapter Eight

1. Transcription reprinted by permission of University of North Carolina Press.

Chapter Twelve

1. [Horsmanden's note] Jack's description of Ben:—His master live in tall house Broadway. Ben ride de fat horse.

2. [Horsmanden's note] Probably alluding to the conspiracy at Antigua, for which many negroes were executed four or five years ago.

Index

Indexes are traditionally organized by the surname of those mentioned in a given text. Because many of the people this anthology restores to our collective historical consciousness were never given a last name, never had an opportunity to choose one for themselves, or were identified by the last name of those who enslaved them, we include all such persons listed in this index under the heading "no last name given." Their inclusion is a reminder that many publication processes have worked to erase the presence of racialized persons, including those who—like Black Peter, here Peter$_{(1)}$—helped to compose and set type.

Abenaki, 17. *See also* Native Americans
Abraham, 43
Addison, Joseph, 7
advertisements, 7
Africa, 177–88, 189n3
African American literature, 1–2, 4, 8, 15–16, 18, 177, 189n2, 191n18
Africans, literary black, 1, 3, 5–6, 9–10, 14–16, 18
Ais, 23
Aljoe, Nicole, 190n8
amanuensis, 15, 19, 153
Anglican Church, 34–35
Annapolis, 143–44, 180
antislavery, 42–44, 61, 125
archive, 5, 10
arson, 14, 72–87 passim, 102, 143, 149, 151–52, 156
Atlantic, 11, 15, 117, 119, 133, 153, 167
authorship, 3–5, 155, 191n15; Black, 16–17; corporate, 5–6; and invention, 6–7; as ownership, 4; of women, 5, 11
autobiography, 3, 61; Black, 10, 153, 174. *See also* life writing

baptism, 34–35
Barbados, 57–58, 146
Barthes, Roland, 4, 7
Bennett, Andrew, 3
Beverly, MA, 123

Bible, 29, 36, 42–44, 72, 81, 85–87, 94, 101; Exodus, 43; Genesis, 43; Isaiah, 37, 40; Jeremiah, 44; John, 38; I Kings, 43; Proverbs, 43; slavery in, 42–44, 129; Song of Solomon, 37
black Africans, 1–18 passim; agency of, 2, 7, 23, 34, 135, 139, 163; and Blackness, 34, 37, 47; conversion of, 21–22, 34, 37–40, 159–60, 174; and criminality, 11, 27, 45–46, 57–60, 66–67, 70, 72–87 passim, 94–111 passim, 113, 143, 153–54, 174–76; dialects of, 57–58, 75; executions of, 27–33, 72, 74, 94, 143, 149–52, 174–76; and gender, 72, 91, 117, 120, 154; labor of, 9, 61–67, 91–92, 117, 133, 163, 183; literary representation of, 1–3, 5–6, 113, 155, 190n4; marriage of, 10, 16, 27, 35, 88–90, 179; medical knowledge of, 133, 159, 162; national identity of, 14; as property, 12–13, 23, 50, 135, 141, 143, 147; as property owners, 13, 91–92; racial identity of, 8, 10, 19–20, 35, 37, 117, 139, 189n3; reading, 8–9, 27, 28–29, 36, 70–71, 94, 159, 175, 177–78, 184; souls of, 21, 27; spirituality of, 16, 19–44 passim, 177; as subjects, 4–5, 7, 18; as submissive, 23
Bluett, Thomas, 15, 177–78
Boston, Jethro, 88–90

Boston, MA, 27, 70–71, 89, 99, 103, 106, 140, 141–42, 146, 163–64; North Church in, 159; smallpox outbreak in, 159–62
Boston Evening-Post, 9, 91
Boston News-Letter, 7, 117
broadsides, 9
Broomfield, Edward, 89

Calcaterra, Angela, 190n4
Calvert, Benedict, 143
Calvert, Charles, 143
Campbell, Joseph, 117
Canaan, 43–44
Canterbury, CT, 42
captivity narrative, 11, 17, 19, 23, 192–193n39. *See also* Native Americans
Caribbean, 6, 14, 163–65, 190n8, 191n23, 192n38
Cartagena de Indias, 9
Casor, John, 47–49, 153
Charlestown, MA, 95, 100, 103, 118
Chesapeake Bay, MD, 5
Christmas, 143, 150
Church of England. *See* Anglican Church
Clark, Charles, 6
class, 8, 154
Cleaveland, John, 37
Codman, John, 94–95, 103
Colombia, 9
Colson, Elizabeth, 5, 10, 174–76
Connecticut, 8, 12, 121, 123. *See also* Canterbury, CT; Fairfield, CT; Norwalk, CT
conversion narratives, 21–22, 37–40
copyright, 3

Dedham, MA, 68–71
Deerfield, MA, 16–17
DeLombard, Jeannine Marie, 1
Devil, 30, 58, 175. *See also* Satan
Diallo, Ayuba Suleiman, 5, 15, 177–88; appearance of, 183; character of, 184–85; devotion of, 177, 179–81; kidnapping of, 177; marriages of, 179; Muslim, 177; and Wolof language, 181

Dickinson, Jonathan, 23–26
Dorchester, MA, 21–22
Douglass, Frederick, 143

Egypt, 35, 43
Eliot, John, 21
Eliot Tracts. See "New England's First Fruits"
emancipation, 133, 155, 159. *See also* freedom
England, 14, 34, 167, 178, 181–82, 186–88
Equiano, Olaudah, 1, 3, 18, 19, 177
Ethiopians, 28
execution, 27–33, 72, 74, 94, 143, 149–52, 174–76

Fairfield, CT, 133
First Great Awakening, 16, 19, 37, 42
Fleet, Thomas, 9, 91
Florida, 23
Foucault, Michel, 4
Fox, George, 125
France, 14, 80–81, 86; French subjects, 163–64
freedom, 42, 121–22, 132, 133, 141, 149; desire for, 42–44, 47; suits for, 50–55. *See also* emancipation
Futa, 179–80

Gambia, 15, 182; River, 177, 180, 186
genre, 10–13, 15, 19, 189n2; conventions of, 11–13, 174; as organizing principle, 10–11
Georgia, 182
Gibson, Edmund, 34–35
Ginsberg, Elaine, 8
Gold Coast, 159
Goldsmith, Samuel, 48–49
grace, 22, 30–31
Greenblatt, Stephen, 2, 5
Green Spring, VA, 130
Grinstead, Elizabeth Key. *See* Key, Elizabeth
Grinstead, William, 53, 55
Guinea, 146
Gyles, John, 89–90

Hall, David, 5
Hammon, Briton, 1, 11, 15, 17–18, 167, 177, 192n38
Hammon, Jupiter, 1, 18
Hanno, Joseph, 27–33, 174
Harvard College, 18
Higginson, Humphrey, 51, 53
Hirschfeld, Heather, 5
Hispaniola, 163, 165
Horsmanden, Daniel, 72
Hubbard, William, 155–56
Hughson, John, 72–78, 80–86

indentured servitude, 47–49, 50–51, 61–65, 121, 131, 141, 158, 167, 174
Indians. *See* Native Americans
infanticide, 174, 176
integrationism, 17–18
Ipswich, MA, 37
Islam, 15, 177. *See also* Diallo, Ayuba Suleiman; Mohammed; Qur'an

Jamaica, 23, 146
Jarrett, Gene, 2
Jesus Christ, 22, 28, 31–32, 36, 38–39
Jim Crow, 4
Johnson, Anthony, 47–49

Keimer, Samuel, 8
Kelly, William, 88–89
Key, Elizabeth, 50–55, 153
Key, John, 52
Key, Thomas, 51–53
King Philip's War, 155–58
Kingston, RI, 128
Kneeland, Samuel, 6

legal records, 45–111 passim, 167, 170–73; contracts, 88; wills, 13, 91–93
life writing, 14–16, 34, 61, 113, 153–88 passim
Lindsay, Lisa, 14
literariness, 5–8
Locke, John, 45
London, 15, 35, 159, 177

Madagascar, 117
Maine, 121–22
Mallott, John, 145–46
Mandinka, 177, 180, 186
Manuel, Fransh, 133–34
Marblehead, MA, 168–69, 172
Marrant, John, 18, 177
marriage, 10, 16, 27, 35, 88–90, 179
Maryland, 15, 132, 147–48, 149–52, 177, 180–81. *See also* Annapolis
Massachusetts, 8, 15, 16–18, 42, 61, 63, 89, 119, 149, 167–68, 170–71. *See also* Beverly, MA; Boston, MA; Charlestown, MA; Dedham, MA; Deerfield, MA; Dorchester, MA; Ipswich, MA; Marblehead, MA; Plymouth, MA; Salem Witch Trials; Scituate, MA; Swansea, MA; Taunton, MA; Weymouth, MA
Mather, Cotton, 8, 27, 159; "The Negro Christianized," 27; *Tremenda*, 28–33
Mather, Increase, 155–56
mediation, 2–3, 5, 21, 27, 57, 133; freedom from, 34
Metacomet, 155
Middle Passage, 15, 16
Moffatt, John, 167
Mohammed, 180, 186. *See also* Islam
Molson, Richard, 131–32
Moore, Francis, 177, 185–88
Morrison, Toni, 2, 7
Mottram, John, 50–52, 55
murder, 27, 29, 94–111 passim, 149–52, 174–75
Muslim. *See* Islam

Narragansett, RI, 120, 127
Native Americans, 11, 16–17, 23, 121, 156–58, 190n4; their conversion to Christianity, 21–22; and criminality, 68–71. *See also* Abenaki; Ais; captivity narrative; King Philip's War; Metacomet; Peter$_{(3)}$; Pummatick, Isaac; and Wampanoag

Neau, Elias, 8
Nevis, 165
"New England's First Fruits," 18, 21, 153
New-England Weekly Journal, 6, 174
New Jersey, 134
Newport, RI, 126
Newspapers, 9–10; popularity of, 6
New York, 8, 14, 72–87 passim
no last name given:
    Anthony, 76, 78, 79, 82
    Bastian, 14, 72, 76, 78, 80–84, 192n37
    $Ben_{(1)}$, 23–26
    $Ben_{(2)}$, 75–79, 81, 82, 84, 85, 194n1
    $Caesar_{(1)}$, 73–74, 76–77, 79, 85
    $Caesar_{(2)}$, 79, 81–82, 84
    $Caesar_{(3)}$, 84
    $Caesar_{(4)}$, 80–81, 85
    $Caesar_{(5)}$, 91
    $Caesar_{(6)}$, 145, 146
    $Cato_{(1)}$, 76–77, 79–80, 82, 84
    $Cato_{(2)}$, 76–77, 79, 82–83, 84
    $Cato_{(3)}$, 79, 82, 83–84
    $Cato_{(4)}$, 84, 86
    $Cato_{(5)}$, 108
    Cora, 143, 149–52
    Curacoa Dick, 77, 79, 82–84
    Daniel, 125–26
    Francis, 78–79, 82
    George, 119
    Hagar, 88–90
    Harry, 123
    Irankilo, 123
    $Jack_{(1)}$, 12–13, 193n44
    $Jack_{(2)}$, 72–76, 77–78, 81–82, 84, 86–87
    $Jack_{(3)}$, 79–80, 82
    $Jethro_{(1)}$, 127–28
    $Jethro_{(2)}$, 155–58
    Joe, 149, 152
    John, 129–30
    $London_{(1)}$, 24
    $London_{(2)}$, 77, 79, 82, 84
    Love, 91–92
    Nanny Negro, 27
    Old Pharoah, 57
    Onesimus, 159–62
    Pawpaw, 133
    Penelope, 117–18
    Pero, 127–28
    $Peter_{(1)}$, 9–10, 13, 91–93
    $Peter_{(2)}$, 113, 121–24
    $Peter_{(3)}$, 123
    Phoebe, 94, 96–106, 108–111
    Powlus, 76, 79, 82, 83
    Primus, 68–70
    $Prince_{(1)}$, 73
    $Prince_{(2)}$, 82
    $Prince_{(3)}$, 84–86
    $Prince_{(4)}$, 85
    Quack, 72–74, 82
    Quam, 135–36
    Quamino, 83
    Quash, 76–77, 78, 79, 82, 84, 85
    Robbin (Vassall), 96, 98–100, 103–109
    $Robin_{(1)}$, 73, 79, 82–82, 84
    $Robin_{(2)}$, 91–92
    Sandy, 72–74, 79–80, 82
    Sarah, 79, 82–83
    $Scipio_{(1)}$, 76–77, 79
    $Scipio_{(2)}$, 84–86
    $Scipio_{(3)}$, 108
    Stephen, 143–44
    Tickle, *also* Ticklepitcher, 73–74, 76, 78, 82, 84
    Timothy, 139–40
    Tituba, 57
    $Titus_{(1)}$, 68–70
    $Titus_{(2)}$, 86
    $Titus_{(3)}$, 163–65, 167
    $Tom_{(1)}$, 137–38
    $Tom_{(2)}$, 73
    $Tom_{(3)}$, 83
    $Tom_{(4)}$, 96, 108, 110
    Tom Peal. *See* Bastian
    $Wan_{(1)}$, 76, 79, 82
    $Wan_{(2)}$, 83
    $York_{(1)}$, 76–79, 82, 84, 86
    $York_{(2)}$, 84–86
Norwalk, CT, 133
novel, 5

Oglethorpe, James, 177, 182, 186

Parker, George, 48
Parker, Robert, 47–49
passing, 8
Peal, Tom. *See* Bastian
Pennsylvania, 136, 137–38, 181
Peters, Phillis Wheatley, 1, 3–4, 18, 42
Plymouth, MA, 171–72, 174
poetry, 9, 16–17
Portugal, 171
Prat, Ebenezer, 175
Prince, Abijah, 16
Prince, Lucy Terry, 1, 16–18
property, 12; text as, 3
Pummatick, Isaac, 122
Puritans, 15, 17, 18, 19, 27, 155, 174; missionaries, 21

Quakers, 23, 125
Qur'an, 179, 184

racism, 4, 11, 20, 68
rape, 8, 88, 120
reading, 7, 113; of black Africans, 8–9, 27, 28–29, 36, 70–71, 94, 159, 175, 177–78, 184; generically, 12
rememory, 7
Rezek, Joseph, 191n15
Rhode Island, 16. *See also* Kingston, RI; Narragansett, RI; Newport, RI; Warwick, RI
Royal African Company, 177, 182, 185, 186
Royal Society, 159
runaway slave advertisements, 7, 10, 12–13, 113–52 passim, 167–68; and celebrity, 149–50; and clothing, 12–13, 113; and language, 128, 137–38, 140, 142; and physical deformity, 111, 121–23, 127–30, 135–36, 141–42

Saffin, John, 42, 61–67, 158
sailors, 5, 163, 165, 167–72, 185
Salem Witch Trials, 57–60
Satan, 38–39, 174. *See also* Devil

Scituate, MA, 126
sea providence narrative, 5
Sekora, John, 4
Senegal, 15, 177, 179
Sewall, Samuel$_{(1)}$, 10, 42, 45, 61, 145, 155
Sewall, Samuel$_{(2)}$, 88
shipwreck, 163, 165
Shirley, William, 89
Sievers, Julie, 5
sin, 22, 28–33, 38–40, 175–76
slave codes, 13, 45, 149, 151–52, 181
slave-for-sale advertisements, 10
slave narrative, 1, 6–7, 10–11, 113, 131, 133, 137, 177, 189n2, 191n23
slavery, 9, 15, 35–36, 145, 177, 181–83, 186; geography of, 131–32; heritable, 50; by law, 35; and race, 47; and war, 42, 45
slave trade, 3, 15–16, 180, 186–87; Black participation in, 47–49, 159, 180, 186
Small Pox, 159, 162
Society of Friends. *See* Quakers
Solomon, 43–44
Solomon, Job Ben. *See* Diallo, Ayuba Suleiman
South Carolina, 121, 123, 132
Spain, 14, 72, 80–81, 86, 167; Spanish subjects, 23–26, 76–78
St. Kitts, 164–65
St. Martinique, 163–64
St. Thomas, 165
Swansea, MA, 155
Sweet, John, 14

Taunton, MA, 155–57
testimonio, 190n8
theft, 8, 135–36, 143–44, 147–48, 159–60, 163, 165, 174, 175
Thomas, Isaiah, 91
Thorne, Francis, 167

Ulrich, Laurel Thatcher, 11
unfreedom, 15, 91, 121, 131

Vernon, Edward, 9
Virginia, 34–35, 47–49, 50, 133. *See also* Green Spring, VA

Waldstreicher, David, 7
Wampanoag, 155
War of Jenkins' Ear, 14, 72. *See also* England; Spain
Warren, Kenneth, 4
Warwick, RI, 140

Weymouth, MA, 174
Whitefield, George, 37
whiteness, 37
Williams, John, 167–73
Winslow, John, 11, 192n38
witchcraft, 57–60
Woolman, John, 10

Yoas, Loumein, 180

www.ingramcontent.com/pod-product-compliance
Lightning Source LLC
Chambersburg PA
CBHW021857230426

43671CB00006B/419